COMMUNITY WAGE PATTERNS

PUBLICATIONS OF THE
INSTITUTE OF INDUSTRIAL RELATIONS
UNIVERSITY OF CALIFORNIA

COMMUNITY
WAGE PATTERNS

By

FRANK C. PIERSON

UNIVERSITY OF CALIFORNIA PRESS
BERKELEY AND LOS ANGELES
1953

UNIVERSITY OF CALIFORNIA PRESS

BERKELEY AND LOS ANGELES

CALIFORNIA

◇

CAMBRIDGE UNIVERSITY PRESS

LONDON, ENGLAND

FOR
RITA

FOREWORD

IN *Community Wage Patterns* the Institute of Industrial Relations presents an original contribution in the field of wage analysis. The author has examined some of the basic assumptions of economic theory in the light of what has actually happened to wages in a particular community, Los Angeles County. Although the monograph will have a special interest for those concerned with wage rates and wage structures in the Los Angeles community, Professor Pierson's analysis of the forces which control wages at the local area level has a much broader application.

The monograph begins with a general examination of the factors bearing on community wage levels and wage structures. This is followed by a discussion of early wage history in the Los Angeles area up to 1940 and then an analysis of Los Angeles wages during the decade of the 1940's. Other chapters deal specifically with those factors which have been most influential in determining the level and pattern of wages in this area.

Throughout the monograph particular attention is given to the Los Angeles situation, but at every step in the discussion comparisons are made with wage developments in other communities and in the country as a whole. The investigation points to a number of conclusions about the behavior of wages in local areas which are also applicable to other large population centers. The findings, in general, support the view that wages in different industries and localities form a well-knit structure largely controlled by economic and social forces operating on a broad regional or national basis. At the regional level, for example, the physical characteristics of the area, including productive soil, favorable climate, and such outstanding resources as crude oil supplies, have been important determining factors in the relatively high Los Angeles wage rates and earnings. Although shifts in local industry wage levels are generally related to broad economic and social developments, fluctuations in local business conditions do cause short-term changes in the community's relative wage position.

Professor Pierson was a Research Associate on the staff of the Institute for two years, on leave from Swarthmore College. The major part of the statistical work for the study was done at that time. His monograph is a significant addition to the publications of the Institute, which seeks to promote independent scholarly research of this kind.

EDGAR L. WARREN, DIRECTOR
Southern Division
Los Angeles, California

ACKNOWLEDGMENTS

THIS STUDY is the result of a group research project undertaken in 1949 and substantially completed in 1950. As a coöperative undertaking it reflects the thought and effort of a number of persons, most of whom are on the staff of the Institute of Industrial Relations at the University of California, Los Angeles. I am chiefly indebted to Hugo M. Morris, who assumed major responsibility for the statistical work in chapter vi, and who aided me in the preparation of the rest of the study at every turn. I also benefited greatly from the suggestions and criticisms of the following: Armen A. Alchian, Irving Bernstein, George H. Hildebrand, and Philip Neff, all of the University of California, Los Angeles, Gladys L. Palmer of the University of Pennsylvania, and Lloyd G. Reynolds of Yale University.

Maurice I. Gershenson and the staff of the Division of Labor Statistics and Research, California State Department of Industrial Relations, were most helpful in supplying information from their files. Harry M. Douty of the United States Bureau of Labor Statistics also provided me much valuable material. The figures appearing in the study were prepared by Eleanor M. Gold, with final execution by Henry W. Schloten. The work of editing the manuscript and preparing the index was done by Anne P. Cook. I wish to express my appreciation also to the reading committee of the Institute, consisting of Professors Paul T. Homan, George H. Hildebrand, and Robert Tannenbaum of the University of California, Los Angeles, for their careful review of the manuscript, and to Edgar L. Warren for his continuing interest and help. Finally, I am grateful to my wife, Marguerite T. Pierson, who served as my unofficial assistant throughout the investigation and who bore more of the brunt of this undertaking than I care to think. Responsibility for any errors, as well as for the opinions expressed in the study, is solely mine.

FRANK C. PIERSON

Swarthmore, Pa.
March 10, 1952

CONTENTS

Text Tables

Appendix Tables

Figures

I. COMMUNITY WAGE STRUCTURES

ECONOMISTS, in explaining the behavior of wages, have long given prominence to local area influences and conditions.[1] This follows from the fact that job openings are generally filled by workers living within a rather narrow geographical radius, employers rarely finding it necessary to go beyond "daily commuting zones" to meet staffing requirements. Competition among firms for labor, to the extent that it exists, is thus largely a local area phenomenon. An employer who is losing key workers to other plants looks first at the wage rates paid by other employers in his own community and then determines whether he can afford to put his wages and other working conditions on a par with theirs. This applies also to the employer who is starting a new plant or adding new workers to his pay roll. Such wage comparisons may be limited to competitors in their own industry in the area, but most types of labor are used in more than one field, and so account must be taken of going rates in other industries in the vicinity as well. Not infrequently, employers try to cut through these difficulties by establishing a certain relationship between their wages and those of some other firm or group of firms, simply moving their rates up or down in step with the leader. Whatever the means employed, the major objective is to achieve a position in the local community which, on the one hand, makes adequate staffing possible and, on the other, yields a satisfactory return on investment.

Analysis of wage behavior from the viewpoint of workers also underscores the importance of local area conditions. Any influence on comparative wage rate levels resulting from the interjob and interfirm movement of workers is largely confined to a particular locality. Actually, students of labor markets have become increasingly doubtful if there is even enough mobility within single communities to have a significant effect on the wage levels existing within local areas, since both the external and internal (i.e., objective and personal) barriers to the movement of labor are so formidable.[2] All are agreed, however, that mobility *among* communities is still more limited and hence a factor to be given even less weight in explaining wage rate phenomena.[3] So far as labor

---

[1] In analyzing the conditions of supply and demand which determine wages, Hicks, for example, based most of his discussion on community-wide markets. J. R. Hicks, *The Theory of Wages* (New York: Macmillan, 1935), especially chap. 4.

[2] A summary of studies of wage differences for the same job titles within local areas is given in Richard A. Lester, "Wage Diversity and Its Theoretical Implications," *Review of Economics and Statistics*, XXVIII (August, 1946), 152–159.

[3] Lloyd Reynolds states: "Almost all manufacturing plants in the United States could find many times their present working force within a radius of a hundred miles, and

supply factors affect pay levels, attention should therefore be centered on conditions within specific localities.

It would be a serious error to infer from the foregoing that the wage rate structure of a community is wholly, or even in large measure, the product of local circumstances. Rather, the community is simply the point at which a wide variety of influences, some local and others non-local, come into focus. If competition between employers in the hiring of labor tends to be local, competition in the sale of products is frequently regional or even national. The extent to which a particular group of employers can raise wages in such industries may therefore be closely related to rates paid by competitors in other communities. Industries with narrow selling areas, like most of the service trades, are less subject to these outside influences, and in such fields differences in wage levels among areas tend to be somewhat greater. Even in their case, however, wage rate movements exhibit a marked degree of uniformity because in an economy as closely knit as that of the United States, changes in output and income in one industry or area tend to spread rapidly to all other parts of the system.

These interarea leveling tendencies of a strictly economic character are paralleled by influences of a more institutional or organizational nature.[4] Large corporations with branch plants in many parts of the country frequently grant general wage increases on a company-wide basis.[5] Wages in small firms are more likely to move apart, though group bargaining through employer associations may achieve for small employers what the large enterprise can do on its own. Similarly, the rise of national unions has, on balance, made for greater uniformity in wage behavior. This result is seen most clearly in industries selling in broad markets and hiring mostly unskilled or semiskilled labor, but even the so-called craft organizations representing skilled groups in local market

---

most of the labor migration which actually occurs involves movement of a hundred miles or less." Richard A. Lester and Joseph Shister, eds., *Insights into Labor Issues* (New York: Macmillan, 1948), p. 277. See also John T. Dunlop, "Allocation of the Labor Force," *Proceedings of the Conference on Industry-Wide Collective Bargaining* (1949), p. 44. Hicks, however, says that movement of labor from place to place does occur, and furthermore that "... recent researches are indicating more and more clearly that differences in net economic advantages, chiefly differences in wages, are the main causes of migration." Hicks, *op. cit.*, p. 76.

[4] For an excellent discussion of some of these "non-market" influences as they affect the determination of wages in local areas, see Lester and Shister, eds., *op. cit.*, chapter by Clark Kerr and Lloyd H. Fisher, especially pp. 48–53.

[5] In a survey covering eighty-eight multiplant corporations, three-fifths were found to make general wage changes on a company-wide basis, but only thirteen reported that their scales were absolutely uniform in every location. Richard A. Lester, *Company Wage Policies* (Princeton: Industrial Relations Section, Princeton University, 1948), p. 43.

industries exert a similar influence. Trade union leaders, because of both internal and external rivalries, are under heavy pressure to maintain or improve the relative wage standing of their constituency.[6] A craft organization in one section of an industry cannot permit the wage standards of its members to fall much below those of other sections in the same field without causing adverse reactions. This can even be true of industries in which competition in the sale of products is highly localized and in which the movement of labor between branches of an industry or between areas is negligible. Wage rates in any one locality, therefore, are affected by a crosscurrent of influences, many of which come from outside the immediate area. The resulting structure, however, is unique in the sense that the particular combination of circumstances that determines wages in one community is never exactly duplicated elsewhere.

This study presents a description of community wage structures and an analysis of the forces which control general wage movements at the local area level. Chief attention is given to a single community, Los Angeles County, but at every step in the discussion comparisons are made with wage developments in other large population centers and in the country as a whole. In this way it is possible to highlight those influences having uniform effects and those having differential effects on wage levels, and, with respect to the latter, to explain why wages behave differently not only between areas but within areas as well. On the "policy" level, the investigation throws light on the conditions which underlie improvements in wage standards and also serves to point up the limits to which increases in wages are subject. Attention now is turned to a more detailed examination of some of these issues.

NATURE OF COMMUNITY WAGE STRUCTURES

Wages in a given locality, just as in a region or the country as a whole, form a complicated though clearly discernible set of relationships. Actually, it is almost impossible to set any clear-cut boundaries to local areas for wage comparison purposes.[7] For some skills and industries the markets in which the buying and selling of labor takes place are quite broad; in others, extremely narrow. The concentration of job opportunities in different urban centers, of course, affords a rough measure of market

---

[6] Arthur M. Ross, *Trade Union Wage Policy* (Berkeley and Los Angeles: University of California Press, 1948), chap. 3.

[7] In analyzing the nature of labor markets, Kerr distinguishes between at least five major types: (1) the perfect market, (2) the neoclassical market, (3) the natural market, (4) the institutional market, and (5) the managed market. "The trend," he believes, "is unmistakably toward the institutional market." Clark Kerr, "Labor Markets: Their Character and Consequences," *Proceedings of the Industrial Relations Research Association* (1949), p. 83.

boundaries, though the growing importance of satellite communities makes this test hard to apply. Probably the criterion of normal commuting distances as measured from the central business or industrial section of a city is the most satisfactory test under the circumstances.[8] The boundaries in any case are necessarily arbitrary and are useful only in providing a way of looking at wage phenomena.

The term "wages" itself is not easily defined either, but in most studies comparisons are based on rates or earnings per hour; local area wage data are usually published in the form of average earnings per hour from which overtime is not excluded. Unless otherwise noted, this is the measure of wage levels employed in this study.[9] Still another troublesome question is what is meant by the phrase "community wage structure." Several definitions suggest themselves. One is the distribution of earnings among individuals or family units, regardless of the occupation or industry in which they work; this might be termed the personal or individual wage structure of a community. Another is the comparative level of earnings among jobs or grades of labor in a given community. Although such comparisons become extremely difficult when they cross industry lines it is at least theoretically possible to construct the job wage structure of a community on this basis. Still another is the relationship between average hourly earnings of individual industries, which in turn are based on earnings data collected from individual firms weighted by the number of employees in each job classification; this can be thought of as the industry wage structure of a community. Finally, it is possible to compute a weighted average of the different industry earnings and arrive at an estimate of the general wage level of the community as a whole. Calculations in other communities on a similar basis permit intercommunity comparisons at each of these four levels of investigation.

The most precise measurements of community wage structures are based on wage rate reports for identical jobs, but unfortunately there is not enough information of this nature over a sufficient period of time to carry us very far. To get an over-all picture it is necessary to fall back on industry averages, using specific job rate data as a check on our findings. For present purposes the use of industry averages is justified

---

[8] Reynolds puts the matter in these terms: "The labor market is best conceived, then, as an outer circle defined by geography (really, distance per se), within which are many smaller circles or nuclei consisting of individual employing units." He is using the term "labor market" here in connection with the movement of labor, not in connection with the determination of wages. Speaking realistically, there is no single market in which wages are set but a plurality of markets ranging all the way from the individual firm to the national economy. Lloyd G. Reynolds, *The Structure of Labor Markets* (New York: Harper, 1951), p. 42.

[9] Under normal conditions, gross earnings can be used for measuring differences in rates per hour, but in periods when there is much overtime, such as during World War II, this assumption is not warranted.

since our main interest is in explaining broad changes within and between community wage structures. Minor movements or temporary shifts in community wage relationships may not be reflected in the industry figures, but it seems reasonable to assume they will mirror changes of a more enduring sort. For these reasons most of the data analyzed in this investigation are industry average hourly earnings.

Great care, however, has to be exercised in interpreting wage figures of this type since they are affected by a variety of influences. Usually changes in an industry's average hourly earnings result from a rise or fall in the general level of hourly rates.[10] But, of course, the hourly earnings of an industry can vary even though rates remain unaltered. Speaking of gross as opposed to straight-time earnings, changes in the amount of overtime, night-shift premiums, and other forms of extra pay may have an important bearing on the final result. Similarly, even the level of straight-time average earnings in an industry may change if there is a substantial shift in the distribution of employees between low- and high-paying jobs or between low- and high-paying firms. Variations may also occur as a result of changes in job duties and requirements, though, strictly speaking, this influence should be regarded as no different from wage movements due to changes in rates of pay for particular jobs. Especially in periods of economic instability or rapid change, these nonrate influences can be of great importance, but at all times their effects should be kept in mind.

The matter of interpretation becomes still more complicated when comparisons are made between communities. A difference in the wage level of an industry, as among localities, may arise because the operations, though they are considered to be part of a single industry, may be essentially different. This source of difficulty can be troublesome enough even within a particular community, but it is likely to be compounded when intercommunity comparisons are attempted. An industry like lumber and timber products, for example, is divided into a number of distinct branches such as logging, sawmill, and planing mill operations, and the relative importance of the various branches is greater in some communities than in others. As a rough measure of *changes* in hourly earnings over a period of time, the use of industry averages, by communities, is permissible, but they obviously cannot be used to compare *absolute* levels in different communities at given moments of time.

Speaking broadly, as already indicated, it is possible to construct a measure of a community's general wage level. This involves combining

---

[10] The comparable adjustment in industries on a piecework basis would be a general change in the rates at which incentive pay is figured, though the more usual practice is to leave incentive rates unchanged and simply to add a cent-per-hour increase to the workers' pay.

the average hourly earnings of individual industries in a weighted average. In addition to the various influences listed above as bearing on industry wage levels, estimates of community wage levels can be affected by shifts in employment between low- and high-paying industries. Again, a warning is in order. Community wage level comparisons are only justified as a means for bringing out major contrasts and long-term trends. They are much too inclusive to be used as precise measures of community wage standings, much less as a basis for explaining the reasons for shifts in the wage rankings of different localities over short periods of time. Data of this type are somewhat more meaningful so long as a distinction is made between manufacturing and nonmanufacturing, since fields within these two categories form more nearly homogeneous groups.

CONTROLLING INFLUENCES

Many of the concepts and findings developed by economists pertain, at least indirectly, to wage relationships at the community level and therefore merit our attention. Their conclusions are particularly helpful in framing hypotheses and in providing guides for further analysis. Although the views summarized in the rest of this chapter would not be acceptable to all present-day economists, it seems safe to conclude that the differences would principally concern matters of emphasis and terminology.[11] The main purpose of this investigation is to test these general ideas against the experience of particular communities.

Most discussions of wage phenomena begin with a consideration of supply-and-demand relationships under various market conditions. Thus, if the wage level of one industry is higher than another, or if wages within an industry are generally higher in one locality than another, the presumption is that the relationship between demand and supply is more favorable from the viewpoint of job holders and job seekers in the one case than in the other. The same reasoning would also apply to a rise in the wage level of one industry, or one area, relative to another.

This seems straightforward enough, but differences in viewpoint (or at least in emphasis) begin to arise when an attempt is made to explain what lies behind these supply-and-demand relationships. Most present-day economists stress the wide variety of influences impinging on wages, many of which are of a psychological or sociological nature. Nonetheless, though emphasis is placed on the diversity of circumstances surrounding the determination of wages, the predominant view is that wages in different industries within a locality, as measured by average

---

[11] This summary of the literature has been greatly benefited by a number of suggestions made by George H. Hildebrand.

hourly earnings, form a certain structure which is subject to little change over long periods of time. Similarly, wages in the same industry in different localities are viewed as forming an interarea (as distinguished from an intra-area) structure which also persists over time.

Some changes within and between these community wage structures, of course, occur, and under certain circumstances a clearly discernible shift in relative wage levels may come about. Such shifts are likely to result in a narrowing of certain differentials and a broadening of others, so that the predominant movement during short periods may be far from clear. Over a period of time, however, shifts in wage levels are likely to form clear-cut patterns of change.[12] In this investigation an important distinction is drawn between persistent, as opposed to changing, characteristics of community wage structures; also between influences which affect all communities and all industries more or less uniformly, as against those having differential effects. Although some of the factors discussed operate in the short run, chief attention is given to those having a long-run significance.

INDUSTRY WAGE COMPARISONS

Students of wage relationships repeatedly emphasize that comparisons of hourly rates or hourly earnings can be most deceiving unless account is taken of a variety of other elements affecting incomes, including differences in the length of the work week or work year, in physical conditions of work, and even in nonwage satisfactions derived from particular jobs. It seems highly doubtful, however, whether these non-rate elements tend to equalize the total rewards of employees doing similar work within a given locality. Recent investigations suggest that employers paying the highest rates for a given job, far from providing below-average conditions, often provide above-average conditions of work and thus accentuate rather than lessen disparities in pay levels.[13] Interarea comparisons are subject to a still wider variety of nonrate

---

[12] Dunlop observes: "Over the long pull wage rates have increased somewhat more rapidly in industries with high rates of increase in productivity and employment. Wage rates have increased somewhat less rapidly in older and more mature industries with relatively constant employment and with less rapid increases in productivity." John T. Dunlop, "American Wage Determination: The Trend and Its Significance," paper presented at a meeting sponsored by the U. S. Chamber of Commerce, January 11, 1947.

[13] In his recent study of wage differences among firms in a local area, Reynolds reports that "... supplementary wage payments and physical conditions of work seem to be positively correlated with wage level, thus tending to make the differentials in aggregate return from the job larger than the differential in wage rates alone." Reynolds, *op. cit.*, p. 234. This confirms the findings of previous investigations. See, for example, W. Rupert Maclaurin and Charles A. Myers, "Wages and the Movement of Factory Labor," *Quarterly Journal of Economics*, LVII (February, 1943), 251.

influences, though it is generally assumed that these influences at least
partly offset rate differences among areas. In any event, an analysis
of total rewards which takes account of such factors as annual earnings,
physical environment, and other nonwage satisfactions may yield conclusions quite different from comparisons based on hourly earnings
alone. In explaining intercity wage relationship it is especially important to bear differences in living costs in mind, although this is a factor
which has more to do with persistent differences in wage structures than
with changes over time.[14]

In this connection, writers on wage economics repeatedly emphasize
that labor markets (whether narrowly or broadly defined) are characterized by many barriers to movement and by serious limitations on the
equalizing influences of competition. Occupations have long been viewed
by economists as divided into noncompeting groups, with little possibility of movement from one general grade of labor to the next.[15] The
movement of labor among communities, not only because of transportation costs but because of ignorance and personal attachments, is
also subject to severe limitations, some economists holding to the opinion that interarea shifts, to the extent they occur, do not come as much
in response to differences in pay levels as in job opportunities and other
considerations.[16] Even within a given locality differences in pay for the
same job can persist indefinitely since most workers neither desire nor
are able to take advantage of such discrepancies.[17]

On the side of demand, the picture is less clear though the prepon-
derant opinion is that employers generally differ as to how high they
can go in setting wage rates and that, at least under nonunion conditions, they usually have some leeway in determining where the actual
level falls. Thus, some employers may be both able and willing to pay
higher rates than competitors in the same area, their purpose being
to attract or retain the best quality of labor, to minimize labor difficul-

---

[14] Comparison of long-term changes in the Consumers' Price Index of the Bureau of
Labor Statistics, for example, reveals very little variation in the movement of the index
in different communities.

[15] Cairnes is generally credited with introducing this concept into the literature. J.
E. Cairnes, *Some Leading Principles of Political Economy* (London: Macmillan, 1874),
p. 72.

[16] Thus, Lester states: "Often the availability of jobs seems to have been more influential than relative wage levels in determining the direction of worker migration
or the lack of such migration." Richard A. Lester, *Labor and Industrial Relations*
(New York: Macmillan, 1951), p. 49.

[17] Speaking of the manner in which workers hunt for jobs within a community,
Reynolds concludes: "For the most part, however, the job-hunting methods used are
no more likely to lead the worker to a good job than a poor one." Reynolds, *op. cit.*,
p. 211. This conclusion is based on interviews with 800 workers in 1947; the results
are analyzed in detail in Lloyd G. Reynolds and Joseph Shister, *Job Horizons, A Study
of Job Satisfaction and Labor Mobility* (New York: Harper, 1949).

ties, or to achieve a "good name."[18] If these findings hold good for the same work in a given locality, they obviously apply with even greater force to general wage level comparisons among industries and areas. They likewise go a long way toward explaining why wage differences persist with little change over long periods of time.

Once differences in wage rate levels become established, still other forces come into play which serve to keep the differentials unchanged. On the one hand, economists emphasize that both workers and employers become accustomed to certain wage differences between jobs and firms, and even between industries and areas, differences which come to be accepted as in some sense fair or proper. If an employer or group of firms refuses to grant an increase which is in line with established relationships, worker reaction is likely to be adverse. If, on the other hand, an employer grants an increase which violates a tacit agreement not to "pirate" labor from competitors, they are likely to take steps to bring the offending firm back in line.[19] The growth of national labor organizations and the trend toward centralized control over wage policy make deviations of the first type increasingly rare. The formation of national companies with branch plants in many parts of the country, together with the development of strong employer associations, serves to minimize deviations of the second type. It would be a mistake to assume that the growth of national labor and employer bodies tends to eliminate all changes in established relationships; indeed, as shown below, union and employer groups can on occasion be instrumental in bringing about major shifts in wage relationships. In the main, however, their effect is to strengthen the forces making for conformity, as opposed to diversity, in wage structures.

Influences of a more strictly economic character are also viewed as working in this direction. In large measure, conditions of supply and demand in different labor markets are determined by broad changes in the level of national income and national output.[20] A marked rise or

[18] Moreover, some economists seriously question whether profit maximization, even in this broad sense, is the prime consideration in company wage policies. H. M. Oliver, Jr., "Marginal Theory and Business Behavior," *American Economic Review*, XXXVII (June, 1947), 375–383.

[19] As Reynolds puts the matter: "Each firm thus has its own minimum wage which is related to its present and previous actual wage rates. These minima lie one above the other like steps on an escalator. The relative ranking of the various firms doubtless changes gradually over long periods of time but at any one time it is rather firmly fixed in the minds of both workers and employers." Lester and Shister, eds., *op. cit.*, p. 297.

[20] Speaking of recent developments in this country, Boulding observes: "A rise in the quantity of money, or in its velocity of circulation, creates an economic tide which will eventually filter into every creek and cranny in the economic system." Kenneth E. Boulding, "Collective Bargaining and Fiscal Policy," *Proceedings of the Industrial Relations Research Association* (1949), p. 55.

fall in the general level of business activity quickly communicates itself to all parts of the country, causing the same directional change in employment in almost all industries and localities. As communication and transportation facilities have been improved and the economy has grown more interdependent, these influences have become more pervasive. Similarity of wage movements is particularly characteristic of inflationary periods, but in our type of economy wage changes tend to be uniform even in periods of deflation.

THE SKILL MIX

The foregoing helps explain why differences in industry-area wage levels persist unchanged, but it tells little about the reasons for the development of differentials in the first place. One factor generally regarded as important relates to differences in skill requirements, though, of course, this factor has a more direct bearing on wage rate differences among occupations than among industries. The extent to which industries utilize highly skilled labor nonetheless varies, fields like newspaper printing having a definitely higher proportion of such labor than fields like cotton manufacturing. Variations in the "skill mix" can also occur among localities in the same industry, and on occasion this factor may be important enough to cause intercommunity wage differences within a given field. Changes in skill requirements also occur over time, and especially where technological development is rapid, changes in production methods can bring about significant shifts in relative wage levels. By and large, however, it seems safe to conclude, the skill-mix factor is more closely related to differences in industry-area wage levels which are subject to little change over time.[21]

MAN-LAND RATIO

Communities, as well as countries and regions, differ in the amount and quality of physical resources available for the support of their populations. Just as in broader economic areas, an unusually favorable climate or the discovery of a rich resource like oil may cause wages to be markedly higher in one locality than another. Similarly, there may

---

[21] In discussing the factors which bring about changes within the nation's interindustry wage structure, Dunlop includes changes in the skill and occupational content of individual industries. He argues that technological improvements may cause a rise in the skill and occupational rating of employees in some industries and a fall in others. Lloyd A. Metzler and others, *Income, Employment and Public Policy, Essays in Honor of Alvin H. Hansen* (New York: Norton, 1948), p. 360. Other wage influences resulting from improved technology, such as increases in output per man-hour, are so closely related to changes in skill requirements, it is quite impossible to disentangle them. Lewis L. Lorwin and John M. Blair, *Technology in Our Economy* (Washington: Government Printing Office, 1941), T.N.E.C. Monograph no. 22, pp. 142–155.

be differences in the extent to which population presses on physical resources. Economists are chary about the notion of an optimum population, since the expansion of trading areas, the development of technology, and differences in degree of capital intensity per man make it impossible to define the optimum level with any precision. Nonetheless, it is evident that in some communities, such as those in the southeastern part of the United States, the ratio of population to resources is far less favorable than in others, a circumstance which is clearly reflected in interarea wage differences.[22]

Although the relationship between population and resources has an important bearing on wages in particular localities, its principal effect is regional in nature. Modern transportation facilities have brought distant resources much closer to urban manufacturing centers, and also trading areas have broadened greatly, so that the natural advantages of a particular area are quickly extended to other parts of the surrounding region. Although some wage differences among communities of a single region can be attributed to the resource factor, the major effect is an interregional one, the wage level of a community depending on the regional relationship between population and resources and not the other way around. Similarly, this factor has more of a bearing on the comparative wage level of a community considered as a whole than on the wage levels of individual industries within the area. The discovery of an unusually rich resource may, of course, alter the wage ranking of a community's industries, but the principal effect is to raise the area's entire wage level relative to that of other industrial centers. In a highly developed country like the United States, the physical endowments of different sections of the country are for the most part intensively exploited, so that whereas shifts in population-resource relationships may cause gradual changes in the wage levels of communities, this factor makes for permanent rather than for changing differences in wage levels.[23]

As already suggested, many industries, especially in the early stages of processing, are concentrated in certain areas because of the distribu-

---

[22] Reynolds, speaking in broad terms, holds that the relatively low wage level in the southeastern part of the United States arises from the fact that: "The rate of natural increase in the South, particularly in the rural South, is much higher than in the northeastern states. At the same time agriculture, the basic competitor of urban industries for the available labor supply, offers much lower returns than in other parts of the country." Lloyd G. Reynolds, *Labor Economics and Labor Relations* (New York: Prentice-Hall, 1949), pp. 332–333.

[23] Indeed, many wage theorists base their analysis of the forces determining wage levels on the assumption that the population, and hence labor supply, of a given market area is fixed. Hicks, *op. cit.*, pp. 2–3. This, however, should not be construed to mean that these writers believe that population changes can be neglected altogether.

tion of physical resources. If the materials going into the manufacture of a commodity are bulkier or more costly to ship than is the product after processing, net costs of transportation will be lower if the industry locates close to resource supplies rather than to selling markets. The locations of blast furnaces and cotton gin mills, to name but two contrasting examples, clearly reflect the importance of this factor. Since wage levels in some industries are definitely higher than in others, it follows that the location of resources goes a long way toward explaining variations in the wage levels of different areas.[24]

LABOR AND OTHER COSTS

In highly developed economies, proximity to abundant natural resources is only one of many influences on the side of production affecting the location and growth of industries, and hence relative wage levels, in different communities. Costs of processing may be favorable or unfavorable, depending on the proximity of parts manufactures or of material supplies from an earlier stage of production. Once a major industry like the production of automobiles becomes concentrated in a certain area, satellite industries grow up in the same vicinity, making it all the more difficult for new centers in the industry to be developed. The distribution of labor, especially in the more skilled categories, also tends to favor the concentration and growth of different industries in different areas. Adequate supplies of labor in the amount and quality required for efficient production draw new firms to the area and so foster further expansion. Still more workers may then be drawn to the community as expansion proceeds, augmenting the supply of labor on which employers can draw. So long as conditions of market demand permit continued growth, the influx of workers, if and when it occurs, helps to hold down costs and to carry the expansion even further. Employers in other communities, on the other hand, which lack the necessary types of labor, operate at an increasing disadvantage with respect to labor costs. Unless offset by other influences, it follows that wages in the first community will tend to rise above those in the second.

There are still other sources of processing cost differences which affect the location and relative growth rates of industries in different areas. Adequate managerial talent may be more available in some localities than in others. Costs of borrowing or of attracting risk capital may differ. Monopolistic practices, blocking the entrance of new firms or the development of new production methods, may be more prevalent in some communities than in others. As discussed in greater detail below,

---

[24] Edgar M. Hoover, *The Location of Economic Activity* (New York: McGraw-Hill, 1948), pp. 31–35.

differences in the age and efficiency of mechanical equipment may cause cost levels to be lower in some areas than in others.[25] Some of these cost influences are the result of deep-seated differences among areas and are therefore subject to little change, but others are related to variable conditions and hence may lead to shifts in comparative wage levels. Cost reductions may also occur in some industries and not in others, within the same community, thus setting in motion forces which can lead to shifts in relative wage levels among the industries of a single area.

CAPITAL EQUIPMENT AND INVESTMENT

Influences on costs stem from many sources but perhaps the most important grow out of differences in the amount of capital per worker. Other things being equal, it is generally assumed that where the capital/worker ratios are high compared to other industries and areas, pay levels also tend to be high, since under these conditions labor is the relatively scarce factor and its marginal productivity is greater. Because other environmental factors are less likely to intervene, the effects of differing capital/worker ratios on wage levels are more easily measured in industries within a given locality than in industries in different localities. Studies of this problem on an interarea basis have yielded no clear results. In his investigations of North-South wage differentials, for example, Professor Lester uncovered little evidence to support the position that the differentials are due to a deficiency in capital equipment per worker in the South. Indeed, he found that in such industries as furniture, hosiery, cotton textiles, pulp and paper, and rubber, southern plants are newer and more modern than in the North, whereas in manufacturing generally the amount of electric energy used per man-hour has also been definitely higher in this region.[26] His findings, however, do not contradict the generalization that wages tend to be lower in areas where labor is relatively abundant. The predominant view still held by economists is that, other things being equal, industries or areas with high capital/labor ratios also tend to pay high wages.

This factor may not only underlie long-standing differences in wage levels but it may also have an important bearing on changes in wage levels. Industries like petroleum refining have been characterized by

---

[25] For a more detailed discussion of interarea cost differences as they affect the comparative rate of growth of different regions and localities, see Glenn E. McLaughlin, *Growth of American Manufacturing Areas* (Pittsburgh: University of Pittsburgh, 1938), pp. 238–249, and Philip Neff, Lisette C. Baum, and Grace E. Heilman, *Production Cost Trends in Selected Industrial Areas* (Berkeley and Los Angeles: University of California Press, 1948), chaps. ii-iv.

[26] The results of his studies are summarized in Richard A. Lester, "Southern Wage Differentials: Developments, Analysis, and Implications," *Southern Economic Journal*, XIII (April, 1947), 386–394.

high capital/worker ratios from their inception, whereas capital/worker ratios in many of the personal service trades have always been low. At the same time, technological advances occur at uneven rates, and cost reduction from greater use of capital equipment may be much greater in some industries or areas than in others. The rayon industry, in contrast to other branches of the textile field, affords a striking example of this fact, and a comparison of wage movements in this industry over the past twenty-five years bears testimony to its significance for comparative wage analysis. The effects of greater capital utilization on wage rate differentials are closely related to relative growth rates, as measured by data on output and employment. The two influences work together, serving to reinforce each other, and both exert a direct effect on the level of demand and hence on the level of wages paid for labor. A rise in output marked by a greater use of capital per worker is likely to be carried further than where there is no change in the capital/labor ratio, and a greater rise in the wage level is therefore likely to occur.

Underlying the foregoing discussion is the assumption that an increase in the amount of capital equipment per worker will be associated with an increase in demand for the services of labor. In any given situation, economists have long recognized, this is not invariably true, since capital can be a substitute for labor as well as complementary. Where substitution occurs, demand for the particular type of labor involved, at least in the short run, may actually fall rather than rise.[27] Alternatively, with increased mechanization there may be such a dilution of skills that even though total employment rises, the general level of wages declines. It is also easy to exaggerate the differential effects on industry and area wage levels which result from additions to capital. There are both institutional and economic influences, some of which have already been discussed, which serve to keep wage movements uniform. It is especially important to remember that greater capital investment in any one field or area has widely stimulating effects elsewhere. Additions to plant and equipment provide markets for a variety of goods and services, and because of the large outlays which are usually involved, substantial increases in employment follow. As jobs multiply, spending for consumers' goods also rises, and a further broadening of the expansion is likely to get under way. By the same token, the general level of output will rise, causing real wages to increase in all or almost all industries in the area and related areas. In view of these considerations it is

---

[27] In a lengthy discussion of this issue, Pigou concludes: "In other words, the relation between capital as a whole and labour as a whole is predominantly one of co-operation." He notes, however, in particular instances that "... the relation is predominantly one of rivalry." A. C. Pigou, *The Economics of Welfare* (London: Macmillan, 1932), p. 662.

hardly to be expected that additions to capital will always have differential effects on industry and area wage levels.

PRODUCT DEMAND AND MARKETS

Reference has already been made to influences operating on wage levels from the side of demand. Here, as in the case of processing costs, a multiplicity of factors is involved, but the one usually accorded most prominence is the influence exerted by varying rates of change in product demand. Employers in industries and areas in which demand for products is rising rapidly not only are able to offer increased wages but, in order to attract or hold workers, they are put under heavy pressure to do so; whereas employers faced with falling demand are likely to have neither the ability nor the incentive to raise pay levels. In some situations, especially within a given locality, nearly all employers are confronted with a more or less uniform rise in product demand, but more typically there are differences in rates of increase and they may well be large enough to have differential effects on interindustry wage levels. This also holds true among areas, differences in rates of expansion in "old" as against "new" communities being especially marked. In this connection comparative population trends may be an important influence although they are perhaps as much an effect as a cause of varying rates of economic growth.[28]

The geographical scope of product markets is another circumstance affecting wage levels. The wider the geographical area served by an industry, other considerations aside, the higher the wage level tends to be. Similarly, the broader the market area served by employers in a given community, the higher wages in the locality tend to be in relation to other communities. Of course, it is not geographical scope as such, but sales volume which is the important consideration. Nevertheless, firms with the largest sales volume are concentrated in industries selling in national markets, and employers in these industries are more likely to pay high wages than firms limited to narrow selling areas. This distinction applies with special force to situations where employers, having previously sold in a local market only, are able to tap national markets, or where a new product is introduced which sells in all parts of the country. Sometimes, as with new products, national status can be gained quickly, but more often some time is required before this can be achieved. In long-established industries, product market areas are sub-

---

[28] The contrasting effects of a rising population on wage levels are shown in the experience of the southeastern and western parts of the country. In the latter case the environment was such as to make the gains in population a favorable development from the viewpoint of improved wage standards, whereas in the former case the reverse held true.

ject to little change, at least over short periods, and to the extent this is true, any wage differences due to this factor do not vary much over time.

To the degree that sales volume per firm is related to the geographical scope of markets, costs of production are likely to be lower in companies selling in national markets than in local markets. Compared to the latter, employers serving broad market areas are more likely to secure the advantages of large-scale production and highly mechanized processes. In fact, one of the essential conditions underlying the extensive use of mass-production techniques is the development of market areas broad enough to absorb a much enlarged volume of output. This would not be true if the number of firms were large, if they were typically small in size, and if competitive rivalry were keen. In clothing manufacturing, for example, product market areas are broad but firms tend to be small. More frequently, however, employers selling in national markets are few in number and large in size, with sales volume per worker or per firm correspondingly high. Under these circumstances influences both on the side of product demand and production costs foster relatively high wage scales.

A number of studies show how factors related to product demand and production costs combine to explain wage level differences among firms and industries in a given area. In their study of industry wage levels in two medium-sized Massachusetts cities, Maclaurin and Myers found a distinct correlation between wage rate levels and degree of product market competition. At the top of the scale were paper manufacture and machinery, the industries with the largest capital investment and the lowest proportion of wages to total costs. Near the bottom were plastics, converted paper products, and shoe and leather products, all industries in which price competition was keen. As to differences in the wage levels of firms within the same industry, the investigation stressed the importance of differences in size of firm and in the wage-paying capacity of individual employers.[29]

In a study of twenty-eight companies in a New England factory city, mostly metalworking firms, Reynolds concluded that the following circumstances were of chief importance in explaining differences in plant wage levels: nature of the industry; intensity of product competition and wages paid by rival producers; nature of the work and kind of labor force required; presence or absence of unionism; efficiency of plant and equipment; and, in some cases, differences in the efficiency of management.[30] It is the particular combination of factors such as

---

[29] Maclaurin and Myers, *op. cit.*, pp. 253–257.

[30] Reynolds, *The Structure of Labor Markets* (New York: Harper, 1951), p. 187.

these which in any given situation determines the relative wage standing of a firm, industry, and/or area.

DISTRIBUTION OF PRODUCTIVE GAINS

The discussion of comparative wage behavior has thus far been focused on conditions affecting the general level of production and employment in different industries and areas. The factors reviewed above determine the gains in aggregate output out of which higher wages may come. To what extent additions to output are in fact distributed to workers or inure to the benefit of other claimants is another question. Alternatively to higher wages, gains may be taken by buyers of the product through lowered prices or improved quality, by suppliers of materials and other nonlabor agents through increased factor prices, or, finally, by the owners of firms through increased profits. Thus, in considering the relation between increases in capital per worker and living standards, economists stress the advantages of distributing the benefits of more efficient production through lower prices and/or improved quality, which in turn will mean higher real incomes for all consumers.[31] Present-day economists are generally agreed that market conditions fall well short of this ideal, but few would deny that cost savings have important effects on prices and real incomes of consumers.

In dealing with the question of distribution, economists have applied the same principles of supply-and-demand analysis as were summarized above. According to static analysis, demand relative to supply may be much more favorable in the short run for one claimant than for others, and if so, its relative share will tend to rise. Where there is active competition among firms (i.e., "large numbers" and easy entry into the industry), buyers of the product stand to gain through lowered prices. Where there is a monopoly, the benefits are likely to go to owners through higher profits. Similarly, if labor is sold on a noncompetitive basis, as it may be where workers are organized in unions or where supply consists of a small but essential craft, gains tend to be distributed through higher wage rates. Finally, certain nonlabor factors, such as raw material supplies, may be sold on a noncompetitive basis, and if so, any productive gains are likely to be captured by these groups.

These findings are somewhat modified, however, by dynamic analysis. Indeed, in a given situation, these distinctions are usually blurred, the relationships among the four claimants exhibiting a variety of combinations. At a given time, one group may appear to have a distinct advan-

---

[31] Pigou, *op. cit.*, pp. 671–680. For a more recent formulation of this same point of view, see Committee for Economic Development, *How to Raise Real Wages, A Statement on National Policy* (New York: 1950).

tage over the other three, but perhaps the more typical situation is one in which two or more of the groups are gaining the lion's share. In the long run, the view of classical economists was that increases in output resulted in lower prices or improved quality so that the principal bene-ficiaries were the consumer group.[32] This view rested on the assumption that competitive influences could be counted on to erase any inordinate gains received by owners, workers, or suppliers. The modern view is that this assumption is unwarranted, and that particular producer groups may enjoy monopoly gains indefinitely.[33] The extent to which the various producer groups can dam up competitive pressures varies markedly, industry to industry, so that this factor has an important bearing on interindustry wage relationships. In the main, however, the forces controlling the distribution of income operate on a broad national scale and so are rather difficult to study on the local community level.

Union and Employer Organizations

Contrary to the analysis presented here, recent discussions of wage rate phenomena have often focused on market control policies of union and employer organizations. This was a natural outgrowth of the spread of unionization, on the one hand, and the development of restraints on competition among employers, on the other. In fact, in no small measure, the impact of union and employer organizations on wage levels can be explained in terms of various noncompetitive models ranging from bilateral monopoly to different types of oligopolies. It would be a gross oversimplification, however, to conclude that the wage rate effects of organizational controls can be neatly subsumed under a branch of economic theory, even of the most sophisticated variety. Union and employer groups, as recent investigations bring out, are not simply

[32] Alfred Marshall put the distinction between short-period analysis, in which bar-gaining power considerations are important, and long-period analysis, in which the marginal contributions of the factors of production are controlling, in these terms: "And indeed the theory of wages ... has no direct bearing on the issue of any partic-ular struggle in the labour market: that depends on the relative strength of the com-peting parties. But it has much bearing on the general policy of the relation of capital to labour; for it indicates what policies do, and what do not, carry in themselves the seeds of their own ultimate defeat; what policies can be maintained, aided by suitable organizations; and what policies will ultimately render either side weak, however well organized." Alfred Marshall, *Principles of Economics* (8th ed.; London: Macmil-lan, 1920), App. J, p. 825.

[33] Garbarino's study of the country's interindustry wage structure revealed a high correlation between degree of concentration in output and relative wage gains. He reasoned that these industries tend to receive "monopoly" profits, but the combined effect of union pressure, government policies, and public opinion has resulted in the distribution of these gains in the form of higher wages. Joseph W. Garbarino, "A Theory of Interindustry Wage Structure Variation," *Quarterly Journal of Economics*, LXIV (May, 1950), 299–300.

economic mechanisms operating in different market situations. They are subject to a variety of institutional pressures which are as much political as economic in character.[34] Especially in the case of trade unions, questions of organizing strategy, bargaining status, membership reactions, and power drives of rival leaders may dominate negotiations over wage settlements. Under these circumstances survival requirements of an organization may compel wage settlements which cannot be defended on strictly economic grounds. Wage rates may be pushed up to "uneconomic" levels in order to retain member acceptance. Wages may be tied to settlements in other companies or industries, not because of any economic logic, but because of internal or external union rivalries. Although less compelling, it seems safe to assume that similar considerations operate on the side of employer groups as well. The upshot is that interindustry and interarea wage phenomena are the result of a wide variety of influences, only some of which are economic in origin.[35]

These observations should help to dispel the notion, which may have been derived from the rest of the discussion, that wage rates are subject to widely divergent forces in differing industries and areas. Since wage differentials constitute the subject of the present study, this impression was hard to avoid. The truth is that wages in different fields are held together by a host of circumstances, of which interorganizational ties are only one. Increasingly in our society, worker and employer groups confront common conditions and common problems. Swings in prices, production, and employment affect all sectors of the economy and induce much the same response in all parts of the country. Variations in wage rate behavior only occur within narrow limits, cohesion rather than separatism being the dominant characteristic of our economic and social system.

Although the spread of trade unionism has helped to tie wage levels more closely together, it is an open question whether unions have had much effect on relative wage levels. Studies of individual industries or areas almost invariably show that the highest-paying firms are unionized or that the high-wage employers are paying above average rates to forestall unionization. But how much of the difference, if any, can be

---

[34] Arthur M. Ross, "Trade Unions as Wage-Fixing Institutions," *American Economic Review*, XXXVII (September, 1947), 566–588. In evaluating Ross's findings, it should be remembered that he was dealing with an inflationary period.

[35] On the other hand, in weighing the relative importance of economic influences on a local labor market, Myers and Shultz conclude: "Yet a sober reconsideration shows that economic analysis has much to contribute in explaining the behavior we have observed in this community. As job opportunities changed, workers, employers, and unions acted in ways that are consistent with the market analysis developed by economists." Charles A. Myers and George P. Shultz, *The Dynamics of a Labor Market* (New York: Prentice-Hall, 1951), p. 204.

attributed to the fact of unionization? Other factors, such as size of firm, plant location, or productive efficiency, may be far more important in explaining the disparity in wage levels. Studies of interindustry wage movements on a nation-wide basis are hardly more conclusive. One approach is to group industries by degree of unionization and compare changes in the earnings of the various groups over a period of time. Differences within each group, however, are likely to be so great as to nullify the results.[36] After carefully reviewing national wage data for manufacturing, Ross and Goldner concluded that between 1933 and 1946 wages in newly organized industries rose more in absolute terms than in unorganized industries, but that wages in industries that were already organized in 1933 lagged behind. As they put it, "... the question of how continuing unionism affects wages is in a rather confused condition, there being no way to disentangle the effect of unionism from the other influences which control relative wage movements."[37]

CONCLUSION

The foregoing analysis has by no means touched on all the influences bearing on community wage levels and wage structures, the objective being only to single out those factors which economists have emphasized most. Even so, the discussion has dealt with a rather bewildering variety of issues which it will be useful to summarize here. The various influences bearing on a community's wage level and interindustry wage structure can be thought of as assuming highly favorable or unfavorable combinations. An "ideal" environment would in the main consist of the following elements: (1) rich, readily accessible natural resources, (2) cheap, efficient transportation facilities, (3) a large, well-trained labor force, (4) plentiful supplies of savings and credit, (5) a rapid and sustained growth in investment in new plant and machinery, (6) prevalence of industries with high labor skill mix and large amounts of capital equipment per worker, (7) continued rapid expansion in markets for consumers' and producers' goods, (8) a strong, enlightened trade union movement, and (9) large-scale business enterprises under skilled, forward-looking managements.

In a community enjoying all these advantages, demand for a wide range of labor skills would be continuously rising, and the value of labor's hourly output would be steadily increasing. At the same time, the existence of strong unions and vigorous business enterprises, both under progressive, broad-gauged leadership, would keep wages in line with the mounting volume of output without destroying incentives to

---

[36] Garbarino, *op. cit.,* pp. 287–290.

[37] Arthur M. Ross and William Goldner, "Forces Affecting the Interindustry Wage Structure," *Quarterly Journal of Economics,* LXIV (May, 1950), 269.

expand production still further. At the other extreme, it is possible to conceive of a community in which these factors would be uniformly unfavorable to high wage standards. Classical economists emphasized that, as between two such localities, forces would be set in motion which would tend to equalize the "net economic advantages" of employment in the two places. On similar reasoning, an area which possessed a relative abundance of labor and a relative deficiency of capital would experience an outmigration of workers and an inmigration of capital until rewards in this and other areas were equalized.

Although not denying that movements of labor and capital exert a certain leveling influence, the modern view is that barriers to mobility make this a long-term tendency at most. In explaining wage relationships among areas, present-day economists place greater emphasis on (1) the pervasive influence of changes in economic conditions in the country as a whole, (2) the force of custom, and (3) the spread of administered wage-price policies attendant on the growth of national unions and the rise of giant business organizations. In such an environment, absolute differences in pay levels may persist indefinitely which in a perfectly competitive system would necessarily be ironed out. Similarly, wage changes in two areas may be kept uniform, even though, from a strictly economic point of view, market conditions would appear to justify differential adjustments. Although the foregoing pertains especially to separate localities, it is also applicable with certain modifications to wage relationships between industries and jobs within a given community.

The general aim of this investigation is to examine the wage structure and wage behavior of particular communities, with special reference to Los Angeles County, in the perspective of these concepts and findings. It can be taken for granted that in concrete situations both favorable and unfavorable wage factors will be found to exist, just as it may be assumed that influences making for both similarities and differences in relation to wage movements elsewhere will also be discovered. The pages which follow bear the imprint of these crosscurrents and conflicting tendencies, but certain broad relationships nonetheless emerge. Succeeding chapters provide a general review of wage changes in the Los Angeles area, followed by an analysis of the relation between wages on the one hand, and product markets, employment, investment, productivity, and unionization in selected communities on the other. A brief chapter summarizing the principal findings concludes the study.

II. LOS ANGELES WAGE LEVEL: PRE-1940

IN INTERPRETING wage changes in a particular community, it is appropriate to consider first the long-term trend in the area's general wage level. This involves combining hourly earnings data from a variety of industries in a single figure and analyzing the results over a period of time and in relation to general wage movements in other communities. The preceding chapter pointed out the pitfalls in such a procedure, and all the strictures noted earlier need not be repeated here. Special mention, however, should be made of the significance of comparisons with national wage data since this method of analysis is employed at a number of points in the study. The figures for the country as a whole, being a composite of wage reports from many localities, can only be used to measure the trend in wages in the most general sense. Thus, although comparisons of the wage level of a·particular community, or even of a particular industry within a community, with the national average at a given point of time have little or no meaning, such comparisons can be useful in bringing out *changes* in comparative wage levels over a period of time. But again, the reader is cautioned that an analysis of this type does not yield precise conclusions, only measures of general tendencies and relationships.

The area chosen for study, Los Angeles County, is different in many ways from almost every other community in the country.[1] In terms of population growth alone, its record is unique. Between 1890 and 1920 it grew from a community of about 100,000 to 1,000,000 inhabitants, and by 1950 it had risen to over 4,000,000, the fourth largest metropolis in the United States. Although much greater in some periods than others, the percentage gain in the area's population has been well above the rest of the country in every decade since 1870 (table 1). Other characteristics of the area, including its climate, geographical location, and physical resources, have been no less important in giving this locality its distinctive character. Accordingly, it may be assumed that the wage structure of Los Angeles will exhibit certain unusual features and that any generalizations about its wages will not be directly applicable to other areas. On the other hand, the very fact that Los Angeles has grown so fast and has followed a pattern rather different from most other communities will make it all the easier to identify the circumstances which control wages in this market. Although Los Angeles is an extreme case, the difference between its economic and social development and that of most other large urban centers is, after all, one of degree and not of kind.

---

[1] Throughout this study, unless otherwise noted, Los Angeles will be assumed to mean Los Angeles County. The latter is an area of about 4,000 square miles.

This community has compressed into a relatively short period economic and social changes which elsewhere have taken much longer periods to work out. Thus, McLaughlin reports that in a period of about fifty years Los Angeles passed through the stages of economic development that required one hundred and fifty years for New York City.[2] With judicious handling, this contrast in environment can be turned into an advantage, rather than a disadvantage, in explaining the area's wage history.

TABLE 1

POPULATION OF LOS ANGELES COUNTY AND UNITED STATES, 1870–1950

| Year | Los Angeles County | | United States | |
	Population	Per cent change over previous 10 years	Population	Per cent change over previous 10 years
1870...........	12,394	.....	39,818,449	....
1880...........	27,025	118.0	50,155,783	26.0
1890...........	101,454	275.4	62,947,714	25.5
1900...........	170,298	67.9	75,994,575	20.7
1910...........	504,131	196.0	91,972,266	21.0
1920...........	936,455	85.8	105,710,620	14.9
1930...........	2,208,492	135.8	122,775,046	16.1
1940...........	2,785,643	26.1	131,669,275	7.2
1950...........	4,125,164	48.1	150,697,361	14.5

SOURCES: Glenn E. McLaughlin, *Growth of American Manufacturing Areas* (Pittsburgh: 1938), p. 51. Sixteenth Census of the United States, 1940, *Population*, Vol. II, pt. I, pp. 19, 547.
    U. S. Dept. of Commerce, *1950 Census of Population, Preliminary Counts*, Series PC-3, no. 4, p. 2 and Series PC-9, no. 1, p. 2.

Before attention is turned to wage trends in this community, some further observations about the development of the area are in order. Accompanying its prodigious increase in population since the 1870's, most of which, of course, was due to heavy inmigration, economic activity in the locality expanded on a broad front. Construction, home furnishings, food processing, wholesale and retail trade, and personal services were some of the industries most directly affected, but a larger number of other fields, especially in light manufacturing, grew almost as rapidly. As a consequence, there was a mounting demand for a variety of labor skills, job opportunities in most lines generally keeping well abreast of the rise in labor supply.

At least before World War II, Los Angeles was not heavily industrialized; the 1940 census showed a lower proportion of its total employment in manufacturing than in the country at large. By the same token, it had

[2] Glenn E. McLaughlin, *Growth of American Manufacturing Areas* (Pittsburgh: University of Pittsburgh, 1938), p. 205.

a greater concentration of employment in such fields as construction, finance, business and repair services, and amusements. Comparisons with other communities of similar size, like Chicago, Pittsburgh, Cleveland, and Detroit, reveal these same contrasts even more sharply.[3] Within manufacturing, firms in Los Angeles were predominantly small in 1940, especially in relation to major industrial centers in the East. In output of nondurable manufactures, it stood among the highest at this time, but as a producer of durables it was well down in the list of the nation's major industrial centers.[4] The heavy, mass-production fields, such as steel, automobiles, and electrical equipment, were not important influences in prewar Los Angeles, and even a number of light manufactures, like leather, textiles, and clothing, were almost wholly undeveloped. In contrast to many cities in which a high degree of specialization in particular manufacturing fields had been achieved, activity in this community was scattered among many different industries serving the consumption requirements of a rapidly growing population.

Geographical location and other physical characteristics of the area have been most important in shaping the Los Angeles economy. Before World War II, most of its employers could not hope to compete with more centrally located producers for the major markets in the Middle West and East. At the same time, the very fact of remoteness made Los Angeles the natural center for the new and growing trading area of southern California and the Southwest. As settlement of this region proceeded, more large-scale operations became possible, but most of the community's economic activity remained centered in consumer-oriented industries. Even in this early period, a few local industries achieved nation-wide standing, notably motion pictures, petroleum refining, and certain food-processing lines, but in every instance special environmental factors, such as advantages of climate or the presence of an abundant natural resource, were responsible for the result. Not until the wartime expansion of the 'forties were many mass-production industries, serving broad product markets, established in Los Angeles. Though less serious than expected, it was in these fields that the most acute economic difficulties occurred in the postwar period.

Much of the Los Angeles experience with respect to wage changes, as well as many other phases of its economic development, can be attributed to the fact that it was only recently an economically young community in which labor commanded premium prices and in which the

[3] Philip Neff and Annette Weifenbach, *Business Cycles in Selected Industrial Areas* (Berkeley and Los Angeles: University of California Press, 1949), pp. 21–22.

[4] Philip Neff, Lisette C. Baum, and Grace E. Heilman, *Production Cost Trends in Selected Industrial Areas* (Berkeley and Los Angeles: University of California Press, 1948), pp. 21–22.

risks and rewards of business enterprise were high. Because of the speed with which the area was developed, these influences were still very much in evidence even when the city had become a major metropolis. Similarly, business practice in the field of labor relations, as in other spheres, continued to be highly individualistic at a time when other communities like San Francisco, only five hundred miles to the north, had moved in a quite different direction. The independent attitude of employers was all the more easily retained because of the community's rapid growth, just as the "booster" spirit was a natural concomitant of the area's phenomenal economic expansion.

WAGES IN THE LOS ANGELES AREA

From this thumbnail sketch of the Los Angeles area it is evident that any analysis of the local wage structure must distinguish sharply between the periods before and after World War II. Hence, the year 1940 serves as a convenient dividing line for this investigation. In that year the general level of hourly earnings, in money terms, was definitely higher in this community than in the country as a whole. Thus, hourly earnings in Los Angeles manufacturing averaged about $.74 in 1940 against a national average of approximately $.66 per hour. The discrepancy in favor of Los Angeles was much greater in the case of nondurables ($.72 vs. $.60 per hour) than in the case of durable manufactures ($.75 vs. $.72 per hour), but the differential was apparent in almost all branches of factory work. Likewise, in the few industries in nonmanufacturing for which data are available, Los Angeles wages in 1940 were somewhat above national averages. This was true of the laundering, cleaning, and dyeing industry as well as of wholesale trade, retail trade, hotels, and the production of crude petroleum, though in all but the last industry the difference did not exceed $.05 per hour.[5]

Relative, however, to many communities of comparable or even smaller size, Los Angeles wages in 1940 were low. Earnings in San Francisco, for example, were markedly higher at this time, averaging $.82 per hour in manufacturing as against $.74 in Los Angeles. The differential between the two cities was twice as great for durable as for nondurable manufacturing ($.12 as against $.06 per hour), the relationship one would expect to find in view of the relatively high wage rates paid in

---

[5] In the following discussion, these four industries (excluding crude petroleum) are referred to as consumer services. The data on 1940 earnings are taken from California State Department of Industrial Relations, Division of Labor Statistics and Research (hereinafter referred to as Calif. State Dept. of Indus. Relations), *Labor in California, 1945–1946* (San Francisco: 1947), p. 44, and United States Department of Labor, Bureau of Labor Statistics (hereinafter referred to as U. S. Bureau of Labor Statistics), *Handbook of Labor Statistics*, Bull. no. 916 (Washington: Government Printing Office, 1947 ed.), p. 54.

Los Angeles in the nondurable field. In four nonmanufacturing trades
for which data are available, San Francisco earnings exceeded those in
Los Angeles by a substantially greater margin than in manufacturing.
Of the four—wholesale trade, retail trade, hotels, and laundering, cleaning, and dyeing—the smallest differential ($.09 per hour) existed in the
first field and the largest ($.15 per hour) existed in the last.[6]

Wage rate index

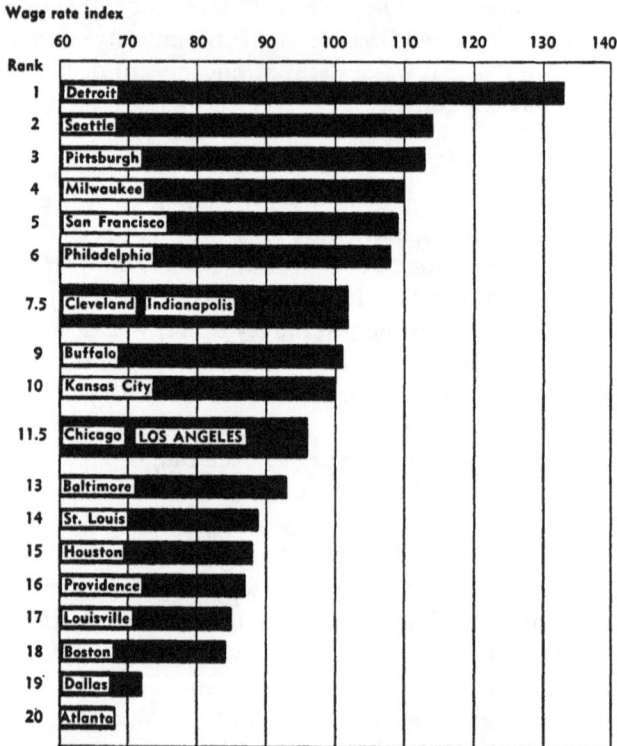

Fig. 1. Ranking of manufacturing wage rate indexes, Los Angeles County and nineteen
urban areas, January, 1941.

SOURCE: Appendix table 1.

Hourly earnings comparisons with other urban centers for 1940 are
not possible because of lack of information, but figures on rates, as contrasted with earnings, show that Los Angeles was well below pay levels
prevailing in a number of other cities. In January, 1941, a study of
manufacturing rates in twenty urban areas ranked Los Angeles 11.5
from the top, with an index of 96 compared to an average of 100 for the
entire group. The results of this investigation are summarized in the
accompanying chart (fig. 1).

_____
[6] Calif. State Dept. of Indus. Relations, *op. cit.*, p. 50.

LONG-TERM TRENDS

The foregoing evidence demonstrates that in 1940, just before war defense preparations revolutionized labor conditions both locally and nationally, wages in Los Angeles were above levels prevailing nationally but well below wages being paid in the highest-wage centers. Some of the circumstances leading to this result become evident when long-term trends in interarea wage relationships are explored.

AVERAGE ANNUAL EARNINGS

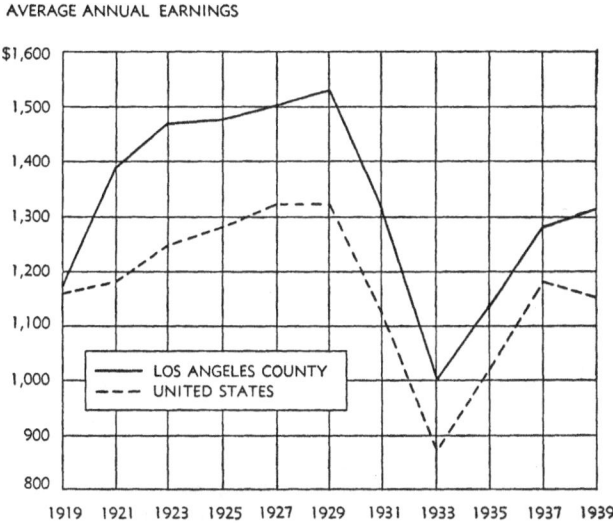

Fig. 2. Average annual earnings of production workers in manufacturing, Los Angeles County and United States, 1919–1939. *Note:* Before 1929, figures include Los Angeles City only. After 1929, motion picture industry excluded from manufacturing category.

SOURCE: Appendix table 2.

Data on annual earnings in manufacturing, which are available by individual cities back to 1919, present much the same picture as the figures on hourly earnings for 1940. As shown in figure 2, annual earnings per worker in manufacturing were consistently higher in Los Angeles than in the country at large between 1919 and 1939, the differential generally ranging between $100 and $200 per year. The margin in favor of Los Angeles widened somewhat during the early part of the 'twenties but narrowed again during the 'thirties. For the entire twenty-year period, however, no well-defined trend, either up or down, is indicated.

The data for Los Angeles become more meaningful when related to the level of annual earnings in other urban centers; comparisons with six major communities (Buffalo, Chicago, Cleveland, Detroit, New York, and San Francisco) are therefore shown in figure 3. Among these cities

AVERAGE ANNUAL EARNINGS

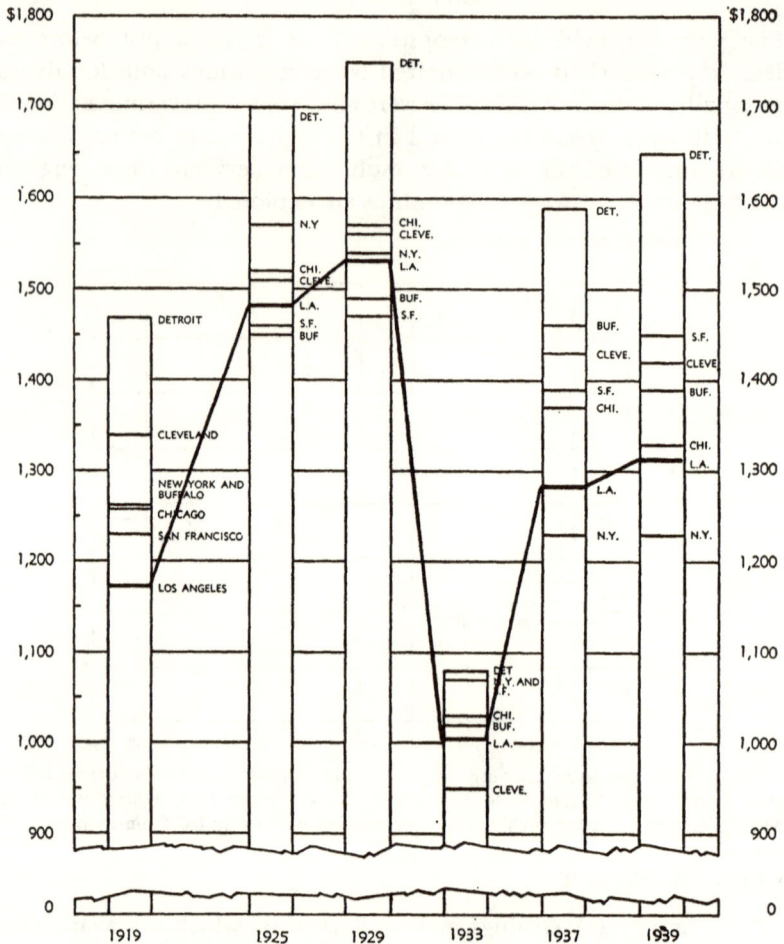

Fig. 3. Average annual earnings of production workers in manufacturing, Los Angeles County and six industrial areas, selected years, 1919–1939. *Note:* Before 1929, figures include cities only.

SOURCE: Appendix table 2.

Los Angeles typically stood second or third from the bottom during this period, registering slight relative gains in the early 'twenties and again after 1929. In the latter part of the 'twenties, however, Detroit, New York, Cleveland, and Chicago stood well above Los Angeles, the latter about equaling San Francisco and Buffalo. After 1929 the annual wage levels of these cities were brought much closer together. Detroit and New York dropped to about the same level as San Francisco; Cleveland now stood lowest; and Chicago, Buffalo, and Los Angeles occupied a middle zone position. In the latter half of the 'thirties, the spread in annual earnings widened again; by 1939 the top four positions were occupied by Detroit, San Francisco, Cleveland, and Buffalo in that order, with New York now lowest in the rankings and Los Angeles and Chicago in the next-to-bottom positions.

Conclusions based on annual earnings cannot be applied directly to hourly earnings, the nature of the two series being quite different. It is evident, however, that the annual earnings comparisons for the period 1919–1939 and the hourly earnings comparisons for 1940 yield consistent conclusions.[7] It therefore seems reasonable to conclude, first, that the findings would not have been much different if hourly figures had been available for the longer period and, second, that although there were some short-term fluctuations in the relative wage level of this community, its position did not vary markedly between the two wars. Such information as can be obtained on hourly wages corroborates these findings, but the data are based on broad regional comparisons and so have only an indirect bearing on the issues considered here. A careful study of wage differentials in manufacturing compares job rates in the Northeast, South, Middle West, and Far West for four periods, 1907, 1919, 1931–1932, and 1945–1946. The major conclusions are: (1) the Far West was much higher than any of the other three regions throughout these years; (2) between 1907 and 1919 there was a substantial reduction in the position of this region relative to the other areas; and (3) between 1919 and 1945–1946 its relative position remained pretty much unchanged. These relationships are set forth in figure 4.

As this figure shows, the Far West enjoyed an average wage differential over the Northeast and Middle West of 30 per cent in 1907; by 1919 the differential had dropped to 15 per cent and 19 per cent respectively, but between 1919 and 1946 there was little further narrowing in rate relationships. The figures reflect a similar decline in the hourly wage advantage enjoyed by the Far West compared to the South over the period 1907–1919; by 1932, however, the gap between these two regions broadened again, only to narrow once more by 1946.

Judging from this evidence, once the general wage level of a given community or region is established, there is every likelihood that its relative position, vis-à-vis other parts of the country, will remain unchanged over long periods of time. Three possible lines of explanation

---

[7] That broad industry-area comparisons based on annual earnings and hourly earnings will yield similar conclusions is corroborated by a correlation analysis of wage data pertaining to the country as a whole as well as to Los Angeles. An analysis of annual earnings and hourly earnings in eighteen United States manufacturing industries in 1947 yielded a rank correlation value of 0.942. A similar analysis of fourteen Los Angeles manufacturing industries based on average annual earnings in 1937 and average hourly earnings in 1940 yielded a rank correlation value of 0.954.

are suggested by this result: (1) that interarea wage relationships are largely based on deep-seated differences in economic conditions which change little, if at all, over time; (2) that relative pay levels are largely controlled by habit, custom, or so-called institutional factors which also are subject to little variation one year to the next; or (3) that for Los Angeles the expansion of markets and the inflow of capital were great enough to keep wages at the same level in relation to other communities that had obtained when it was a frontier town. Whatever the explana-

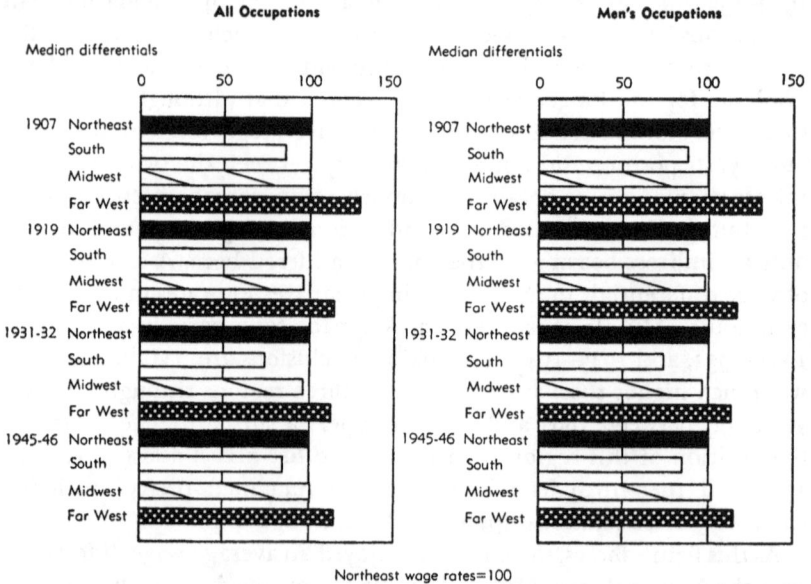

Fig. 4. Regional differences in job rates in manufacturing, United States, selected years, 1907–1946.
SOURCE: U. S. Bureau of Labor Statistics, *Monthly Labor Review*, 66 (April, 1948), 375.

tion, it is clear that the forces controlling the general wage level of a community are related to more or less permanent environmental conditions, and that alterations in a community's wage level only come as the result of far-reaching changes in economic and/or social relationships.

LONG-TERM INFLUENCES

One of the environmental influences which had lasting effects on the comparative wage level of Los Angeles was the severe scarcity of labor characteristic of its early settlement. The "frontier phase" of this community's history can be said to have continued at least until the 1880's, and the facts show that many types of labor commanded premium rates at this time. The earliest statistical comparison obtainable was for the year 1885, and unfortunately it combined data for both northern and southern California. This report, given in table 2, reveals that wages in California were definitely higher than in New York and Pennsylvania for most of the jobs shown. After an intensive study of early labor conditions in Los Angeles, however, one writer concludes that there can be

TABLE 2

DAILY AND WEEKLY WAGES IN CALIFORNIA, NEW YORK, AND PENNSYLVANIA, 1885

Occupation	Wages		
	California	New York	Pennsylvania
	Daily		
Cabinetmaker.................	$2.50–3.00	$2.50	$1.67–3.00
Upholsterer.................	3.00–5.00	2.95	2.25
Millwright.................	3.50	3.00	2.50
	Weekly		
Bricklayer...................	$30.00	$20.00	
Mason.....................	30.00	18.00	
Plasterer...................	30.00	18.00	
Plumber...................	24.00	16.00	
Carpenter...................	24.00	14.00	
Baker......................	18.00	7.00	
Brewer....................	12.50	5.00	
Cooper....................	21.00	12.00	
Teamster..................	15.00	10.00	
Printer....................	12.50–30.00	13.00	
Tailor....................	20.00	7.00–12.00	

SOURCE: *Third Biennial Report, California Bureau of Labor Statistics, 1887–1888* (Sacramento: 1888), pp. 139–144, in Grace E. Heilman, "Early History of the Labor Movement in Los Angeles" (Ph.D. dissertation, University of Pennsylvania, 1949), p. 94.

no doubt that before 1880 wages in both northern and southern California were high when judged by eastern standards.[8] Once established, this wage position was to be maintained with surprisingly little change over the succeeding decades.

With the passing of frontier conditions, counter influences tending to bring local wages more nearly in line with levels in older communities began to make themselves felt. These influences were reflected in the rapid movement of labor into the area, especially following completion of the Southern Pacific and the Santa Fe railroads in 1876 and 1885, respectively. The influx of job seekers eliminated some of the more

[8] Grace E. Heilman, "Early History of the Labor Movement in Los Angeles" (Ph.D. dissertation, University of Pennsylvania, 1949), p. 7.

severe labor shortages, but the effects on comparative wage levels were limited, the demand for labor rising at a sufficiently rapid rate to absorb quickly most of the new arrivals. The first important boom, locally, came toward the end of the 1876–1887 period, which also marked the beginning of the shift of this community from a pastoral to an industrial economy. The first big upsurge in population also occurred at about this time, the number of people in Los Angeles jumping from about 5,700 to more than 50,000 between 1870 and 1890.[9] Given the favorable climate of business conditions existing at the time, the increase in population only served to quicken the forces of economic expansion, and thus any tendency to bring wages more on a par with longer-established communities was greatly mitigated.

This was to be a frequently recurring pattern in subsequent years. A slower pace of economic development would doubtless have resulted in a marked narrowing of interarea wage relationships as the community moved further away from its frontier beginnings. Instead, at least until 1929, the output of goods and services rose at a much faster rate locally than in other important urban areas. In a study of thirteen large industrial areas covering the period from 1899 to 1935, McLaughlin found that the rise in manufacturing output in Los Angeles far exceeded the gains in all the other communities surveyed.[10] Per cent comparisons showing the astronomical rise in Los Angeles manufacturing before World War I are in one sense deceptive since the actual values involved were small. As a measure of the rise in demand for factory labor in relation to available supplies, however, the figures are of great significance. In the 1899–1935 period the only other community which even approached the rate of increase of Los Angeles manufacturing was Detroit. As an indication of the comparative growth rate of Los Angeles, the data for these two areas, together with information on four other important industrial centers, are given in figure 5; this figure covers the forty-year period 1899–1939.

Judging from figure 5, the contrast between Los Angeles and these five communities became especially pronounced between 1919 and 1929. Comparisons based on employment show this was even more applicable to fields outside manufacturing. These developments were quickly reflected in comparative wage movements. As noted earlier, annual earnings in Los Angeles manufacturing rose more rapidly during this period than in other urban areas (fig. 3). Data on nonmanufacturing wages are fragmentary, but what evidence can be obtained points to a similar finding. Whereas in most fields before World War I hourly and weekly

---

[9] *Ibid.*, pp. 30, 99.
[10] McLaughlin, *op. cit.*, p. 137.

earnings had been substantially lower in Los Angeles than in San Francisco, the differential was apparently narrowed greatly by 1929. Indeed, state government reports indicate that by the latter year wage rates in a number of trades were about as high in Los Angeles as in San Francisco.[11] These facts demonstrate that the forces pushing up local wages

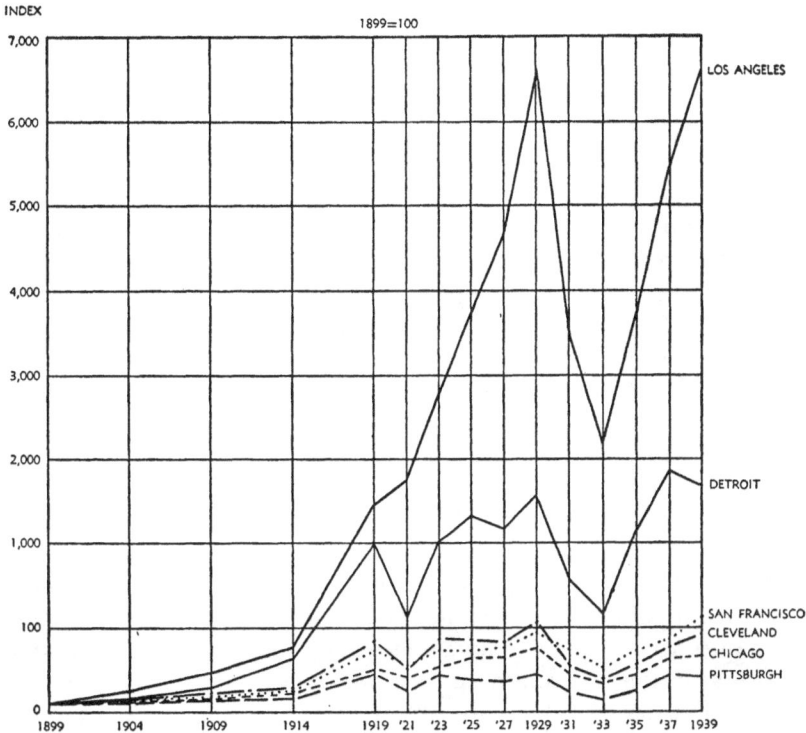

Fig. 5. Indexes of value added by manufacture, Los Angeles County and five industrial areas, 1899–1939.
SOURCE: Philip Neff, Lisette C. Baum, and Grace E. Heilman, *Production Cost Trends in Selected Industrial Areas* (Berkeley and Los Angeles, 1948), p. 17.

were more than strong enough to offset any long-term tendency to narrow previously established differentials.

In the ten-year period between 1929 and 1939, economic developments in Los Angeles more closely paralleled those in other large urban centers than in the preceding decade. With the onset of the depression, there was a sharp drop in local manufacturing output after 1929, followed by a marked recovery beginning in 1933. Compared to the five other urban

---

[11] The biennial reports of the California Bureau of Labor Statistics show, for example, that construction rates in 1927 and 1928 were as high in Los Angeles as in San Francisco.

areas included in figure 5, it appears that during this period manufacturing output in Los Angeles behaved much the same as in San Francisco, Cleveland, and Chicago, a somewhat different pattern occurring in Detroit and Pittsburgh.[12] Similarly, an analysis of cyclical changes in both manufacturing and nonmanufacturing during this same period revealed that ". . . in spite of notable differences in the economic pattern of Los Angeles, Cleveland, and Pittsburgh, the cyclical patterns of these areas are much alike."[13] During this period, in contrast to the previous decade, the wage ranking of Los Angeles in relation to these five urban areas remained substantially unchanged (fig. 3). Comparisons on a national basis yield similar findings. Employment between 1929 and 1939 rose somewhat more in Los Angeles than in the country as a whole, but the slackening in the local area's rate of growth, coupled with heavy inmigration, resulted in a marked amount of unemployment. Under these circumstances, even though employment was expanding somewhat more rapidly locally than in many other communities, employers in Los Angeles could still attract new workers without raising wage rates any faster than in other localities. In short, extensive unemployment together with slackening growth kept wage changes in the Los Angeles area pretty much in line with wage changes in the rest of the country during the 'thirties.

Some students of regional economic behavior hold that communities, like industries, pass through various stages of economic growth. Initially, there is a period of slow growth when settlement is first getting under way; then a period of very rapid expansion when modern production techniques are first applied on a wide scale; then a period of less rapid growth as further gains in output become relatively less easy to secure; and finally, a period of "leveling off" or even of absolute decline as other "newer" regions gain ascendancy. Thus, speaking of the period 1870–1935, McLaughlin concluded that Los Angeles reached its peak of greatest percentage growth about 1919.[14] Whatever the validity of this view (and it certainly is not one to be applied mechanically or under all circumstances), it is obvious that long-term wage relationships do not follow this pattern. On the other hand, the facts summarized above indicate that shifts in the rate of general economic growth of Los Angeles had a direct bearing on the community's interarea wage position.

REGIONAL AND MARKET INFLUENCES

The long-term influences on the local wage level described above were reinforced by broader developments taking place in the surrounding

---

[12] Neff, Baum, and Heilman, *op. cit.*, p. 27.   [14] McLaughlin, *op. cit.*, p. 205.
[13] Neff and Weifenbach, *op. cit.*, p. 163.

region. Although less spectacular in many respects, the growth of the Southwest and the Far West followed much the same course as the Los Angeles area itself. Until recently both were characterized by frontier conditions. If, during the early phase of the development of Los Angeles, there had been a large population in the surrounding region largely dependent on small-unit farms, the upward pressures on wages in the Los Angeles area would have been far less. Instead, the entire region was generally deficient in man power, and the development of its resources (minerals, fuels, cultivable land, and so on) placed a heavy premium on the services of labor. The interurban wage relationships described above were therefore part of an interregional rate structure which in turn rested on basic differences in the economies of the various sections of the country. Interregional differences in resources, population, and industrial structure tend to persist over long periods of time and, because of their importance in determining the wage level of any given community, they tend to perpetuate interurban wage relationships as well.

Regional developments also had an important bearing on this community's wage level through their effects on product markets. The population growth of the immediate area was merely the focal point for a general rise in population throughout this section of the country, and for many local firms the development of regional markets was hardly less important than the growth of the local market itself. In the first part of the century, the trading area of Los Angeles was largely confined to the southern half of California. With the development of modern transportation facilities, however, its trading area was enormously expanded. Today, many of its industries, such as petroleum refining, automobile assembly, rubber tires, and the like, serve the entire eleven western states, and in a few instances, especially motion picture production, even world markets. As this trading area itself developed economically, the forces pushing up wages in Los Angeles also increased in strength.

Further light is thrown on the long-term influences determining this community's wage level when attention is turned to the composition of its industries. As already stated, a higher proportion of its industries in 1940 fell in service and trade categories than in most other large city areas, with a smaller proportion in manufacturing. In fact, comparisons with the United States as a whole reveal a similar contrast despite the fact that national figures cover many nonindustrial centers. Such manufacturing as existed was largely carried on by small plants. Thus, a study of manufacturing industries in six industrial areas concluded that Los Angeles stood at the bottom of the list in terms of average size per establishment, in the manufacture of both durable and nondurable goods.[15]

As shown in figure 6, employment shifts in Los Angeles between 1920 and 1940 followed much the same pattern as in the United States, the most striking development being the drop in relative importance of manufacturing and the rise of the service and trade groups in both areas. These facts indicate that, on this score, Los Angeles stood in about the

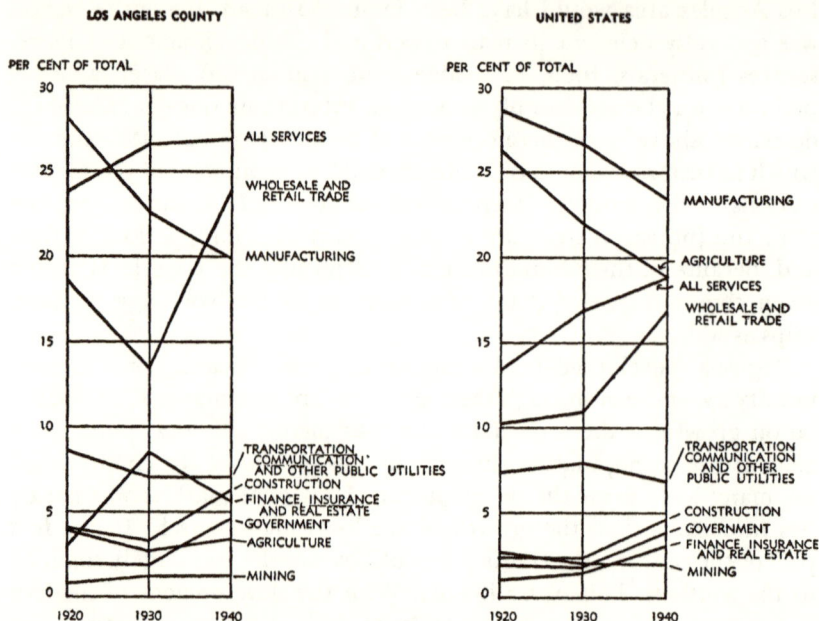

LOS ANGELES COUNTY

UNITED STATES

PER CENT OF TOTAL

PER CENT OF TOTAL

ALL SERVICES
WHOLESALE AND RETAIL TRADE
MANUFACTURING

MANUFACTURING
AGRICULTURE
ALL SERVICES
WHOLESALE AND RETAIL TRADE

TRANSPORTATION COMMUNICATION AND OTHER PUBLIC UTILITIES
CONSTRUCTION
FINANCE, INSURANCE AND REAL ESTATE
GOVERNMENT
AGRICULTURE
MINING

TRANSPORTATION COMMUNICATION AND OTHER PUBLIC UTILITIES
CONSTRUCTION
GOVERNMENT
FINANCE, INSURANCE AND REAL ESTATE
MINING

Fig. 6. Distribution of employment, Los Angeles County and United States, 1920–1940. SOURCE: Appendix table 3.

same position with respect to the rest of the country at the end of this period as at the beginning. More detailed analysis of the manufacturing group, considered alone, corroborates these findings. Employment in Los Angeles manufacturing was about equally divided between durable and nondurable goods, both in 1929 and 1939, roughly the same pattern of distribution which existed in these two years in the country as a whole. In more industrialized areas like Pittsburgh, Cleveland, and Detroit, there was a slight increase in the proportion of manufacturing employment in nondurable goods industries during this period, but the share represented by durable goods still averaged more than 75 per cent, well above the level in Los Angeles.[16] Especially in the period before

---

[15] Neff, Baum, and Heilman, *op. cit.*, pp. 20–22. The data pertain to the year 1939 and, in addition to Los Angeles, cover Chicago, Cleveland, Detroit, Pittsburgh, and San Francisco.

[16] Neff and Weifenbach, *op. cit.*, table 4, pp. 24–25.

World War II, it is evident that heavy manufacturing played a relatively minor role in the Los Angeles economy.

Certain important wage effects followed from the fact that in prewar Los Angeles most of its employment was concentrated in consumer-oriented industries. In spite of its rapid growth, this meant that wages did not rise as rapidly as would have been the case if large-scale, mass-production industries had been developed. True, in some fields directly serving consumers, like printing and publishing and the various construction trades, wage rates have been traditionally high; in these industries the rapidly growing population was a sufficiently favorable factor to bring about substantially higher wages. But in many other industries directly serving consumers, like wholesale and retail trade, labor's position has been traditionally weak and wages comparatively low. Everything considered, despite its prodigious growth, it is perhaps not surprising that between 1920 and 1940 the interarea wage position of Los Angeles changed little, if at all.

Two factors which go a long way toward explaining the wage history of this area were the extent of its markets and the nature of its resources. Although favorable to the growth of certain industries, these two factors were not conducive to the rapid development of large-scale enterprise before World War II. Because of the disadvantage of geographical location and heavy transportation costs, many employers were effectively barred from competing in the national market. The rapid growth of the Los Angeles market, local and regional, assured a favorable demand for most firms, but it limited growth largely to those fields serving consumer needs in the immediate area. Similarly, the natural resources of the Southwest were conducive to the growth of some industries, notably petroleum and various food products, but not to others like coal and steel, industries which are essential to the growth of heavy manufactures. Water-power resources were also a barrier to the development of large-scale industry in this area, though beginning in 1916 the increased availability of low cost electric power led to important industrial development.[17] The climate of the area was a factor favorable to growth, but the dearth of water supplies proved a continuing problem. Moreover, the factor of climate was related to the development of such industries as agriculture, motion pictures, and recreational services rather than to factory trades. On balance, it seems clear that before 1940 the joint influence of markets and resources was not conducive to the development of large-scale enterprise in this area.

These considerations should be borne in mind in interpreting com-

[17] Frank L. Kidner and Philip Neff, *An Economic Survey of the Los Angeles Area* (Los Angeles: The Haynes Foundation, 1945), p. 4.

parative data on employment, new firms, and total capital outlays. Treated simply as aggregates, the reported figures suggest that the pressures on the community's wage level might well have pushed rates substantially above those prevailing elsewhere. Before World War II, however, since most of the new enterprises and new capital were confined to nonmanufacturing lines or to the finishing stages of processing, and since most of the firms were small, the amount of capital equipment per worker was relatively low. Hence, in spite of the over-all rapid growth of the community, the expansion failed to raise wages locally any more than they increased in many other large urban areas.

Another long-term influence affecting the interarea wage position of Los Angeles related to differences in living costs and to certain non-monetary advantages derived from living in this part of the country. Quantitative estimates of relative living costs before 1940 reveal that the prices of goods bought by wage earners in Los Angeles before World War II were somewhat less than in most large or highly industrialized cities of the country. The most comprehensive study dealing directly with this question was an investigation of living costs in fifty-nine cities in 1935, conducted by the Works Progress Administration in coöperation with the United States Bureau of Labor Statistics. According to this report, differences in prices of consumers' goods as between cities were relatively small, the gap between high and low wage-earner budgets being in the neighborhood of $200 to $300 per year, depending on the type of family budget employed.[18] Among the fifty-nine cities covered in the survey, Los Angeles ranked fourteenth from the top with respect to the so-called maintenance level budget ($1,308 per year as opposed to $1,415 per year in Washington, D.C., the highest cost center, and an average of $1,261 for all fifty-nine cities combined). Among the five cities of more than 1,000,000 population which were included, Los Angeles ranked fourth, just slightly above Philadelphia. It was also below a number of smaller, though more highly industrialized, centers like San Francisco, Cleveland, and Detroit.[19] During the 'twenties the cost-of-living advantage enjoyed by Los Angeles over these cities was probably somewhat greater than these figures would indicate, whereas between 1935 and 1940 it was apparently slightly less.[20] Taking the interwar period as a whole, there is no question that differences in consumers'

---

[18] Works Progress Administration, *Intercity Differences in Costs of Living in March 1935, 59 Cities*, Research Monograph XII (Washington: Government Printing Office, 1937), p. xvii.

[19] *Ibid.*, pp. 158, 182. Los Angeles, however, was somewhat above the three other West Coast cities included, Seattle, Spokane, and Portland.

[20] U. S. Bureau of Labor Statistics, *Changes in Cost of Living in Large Cities in the United States, 1913–1941*, Bull. no. 699 (Washington: Government Printing Office, 1941), table 3, pp. 47–78.

goods' prices justified somewhat lower wages in Los Angeles than in other large or highly industrialized centers. Since the price variations were slight, however, it is equally clear that any wage differential based on this ground alone would have been small indeed.

More important is the contention that workers gained special advantages from being employed in the Los Angeles area by reason of its climate, proximity to recreational areas, and other distinctive features of southern California living. No precise measure of the total satisfactions derived from jobs in different areas can possibly be contrived, but differences in working environment are nonetheless important in explaining apparent discrepancies in money wage levels. In the case of Los Angeles, this circumstance was doubtless significant, but again its influence can easily be exaggerated. So far as wage levels are concerned, the principal effect of this type of influence was to draw workers into the area, a development that has already been considered in connection with the rapid increase in the community's labor force. Any direct effect it may have had in keeping wages below the level they would otherwise have attained was probably slight.

Finally, the institutional and sociological characteristics of the area help explain why wages did not rise higher in the prewar period. This is an aspect of the local economy which some observers would probably judge more important than any other in determining the general wage level. The foregoing analysis has led to a rather different conclusion, the comparative level of wages in prewar Los Angeles being quite adequately explained in terms of the economic influences reviewed above. The fact remains that throughout most of the 1900–1940 period, Los Angeles employers were well organized whereas unions were relatively weak. The Merchants and Manufacturers Association, a trade association representing the most influential employers in the area, was established in 1896. At its inception, its principal activities lay outside the field of labor relations, but in the course of the prolonged strike against the *Los Angeles Times* which had begun in 1890 and in other disputes over the union recognition issue, this association became more and more concerned with union organizing efforts and strike situations. By 1920, the M. and M., as it was generally known, was confining itself almost entirely to the field of labor relations.[21]

During most of this period the principal plank of the organized employers in this area was the preservation of the open shop. Speaking of the 'twenties, one of the M. and M. publications reported:

The outstanding fact is that this great city of ours, the greatest on the Pacific Coast,

---

[21] Louis B. Perry, "A Survey of the Labor Movement in Los Angeles, 1933–1939" (Ph.D. dissertation, University of California, Los Angeles, 1950), p. 6.

is getting along considerably better than any other city in the United States, because it is free—free from the domination of organized labor, or the domination of anything else.[22]

Except for a brief period of union growth during World War I, labor organizations remained ineffective in Los Angeles until the mid-'thirties.[23] A few of the old-time crafts like the printers were able to win a few agreements, but even in their case organization was far from complete.[24] The lack of effective union representation was made all the more striking by the high degree of organization in near-by San Francisco where unions had been well established since the turn of the century.

There seems little question that Los Angeles employers joined forces during this period to block the spread of unionism. Whether they also combined to hold down wages is harder to determine. The data presented earlier indicate that wage levels in Los Angeles were generally below those prevailing in San Francisco as well as in many other major urban areas. It is tempting to conclude that differences in degree of unionization explain these wage relationships, but it is important to remember that in most large communities unions were generally weak at this time. The preceding discussion has shown that interarea wage differences reflect deep-seated economic characteristics and that changes in general wage levels result from the interplay of a variety of influences. In Los Angeles, lack of unionization and the presence of powerful employer organizations doubtless strengthened the forces holding down local wage levels, but given a different economic setting it seems equally clear that differences in degree of unionization would not have altered the result materially.

CONCLUSION

The foregoing discussion provides a useful vantage point from which to review the general analysis of local wage rate structures contained in the preceding chapter. The Los Angeles wage experience, before World War II, underscores the stability of intercommunity wage rate relationships. Despite the rapid economic changes of the area, the comparative wage position of Los Angeles in 1940 was not markedly different from what it was forty or fifty years earlier. There is little doubt that the community's phenomenal growth was itself an important factor contributing to this result. At the turn of the century, and earlier, the local wage rate level reflected the conditions of labor scarcity usually asso-

---

[22] *Violations of Free Speech and Rights of Labor,* U. S. Senate, 76th Cong., 3d sess. (Washington: Government Printing Office, 1940), pt. 52, p. 19,300, in *ibid.,* p. 15.

[23] Developments in the latter period are treated in more detail in chap. viii.

[24] The most important newspaper of the area, the *Los Angeles Times,* remained nonunion throughout this period and is unorganized at the present time.

ciated with newly settled, remote areas. With the rise in population, supply and demand for labor more nearly approximated conditions in longer-settled areas, and wage rates moved toward greater equality with levels elsewhere. These equalizing tendencies, however, were never fully realized because of the community's sustained rate of economic growth. The effect of this influence in maintaining relatively high wage rates in the Los Angeles area was especially marked during the 'twenties. During the 'thirties the contrast in economic conditions was less marked, and the pressures pushing local wage rates above those in the rest of the country were greatly reduced. As the period of settlement lengthens, it is only reasonable to suppose that the Los Angeles wage level will gradually move more and more closely into line with wages in longer-established communities.

Another aspect of local wage phenomena highlighted by the Los Angeles experience is the importance of the three factors—climate, physical resources, and geographical location. The development of the petroleum industry, the initial location of motion picture production, and the growth of highly mechanized agricultural industries in the surrounding region can be directly traced to the physical endowments of the area. These industries, because of their unusual productiveness and rapid growth, helped to keep wages in the community comparatively high. Similarly, the physical remoteness of Los Angeles served to perpetuate any differences between its wage rate level and those of other localities. A quite different picture would have emerged if the major sources of labor had been in near-by communities or in surrounding farm areas. Instead, most of the new labor had to come across state lines, and the pressures to equalize pay levels under these circumstances were far from strong. At the same time its geographical remoteness made Los Angeles the center of a new and expanding trading area. The growth of this area exerted an important upward pressure on wages locally, but ties with other communities outside this area were not close, so that the principal effect of the geographical location factor was to accentuate rather than lessen intercommunity wage differences.

As already indicated, the major influence determining the comparative wage level of this area was the rate of growth in demand for labor. Indeed, before World War II, the long-term trend in the demand for labor rose more rapidly in this community than in any other large population center in the country. This high growth rate was associated with a fast-growing population, expanding consumer markets, a mounting number of new firms, and a rising volume of capital outlays. The expansion, however, was largely confined to industries directly serving consumer wants. Heavy manufacturing industries, which played such an important role in raising wage levels in many eastern cities, were for the most part undeveloped. Even airframe manufacturing had yet to be placed on a mass-production basis, and industries like basic steel, automobile manufacturing, and the production of heavy machinery were either nonexistent or extremely limited. In part, the absence of these industries was attributable to certain resource limitations of this general region; in part, to geographical remoteness from major markets; in part, to limitations on the supply of capital and to the other handicaps which any newly developed area confronts in challenging long-established producers in older communities. Hence, the long-term rise in Los Angeles wage rates was subject to severe limitations and, in spite of its phenomenal growth, this community's general wage level in 1940 was still well below the level of many other metropolitan centers. Although less important than these circumstances, the fact that employers were on the whole well organized, whereas labor was not, also imposed a barrier to wage increases.

This discussion has been focused on long-term changes in the wage level of the Los Angeles area. For a more complete understanding of the influences controlling the movement of wage rates in a given locality, consideration must be given to short-term wage changes as well. The decade of the 'forties, with its sharp contrast between wartime and postwar conditions, provides a good setting for such an analysis, and to this period attention is now turned.

III. LOS ANGELES WAGES: 1940–1949

A STUDY of the influences controlling wage movements in the Los Angeles area during the 'forties may be divided into two periods: 1940–1945, when developments associated with the war dominated all aspects of the community's economic life, and 1945–1949, when the aftermath of the war, though still paramount, became an influence of lessening significance. Largely because of its importance as an aircraft and ship-building center, Los Angeles grew overnight into a major industrial area during the early part of the decade. The wartime expansion in fields directly related to the military effort induced greater output in a wide range of industries supplying the armament trades, the increased tempo of activity in these fields leading, in turn, to a marked rise in demand for almost all goods and services. During this period of rapid industrialization, it need hardly be added, there developed an unprecedented competition for most kinds of labor. Wartime production reached a peak locally in late 1943, followed by a general redistribution of employment together with a rise in unemployment. Beginning in 1946, the mounting volume of consumer spending, augmented by a heavy backlog of deferred demand, checked the business decline and, despite the continued rise in the area's labor force, unemployment fell. In 1948, business activity in the local area once again declined and unemployment rose quite sharply, but by the end of the decade the rise in the volume of business was resumed. At the time of the outbreak of hostilities in Korea in June, 1950, most local industries were already enjoying a substantial improvement in business.

HOURLY EARNINGS

During this period, 1940–1949, hourly earnings in Los Angeles industries more than doubled, a greater gain than in most other communities in the country. Earnings of Los Angeles factory workers increased about 115 per cent over the nine-year period, rising from $0.736 per hour in 1940 to $1.582 per hour in 1949. Factory earnings in the United States increased about 112 per cent during this period, and the absolute gain, from $0.661 per hour in 1940 to $1.401 per hour in 1949, was substantially less than in the local area.[1] The comparative movement of factory earnings, both in money and real terms, is shown in figure 7. In consumer service fields, the relative gain in Los Angeles was still greater. Hourly earnings in these fields rose from $0.600 in 1940 to $1.303 in 1949, a gain

[1] Appendix table 4-A.

of about 117 per cent, against a rise nationally from $0.573 per hour to $1.173, a gain of approximately 104 per cent.[2]

HOURLY RATES

The foregoing comparisons, based on gross average hourly earnings, reflect a wide variety of influences, including changes in the amount of

AVERAGE HOURLY EARNINGS

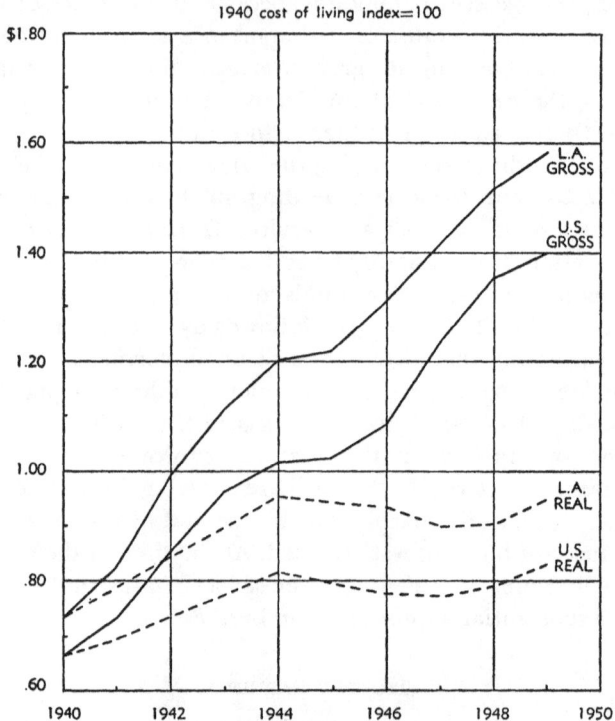

Fig. 7. Gross and real average hourly earnings in manufacturing, Los Angeles County and United States, 1940–1949.
SOURCE: Appendix table 4-A.

overtime and shifts in the distribution of employment between low- and high-paying jobs, industries, and areas. A more precise measure of the relative wage position of the community is afforded by occupational rates, since the latter exclude all influences on wages other than changes in the basic rates themselves.[3] Although the gain in rates was much less

---

[2] Appendix table 4-B. The data for consumer service fields refer to four industries: hotels; laundering, cleaning, and dyeing; retail trade; and wholesale trade.

[3] The data on comparative rate movements summarized below measure changes in straight-time hourly earnings, exclusive of all premium pay for overtime, late-shift

in absolute terms, the rise in rates locally was even greater than the rise in earnings when compared with changes in the country as a whole. Thus, hourly rates rose about 58 per cent in Los Angeles manufacturing between January, 1941, and April, 1948, as against a gain of about 41 per cent in the United States. The earliest figures available on rates in nonmanufacturing lines go back only to April, 1943. Between that date and April, 1948, Los Angeles nonmanufacturing rates rose about 68 per cent as against an increase of about 57 per cent in the country at large.[4] In any event, it is evident that the same forces which raised hourly earnings in Los Angeles had roughly similar effects on the community's general level of rates.

INTERCITY COMPARISONS

A better notion of the significance of these developments is gained by comparing wage changes in Los Angeles and other large urban centers over the nine-year period. In chapter ii, the wage level of this community was found to be well below San Francisco's, in 1940 the differential averaging nearly 10 cents per hour. By 1949, this differential had been narrowed substantially, perhaps by as much as one-third, but the greater part of the change occurred in such fields as wholesale and retail trade, not in manufacturing (figs. 8 and 9).

The only other communities for which comparable hourly earnings data could be secured for the period 1940–1949 are Philadelphia and Pittsburgh, and even here the data are confined to manufacturing industries. Nevertheless, the figures which appear in figure 9 afford striking evidence of the relatively rapid rise in the Los Angeles wage level. In 1940 hourly earnings in manufacturing in the latter community were about on a par with Philadelphia and substantially below Pittsburgh.

---

work, and so on. Before April, 1947, the Bureau of Labor Statistics published an Urban Wage Rate series which reflected only changes in wage rates of time workers and earned straight-time rates of incentive workers. Since then, the Bureau's figures have reflected these same elements, plus the effect on average straight-time hourly earnings of change° in the occupational structure of individual establishments. Since constant weights are employed, both series exclude the influence of shifts in the distribution of employment as between industries and areas, and for present purposes the two series can be considered comparable. Due to shifts in industry definitions, comparable figures are not available after 1948.

The Bureau's figures on straight-time earnings in manufacturing are based on surveys of about 3,000 manufacturing establishments, whereas the nonmanufacturing industries studied included about 2,500 wholesale and retail trade, finance, local utility, and service trade establishments. U. S. Bureau of Labor Statistics, release, November 10, 1948.

[4] Appendix tables 1 and 6. Not much weight can be placed on the greater rise in rate compared to the relative rise in earnings, however, since the coverage of the data is not the same.

By 1949, hourly pay in Los Angeles factories had risen well above the comparable figure for Philadelphia and was even slightly above the level in Pittsburgh.

A comparison of wage trends in a larger number of communities becomes possible when data on occupational rates or straight-time hourly

AVERAGE HOURLY EARNINGS

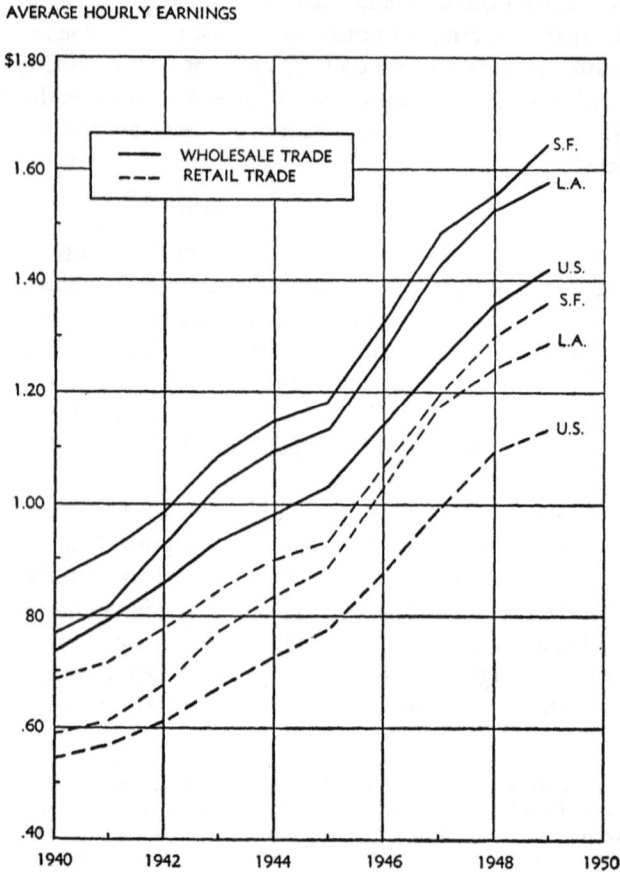

Fig. 8. Average hourly earnings in wholesale and retail trade, Los Angeles County, San Francisco Bay industrial area, and United States, 1940–1949.
SOURCE: Appendix table 4-C.

earnings are employed. As noted in the preceding chapter, in January, 1941, manufacturing rates in Los Angeles stood about halfway down the list of twenty urban centers covered in the government's survey. Figure 10 shows the rankings of these twenty urban areas as of April, 1948 (as explained earlier, later data on a comparable basis are unavailable). In this listing the Los Angeles manufacturing wage rate index stood seventh from the top. To make direct comparisons possible, the rankings for these same twenty cities are also shown for certain earlier years (fig. 11). The gain in Los Angeles was the largest of the cities shown, rising from a rank of 11.5 in 1941 to 7 in 1948. This, of course, does not

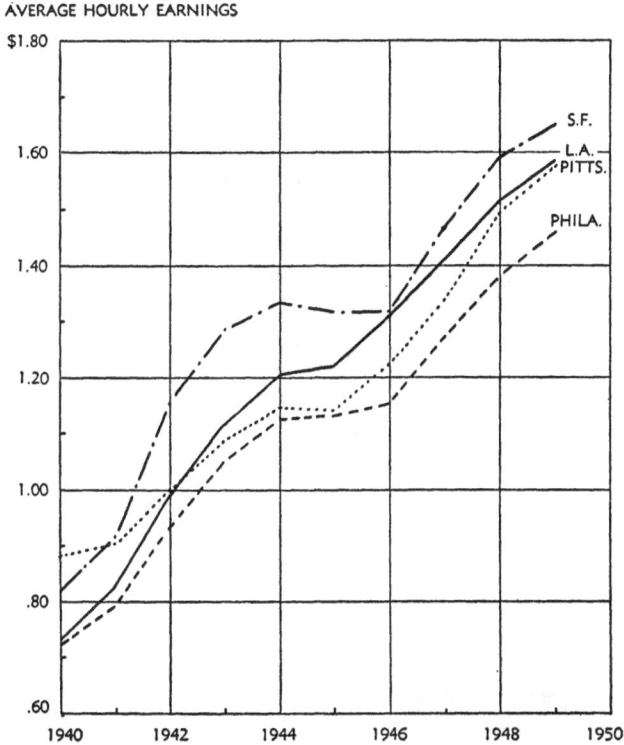

AVERAGE HOURLY EARNINGS

Fig. 9. Average hourly earnings in manufacturing, Los Angeles County and three industrial areas, 1940–1949. *Note:* Los Angeles area: Los Angeles County; Philadelphia area: Bucks, Chester, Delaware, Montgomery, and Philadelphia counties; Pittsburgh area: Allegheny, Armstrong, Beaver, Butler, Fayette, Greene, Washington, and Westmoreland counties; San Francisco Bay area: Alameda, Contra Costa, Marin, San Francisco, and San Mateo counties.

SOURCE: Appendix tables 4-A and 5.

mean that the percentage gain in Los Angeles rates was greater than that of any other community, since some cities, notably in the South, started from a much lower rate level. Moreover, the rise in the ranking of Los Angeles was confined to the first part of the nine-year period, no change in its position occurring after 1943.[5]

Data on rates in nonmanufacturing fields are less adequate than in

---

[5] Contrary to the data on hourly earnings, it should be noted that, on the basis of rates, Los Angeles still ranked below Pittsburgh and Philadelphia in 1948.

manufacturing, and comparable figures are not available before April, 1943. Judging from the available evidence, however, roughly similar conclusions emerge. Thus, of twenty areas, only Philadelphia increased as many rankings as Los Angeles over the five-year period. The result is all the more striking since the latter community stood fairly high even

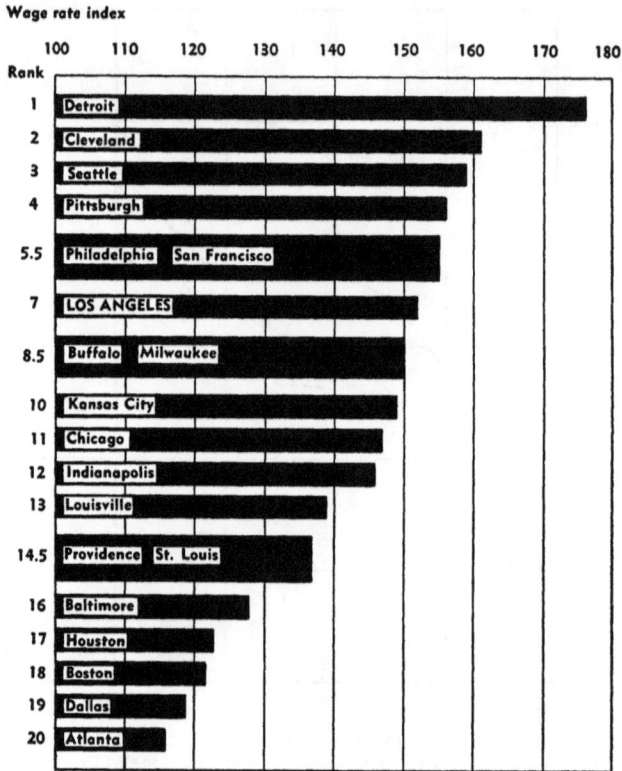

Wage rate index

Rank		
1	Detroit	
2	Cleveland	
3	Seattle	
4	Pittsburgh	
5.5	Philadelphia San Francisco	
7	LOS ANGELES	
8.5	Buffalo Milwaukee	
10	Kansas City	
11	Chicago	
12	Indianapolis	
13	Louisville	
14.5	Providence St. Louis	
16	Baltimore	
17	Houston	
18	Boston	
19	Dallas	
20	Atlanta	

Fig. 10. Ranking of manufacturing wage rate indexes, Los Angeles County and nineteen urban areas, April, 1948.
SOURCE: Appendix table 1.

in 1943. In that year it ranked fifth from the top among the areas covered in the survey, and by 1948 it had risen to second position. Figure 12, as in the case of manufacturing wage rates, shows the shifts in urban rankings only, not the amounts of change in either absolute or percentage terms.

REAL EARNINGS

The foregoing discussion has been concerned with the relative wage position of Los Angeles between 1940 and 1949, considered in terms of money wages. In appraising the record of the period, however, consideration has to be given to a number of other influences bearing on the economic welfare of wage earners, of which the most important are changes in the length of the work week, in the proportion of worker income subject to taxation, and in the prices of goods bought by wage earners.[6] Since the present study is focused on intercity variations in wage behavior, the discussion of these three aspects of the problem can be

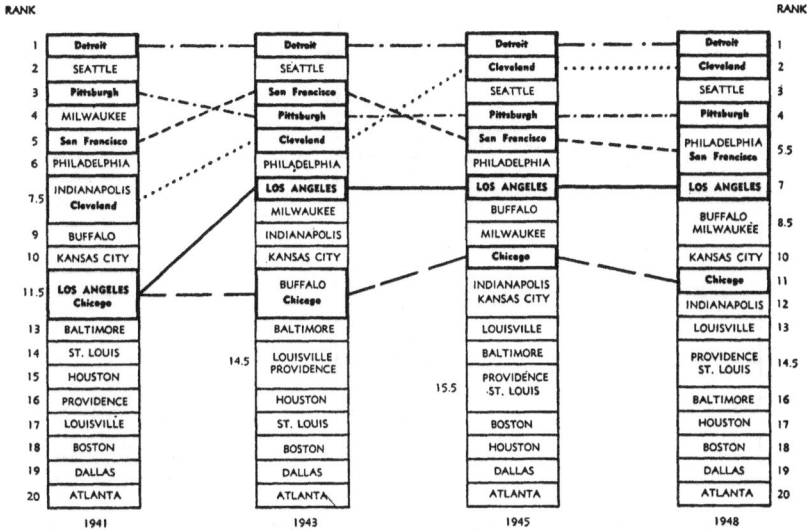

Fig. 11. Shifts in rankings of manufacturing wage rate indexes, Los Angeles County and nineteen urban areas, January, 1941–April, 1948.
SOURCE: Appendix table 1.

brief, in each instance developments in the Los Angeles area paralleling very closely changes in most other urban centers.

By the end of the decade, following the sharp rise in the work week during the war years, average hours in most Los Angeles industries had returned to about the level prevailing in 1940. In manufacturing, for example, the average in 1949 was 38.8, the same as in 1940. In retail trade, wage earners worked an average of 37.7 hours per week in 1940 and 38.7 hours in 1949, whereas in wholesale trade the work week in these two years averaged 40.3 hours and 39.8 hours, respectively. The wartime lengthening of the work week, with overtime pay after 40 hours, raised average weekly earnings between 1940 and 1945 more rapidly than hourly earnings, but after this date the relationship was,

[6] Some writers argue that the tax payments of wage earners, even though involuntary, are a form of consumer expenditure and ought not to be treated as a deduction from income. A more complete picture is nonetheless afforded by estimating changes in the tax burden which workers carry.

of course, reversed. Elsewhere in the country, substantially similar trends prevailed during this period.[7]

Between 1940 and 1949, the proportion of wage earner income deducted for taxes rose markedly, although there was some decline after the end of the war. In 1940, most Los Angeles wage earners were subject to a 2 per cent pay deduction for old age and survivors and unemploy-

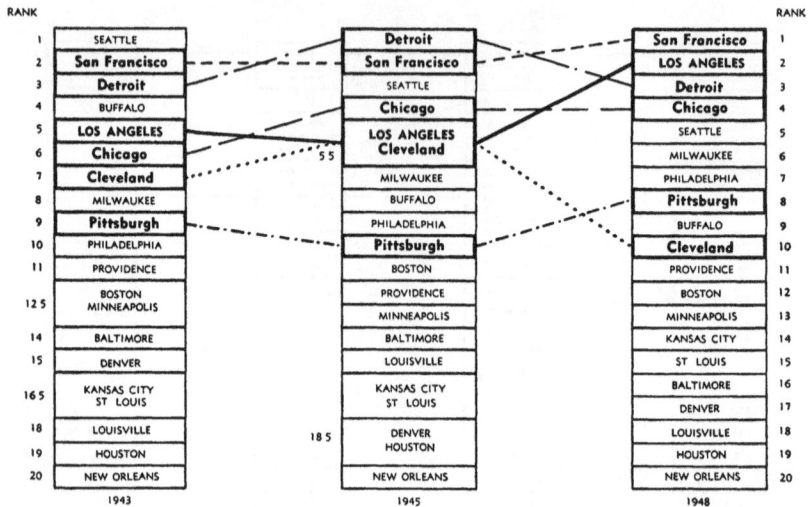

RANK	1943	1945	1948	RANK
1	SEATTLE	Detroit	San Francisco	1
2	San Francisco	San Francisco	LOS ANGELES	2
3	Detroit	SEATTLE	Detroit	3
4	BUFFALO	Chicago	Chicago	4
5	LOS ANGELES	LOS ANGELES	SEATTLE	5
6	Chicago	Cleveland 5 5	MILWAUKEE	6
7	Cleveland	MILWAUKEE	PHILADELPHIA	7
8	MILWAUKEE	BUFFALO	Pittsburgh	8
9	Pittsburgh	PHILADELPHIA	BUFFALO	9
10	PHILADELPHIA	Pittsburgh	Cleveland	10
11	PROVIDENCE	BOSTON	PROVIDENCE	11
12 5	BOSTON MINNEAPOLIS	PROVIDENCE	BOSTON	12
		MINNEAPOLIS	MINNEAPOLIS	13
14	BALTIMORE	BALTIMORE	KANSAS CITY	14
15	DENVER	LOUISVILLE	ST LOUIS	15
16 5	KANSAS CITY ST LOUIS	KANSAS CITY ST LOUIS	BALTIMORE	16
			DENVER	17
18	LOUISVILLE	18 5 DENVER HOUSTON	LOUISVILLE	18
19	HOUSTON		HOUSTON	19
20	NEW ORLEANS	NEW ORLEANS	NEW ORLEANS	20

Fig. 12. Shifts in rankings of nonmanufacturing wage rate indexes, Los Angeles County and nineteen urban areas, April, 1943–April, 1948.
Source: Appendix table 6.

ment insurance taxes, but very few were affected by personal income taxes.[8] In 1949, the latter tax took at least this much again from wage earner incomes, a manufacturing employee with three dependents paying, at average wages, nearly 4 per cent. Estimates of the tax burden on manufacturing wage earners during the period 1940–1949 are given in figures 13 and 14.

Of far more importance was the sharp increase in the cost of living between 1940 and 1949. Over this period the Consumers' Price Index of the United States Bureau of Labor Statistics for Los Angeles rose a little less than 70 per cent. Consequently, the rise in money hourly earn-

---

[7] Similarly, average hourly earnings rose more rapidly than hourly rates between 1940 and 1943, more slowly between 1943 and 1946, and at about the same rate between 1946 and 1949.

[8] In this discussion no account is taken of sales taxes or other types of tax payments. Two per cent is deducted for social security taxes, no allowance being made for workers with earnings of more than $3,000 per year. Both state and federal income taxes were computed, using the rate applicable at different dates. This was the method used by Nedra B. Belloc, *Wages in California* (Berkeley and Los Angeles: University of California Press, 1948), chap. iv.

ings of about 115 per cent in manufacturing, when translated into real terms, was reduced to about 28 per cent. In the case of money weekly earnings in manufacturing, which rose about 115 per cent between 1940 and 1949, the rise in the cost of living, when taken together with the

AVERAGE WEEKLY EARNINGS

1940 cost of living index=100

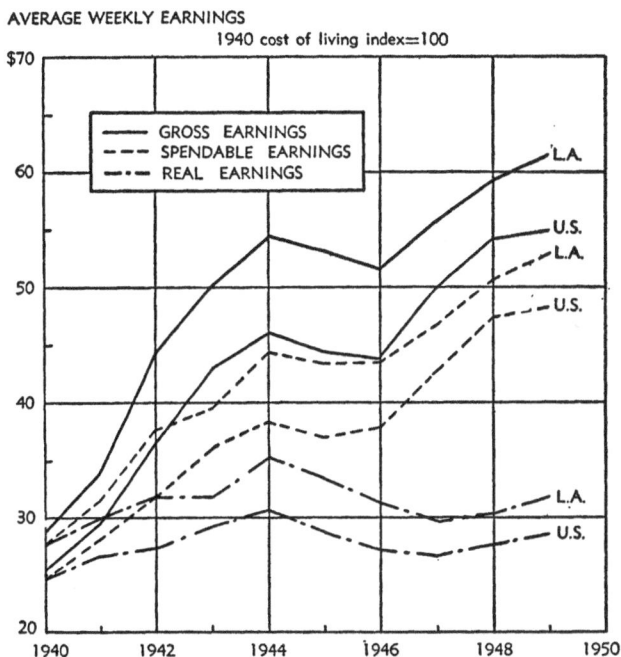

Fig. 13. Spendable real average weekly earnings, single worker in manufacturing, Los Angeles County and United States, 1940–1949.
SOURCE: Appendix table 7.

increase in tax payments, resulted in a net gain of only 16 per cent over the period. These changes, as they affected the level of weekly earnings in manufacturing in Los Angeles and the rest of the country, are also set forth in figures 13 and 14.

SUMMARY OF GENERAL WAGE CHANGES

The foregoing account of changes in the general wage level of Los Angeles between 1940 and 1949 yields the following major conclusions:

1. Broadly speaking, wages followed the same path locally as nationally. Thus, both in Los Angeles and the United States, hourly earnings in manufacturing in 1949 were somewhat more than twice their 1940 levels. In real terms, the rise came to slightly less than one-third in both instances.

2. The gain was greater, however, in Los Angeles than in the country as a whole. In percentage terms, the differential gain in average earnings was slight, but in absolute terms it was quite marked. Moreover, in terms of rates, the rise locally was substantially greater than in the country as a whole, even on a percentage basis of comparison. Also, comparisons with individual communities show that from a position

AVERAGE WEEKLY EARNINGS

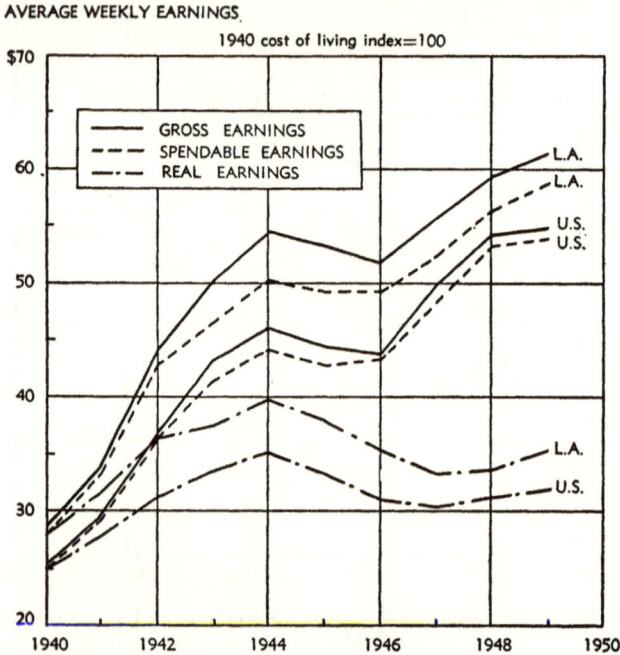

Fig. 14. Spendable real average weekly earnings, married worker in manufacturing, Los Angeles County and United States, 1940–1949. *Note:* Worker with three dependents. SOURCE: Appendix table 7.

more than halfway down a listing of twenty urban areas in 1941, straight-time wage rates in Los Angeles manufacturing rose to a position seventh from the top in 1943 and remained in this position during the balance of the decade.

3. Although incomplete, the data suggest that the rise in Los Angeles wages over the rest of the country was greater in consumer services than in manufacturing. In 1940, gross hourly earnings in consumer services, locally, were about 5 per cent above the national average; in 1949, the differential had increased to 11 per cent. In manufacturing, on the other hand, the differential was about 11 per cent in 1940 and had risen only to 13 per cent in 1949.

4. Similarly, wages in the Los Angeles area registered their greatest gain relative to the rest of the country between 1940 and 1943. In fact, in the period between 1943 and 1949, hourly earnings in manufacturing and nonmanufacturing rose slightly more, percentagewise, in the United States than in Los Angeles. This change in relative wage behavior roughly coincided with the peak in local armament production which occurred in the latter part of 1943.

Major Environmental Influences

The extent to which changes in the Los Angeles wage level paralleled changes in the country at large during this period has already been discussed. Since the general similarity was marked, it may be concluded that the forces which operated nationally also controlled wages locally. This squares with the view that almost all communities will feel the impact of an economic expansion of the type experienced during the 'forties and that wages in particular localities will behave accordingly. Thus, from 1940 until the end of the war in 1945, there was mounting pressure on wage levels for almost all types of labor resulting from the government's heavy armament expenditures. As the income-increasing effects of these outlays spread throughout the local and national economy, raising the level of spending for goods and services generally, and more and more of the labor force was drawn into pursuits immediately related to the war effort, competitive bidding for workers in both war and nonwar industries was intensified. Because of the government's program limiting price and wage rate increases during this period, hourly rates did not rise as rapidly as might have been expected. In large measure, the effects on wages were felt in terms of longer hours with more premium pay, shifts in employment from low-wage to high-wage industries and areas, rapid upgrading within firms, and lowering of skill requirements for new hires.[9] Even so, as shown in the urban wage rate data already referred to, substantial increases in hourly rates occurred in most industries and areas during the war years.

At the beginning of the postwar period, 1945–1949, there was a sharp decline in aggregate spending when the government's outlays for immediate war purposes were cut off, but the postwar contraction proved to be short-lived. By 1946, spending by consumers and business firms, taken together with government outlays, was great enough to reverse the deflation, and seller market conditions were reëstablished in most

---

[9] Of the increase in nonagricultural wages and salaries in the United States between 1940 and 1944, these factors accounted for between one-fourth and one-third of the total. Increases in basic wage-salary rates accounted for about two-fifths and increases in number employed for the remaining third. Board of Governors, Federal Reserve System, *Prices, Wages and Employment,* Postwar Economic Studies, no. 4 (Washington: Board of Governors, 1946), p. 55.

sections of the country. The complete elimination of the government's restrictions on wage rate increases in 1946, together with the ending of price controls, served to focus the inflationary pressures of this period on wage rates and commodity prices. In fact, contrary to the early war years, hours worked per week in manufacturing began to decline as early as 1945 and, with less overtime pay, weekly earnings fell, too. Moreover, in 1945 and 1946, employment shifted back from the higher-wage industries related to the war effort to the lower-wage industries of a peacetime economy, upgrading of labor within firms became less rapid than in the period of intense war activity, and skill requirements for filling jobs more nearly approximated prewar standards.

In Los Angeles, even though rates per hour in manufacturing increased somewhat during 1945 and rose sharply in 1946, average weekly earnings fell. Between 1946 and 1949, the influences tending to reduce weekly earnings became less important, and, since they were more than offset by the rise in rates, weekly earnings once again increased (fig. 13). In such nonmanufacturing fields as wholesale and retail trade, on the other hand, the divergence throughout the 'forties between weekly earnings and hourly rates in Los Angeles was far less extreme than in manufacturing, weekly earnings following the rise in rates quite closely in the war and postwar period. By 1948, production in both manufacturing and nonmanufacturing had increased sufficiently to reduce the pressure of demand on supplies, so that in 1948 and 1949, despite the continued rise in total expenditures, prices fell somewhat. As in most parts of the country, conditions of labor scarcity no longer existed and unemployment increased. In spite of these developments, wage rates continued to rise, though at a somewhat slower pace than in the years immediately preceding. By the end of 1949, locally as well as nationally, the decline in prices had been checked and employment prospects showed definite signs of improving.

The data already presented on wage changes in the Los Angeles area between 1940 and 1949 clearly demonstrate that the same forces operating nationally were also at work locally. The parallelism extended to the behavior of wage rates, hourly earnings, weekly earnings, and real earnings. Viewed broadly, the economic environment was also much the same, the relationships between total spending, available supplies of materials and labor, employment, and unemployment following a rather similar course. In certain particulars, however, the behavior of wages in the Los Angeles area differed from the national pattern, suggesting that the environmental influences were not altogether the same. These distinctive features of the community's wage history become apparent when the period 1940–1949 is examined in more detail.

IV. WAGES AND THE LOCAL
ENVIRONMENT

THE MOST STRIKING development in interarea wage relationships during the 'forties was the greater percentage rise in low-rate, as opposed to high-rate, communities. To a great extent, this simply reflected differences in levels prevailing at the outset of the period, but in part it also reflected the fact that with the general tightening of labor supply conditions and increasing mobility of labor, low-wage areas found it increasingly difficult to retain necessary personnel.[1] On top of this, high rates were frequently "imported" into low-wage areas whenever new factories were established in what had previously been predominantly nonindustrial communities. The spread of aircraft production into certain southern and midwestern cities was a clear example of this development.

At the beginning of this period, Los Angeles was far from being a heavily industrialized community, but it was definitely more advanced in this way than most southern and midwestern cities. Wagewise, though a majority of industrial areas ranked above it, Los Angeles stood somewhat higher than the national average. In the years that followed, this area became a more important industrial center and its wage ranking rose markedly; but the economic changes resulting from the war were even more striking in some of the hitherto undeveloped areas, and the relative wage change in these localities was greater still. Consequently, the wage position of Los Angeles in 1949, relative to that of the country as a whole, was not materially different from its position in 1940.

How sensitive was the wage level of this community to fluctuations in local business activity? Did changes in the prospects for production and employment have any observable effects on wage levels in the area? Some light is thrown on these questions in figure 15, which compares changes in factory hourly and weekly earnings in Los Angeles with changes in the general level of business activity in southern California between 1940 and 1949. To measure the degree of association as closely as possible, the data are shown on a monthly basis. Viewed broadly, the two wage series parallel the business activity index quite closely, but after 1945 the short-term fluctuations in business are not reflected

---

[1] Thus Dunlop writes: "A study of the movement of both geographical and occupational differentials over time suggests that they spread in times of unemployment and are markedly narrowed in times of prosperity." John T. Dunlop, "American Wage Determination: The Trend and Its Significance," paper presented at a conference sponsored by the Chamber of Commerce of the United States (Washington: 1947), p. 7.

MONTHLY INDEX

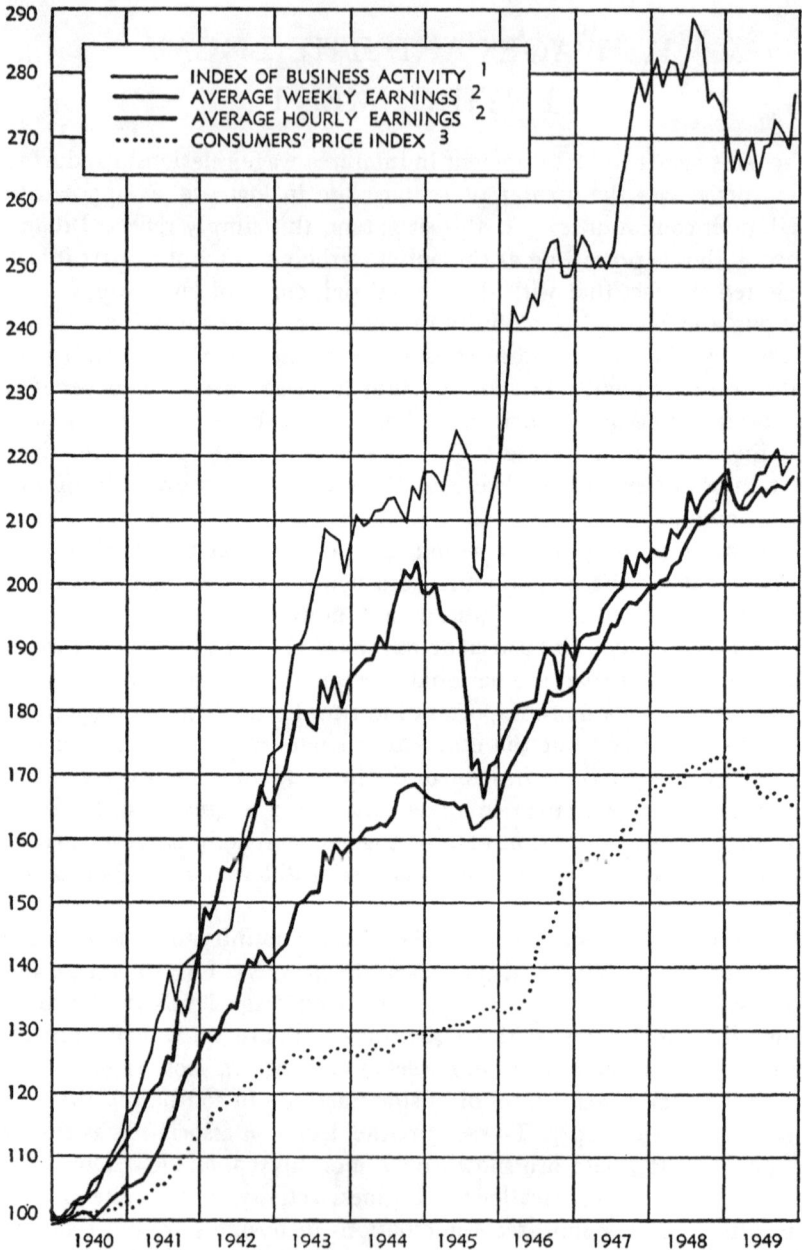

Fig. 15. Wages in manufacturing, consumers' prices, and business activity, Los Angeles area, 1940–1949. *Note:* (1) 1939–1940 = 100. Figures represent southern California. (2) January, 1940 = 100. (3) 1935–1939 = 100.

SOURCES: Calif. State Dept. of Indus. Relations, Div. of Labor Statistics and Research; Research Department, Security–First National Bank of Los Angeles.

in the wage data. Between 1940 and 1945, the series on weekly earnings of factory workers gives a closer fit than the series on hourly earnings, since changes in the length of the work week resulting from the war boom and the immediate postwar adjustment were fully reflected in the former series and only partly in the latter. Beginning in 1946, weekly and hourly earnings moved very closely together.

THE 1940–1945 PERIOD

The index of general business activity, which consists of ten industrial, retail, and financial series covering southern California, shows three rapid upward movements during this nine-year period, each followed by a definite slackening in the rate of increase and/or a sharp decline. The first rise and subsequent readjustment, occurring between 1940 and 1945, was especially marked, so that it is not surprising that the two wage series, including even the average hourly earnings data, followed a roughly similar path at this time. The major point of contrast was that the average hourly earnings series rose less rapidly, and also fell off less rapidly, than the general business index during this five-year period.

Comparisons with changes in hourly earnings in the rest of the country during the decade throw still more light on the forces controlling wage levels in this and other markets. The period of greatest gain in Los Angeles wages, relative to the rest of the country, came between 1940 and 1943. Thus the percentage gain over United States average hourly earnings both in manufacturing and in consumer service fields outside manufacturing was greater in 1940–1943 than in 1943–1945. Indeed, in the latter period, hourly earnings in consumer services rose 14.5 per cent nationally as against 13.5 per cent locally. As to interarea rate comparisons, the data given in figure 11 clearly show that the rise in Los Angeles' ranking in manufacturing occurred in the early phase of the decade.

The explanation of the rapid rise in Los Angeles wages that occurred between 1940 and 1943, both in absolute terms and relative to the rest of the country, seems clear enough. In 1940, the area was comparatively undeveloped industrially. By 1943, the government's armament program had made Los Angeles second only to Detroit as a war production center.[2] This entailed, directly or indirectly, a greater increase in spending per worker than in other areas that were either already developed industrially or that had not become so involved in the war production program. More significant, large-scale industry suddenly, and for the

---

[2] John D. Gaffey, *A Post-War Business Review of the Pacific Southwest* (Los Angeles: U. S. Dept. of Commerce, 1947), mimeo., p. 10.

first time, became an important influence in the Los Angeles labor market, introducing a wage level that contrasted sharply with the scale previously paid. So long as the rapid expansion in war production spending continued, the upward pressures on local wages were aided and abetted by an increasing scarcity of labor as competitive bidding for workers by employers became more intense. These pressures had even greater effects on gross hourly earnings and gross weekly earnings than on occupational rates since, in addition to increases in rates, earnings reflected the lengthening of the work week, interindustry shifts in employment, more rapid upgrading within firms, and the lowering of standards for new hires—all the outgrowth of heavy armament spending in the area. By the same token, these nonrate influences had a much greater effect on manufacturing than on nonmanufacturing wages, since man-power requirements at this time were concentrated in the former field.[3]

Beginning in 1943, hourly earnings and hourly rates in Los Angeles became subject to a conflicting set of influences, the net result of which was to reduce the rise in wages in the area to about the pace of the rest of the country. The most important change was the drop in employment in war production industries which began near the end of the year. The greater part of the decline was due initially to the reduction in the labor needs of local aircraft and shipbuilding factories as production methods in these two fields improved. Employment continued to fall in 1944 and 1945, chiefly as the result of cutbacks in government orders before and after V-E Day in May, 1945. By the end of 1945, employment in the Los Angeles area had fallen to about 250,000 below the peak reached in wartime.

During this period, population in the area continued to rise. In 1943, the population was estimated to be 3,354,000; by the end of 1945, it had risen by about 100,000. The community's civilian labor force, however, declined about 60,000 between 1943 and the end of 1945, the increase in military personnel and the reduction in the number of women available for work more than offsetting the increase in the labor force due to continued inmigration. Conditions of labor scarcity continued in most lines even though the period of keenest competition for workers had passed. Thus, whereas unemployment increased from approximately 25,000 in 1943 to 190,000 at the end of 1945, the rise in joblessness was not enough to offset the upward pressures on wage levels in the area.[4] Nor was the gain in unemployment substantially greater than in other large urban centers which had been paying higher wage rates than Los Angeles. In fact, as already pointed out, local wage rates

---

[3] *Ibid.*, table vi, p. 9.   [4] *Ibid.*, pp. 8–10.

during this period rose somewhat more than in these other communities. The change was nonetheless sufficient to bring wage increases in the area more into line with gains elsewhere, the largest increases now occurring in such hitherto "low-wage" centers as Atlanta and Houston.

Another important change which occurred in 1943 was the introduction of the government's program to control prices and wages. This program limited general wage rate changes to 15 per cent above levels prevailing in January, 1941 (the cost-of-living adjustment established under the Little Steel formula) and to the correction of a few other types of wage inequities. The government's wage controls became generally applicable in the spring of 1943 and, for most practical purposes, were terminated in the fall of 1945.⁶ The effect of the program locally, as well as nationally, was to slacken the advance of wage rates, though substantial gains still occurred. Moreover, hourly earnings, so far as they were affected by overtime pay and other nonrate influences, remained outside the orbit of control. If the local employment market had not changed in 1943, hourly earnings would have continued to rise more rapidly than rates. Instead, during the wage control period, 1943–1945, rates in Los Angeles industries rose somewhat more than earnings. After the peak in wartime employment in the latter part of 1943, the same factors, such as overtime pay and interindustry shifts in employment, which earlier had caused hourly earnings to rise more rapidly than hourly rates, now had a precisely opposite effect. These developments were largely confined to manufacturing industries, rates and earnings moving together quite closely in nonmanufacturing fields.

So far as intercity wage relationships are concerned, the government's program served to lessen geographical differentials somewhat. This effect was particularly evident in connection with the National War Labor Board's policy of granting wage rate increases to correct substandard conditions of employment, since this affected cities in low-wage areas like the Southeast more than in other sections of the country. Since the wage rate position of Los Angeles, by 1943, was already fairly high, the importance of this aspect of the control program for this community was not too great.

In conjunction with influences relating to the armament program and to shifts in the general level of business activity, wages in the Los Angeles area, as elsewhere, reflected changes in the cost of living. During the early years of the decade, as shown in figure 15, the Consumers' Price Index for Los Angeles rose markedly, whereas hourly earnings in local factories rose still more sharply. But in the period 1943–1945, the price

---

⁶ After V-J Day in August, 1945, only wage increases involving higher prices or greater costs to the federal government required approval by the National Wage Stabilization Board. Executive Order No. 9599 (August 18, 1945).

index rose only slightly, from 143.3 to 145.6 (1935–1939 = 100). During the latter period, the rise in factory hourly earnings also slackened measurably but, relative to prices, the rise was much more than between 1940 and 1943. The shift in the course of prices at the beginning of 1943, which followed the imposition of government controls, had the effect of releasing some of the upward pressure on money wage rates in this area, but the continued rise in production for armament continued to pull up the hourly earnings level of the community. Beginning in 1944, however, the rise in business activity slackened and the rise in wages (both earnings and rates) slowed perceptibly.

The influence of trade unions on local wage levels during this early period seems to have been comparatively unimportant. True, it was about this time that the unions won a major place in many Los Angeles industries, but their influence was minor compared to the pressures on local wage levels stemming from the war effort. The course of wages between 1943 and 1945, on the other hand, may have been altered somewhat by union activities, since hourly earnings continued to rise during this period even though the peak of war production had been passed. The upward pressure on wages exerted by unions was especially marked in the last half of 1945 when local cutbacks in war orders caused a marked rise in unemployment. If strong unions had not been in existence, wage rates might well have been lowered and both weekly and hourly earnings reduced much more than was actually the case.

THE 1945–1949 PERIOD

After the cessation of hostilities, there was a rapid expansion in the general level of business activity in the local area in late 1945 and early 1946, followed by a year of slower and more erratic growth. Another rapid rise occurred in the last half of 1947, followed again by a period of less steady growth. In this instance, however, a sharp decline occurred in the last part of 1948, followed by a moderate gain in 1949 (fig. 15). If the five-year period is viewed as a whole, local business activity can be said to have moved ahead far more rapidly than was expected at the war's end.

During this period, the local wage level pursued a steady but rapid upward course, with only a slight slackening toward the end of the decade. Factory hourly earnings in Los Angeles rose about 30 per cent between 1945 and 1949, approximately 10 cents per year with the exception of a 6½ cents rise in 1949. Wages in consumer service fields outside manufacturing rose even more rapidly (44 per cent), though the gains in 1948 and 1949 slackened much more sharply than did earnings in manufacturing.

In explaining the postwar behavior of wages in this area (and this applies to the rest of the country as well), perhaps the most important consideration to keep in mind is that overtime pay and certain other sources of higher earnings largely disappeared at this time, so that changes in hourly earnings largely reflected adjustments in straight-time rates. This explains why the rate of progression shown by the data on hourly earnings was more steady than in the war period. It also has some bearing on the speed at which postwar rates were increased, since overtime and other sources for augmenting earnings were no longer available.

Another important influence operating on both local and national levels to push wages upward at this time was the sharp rise in prices. Between mid-1946 and mid-1948 the Consumers' Price Index for Los Angeles rose from 136 to 169 (1935–1939 = 100), with the result that during this period real hourly earnings, both in manufacturing and in consumer services, fell. The sharp rise in the cost of living placed heavy pressures on local working groups, both organized and unorganized, to secure higher wages. For their part, employers in the local area were not inclined to resist these pressures too stubbornly, since the rise in prices plus the expansion in the volume of business in most lines placed a high premium on the maintenance of steady production. Employer resistance to wage increases, however, was much greater than in the period of wartime when man-power conditions were far tighter. Moreover, the price influence became a deflationary factor in 1949 and, as mentioned above, this coincided with a definite slackening in the rate of increase in the local wage level.

The postwar wage influences discussed thus far affected other urban areas in much the same manner as Los Angeles. There were certain environmental conditions, however, which caused wages to follow a somewhat different course locally than nationally. The facts show that, in contrast to the war period, hourly earnings in Los Angeles manufacturing rose less rapidly than in the United States between 1945 and 1949 (30 per cent as against 37 per cent). In absolute terms, the differential was somewhat less. In consumer service fields outside manufacturing, on the other hand, the rise in hourly earnings in the Los Angeles area was a good deal more sharp than in manufacturing, and local wages kept fully abreast of gains nationally. In both fields, locally, the increases late in the period were less than those which occurred earlier. Comparisons based on hourly rates instead of earnings, and involving individual cities rather than the country as a whole, show these same differences in even more clear-cut form.[6]

---

[6] See figures 11 and 12.

In seeking for an explanation for these wage relationships, both intra- and intercommunity, changes in the number of new business enterprises and in the volume of new capital outlays in the Los Angeles area deserve emphasis. Both provide a sensitive index to conditions in the local labor market since they are closely related to current and pros-

IN MILLIONS

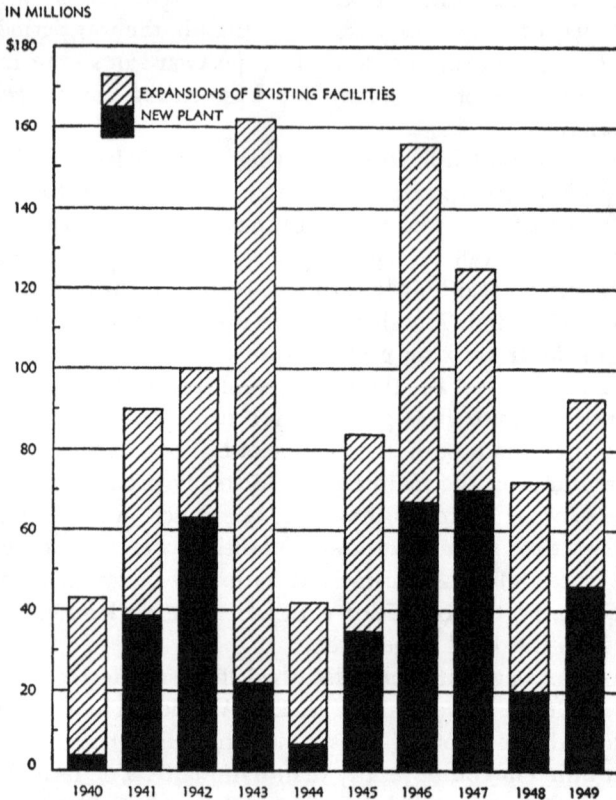

Fig. 16. New capital in industrial plant facilities, Los Angeles County, 1940–1949. SOURCE: Los Angeles Chamber of Commerce.

pective demands by employers for man power. If one considers manufacturing wages alone, capital outlays prove to be especially important as a measure of the movement or direction of the demand for labor. True, the data on new capital in industrial plant facilities, set forth in figure 16, show sharp fluctuations in the 1945–1949 period in contrast to the continued rise in manufacturing hourly earnings throughout this period. Nonetheless, in 1946 and 1947, when hourly earnings in manufacturing were rising most rapidly, new capital outlays were at unusually high levels. By 1948 and 1949, on the other hand, when the

LOS ANGELES
In millions

UNITED STATES
In millions

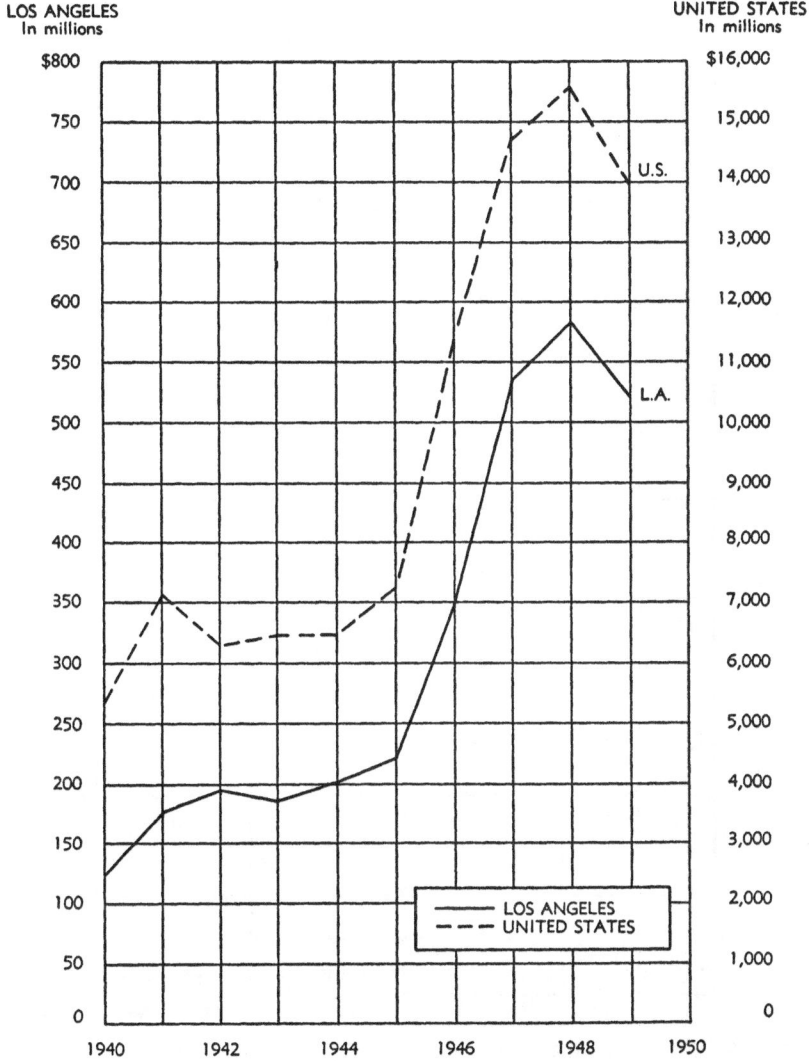

Fig. 17. Business loans held by banks, Los Angeles City and United States, 1940–1949.
Note: United States data for years before 1946 not strictly comparable with data for 1946 through 1949, due to greater coverage incorporated in mid-1946. 1946 figure on old basis: $10,251. United States data represent year-end figures; Los Angeles data represent annual averages.

SOURCE: Research Department, Security–First National Bank of Los Angeles.

rate of increase in earnings had slackened, new capital outlays had
fallen to much lower levels. The data on new investment also square
with local-national wage comparisons in manufacturing. In contrast
to the Los Angeles area, capital outlays in the country at large rose in

THOUSANDS OF ENTERPRISES

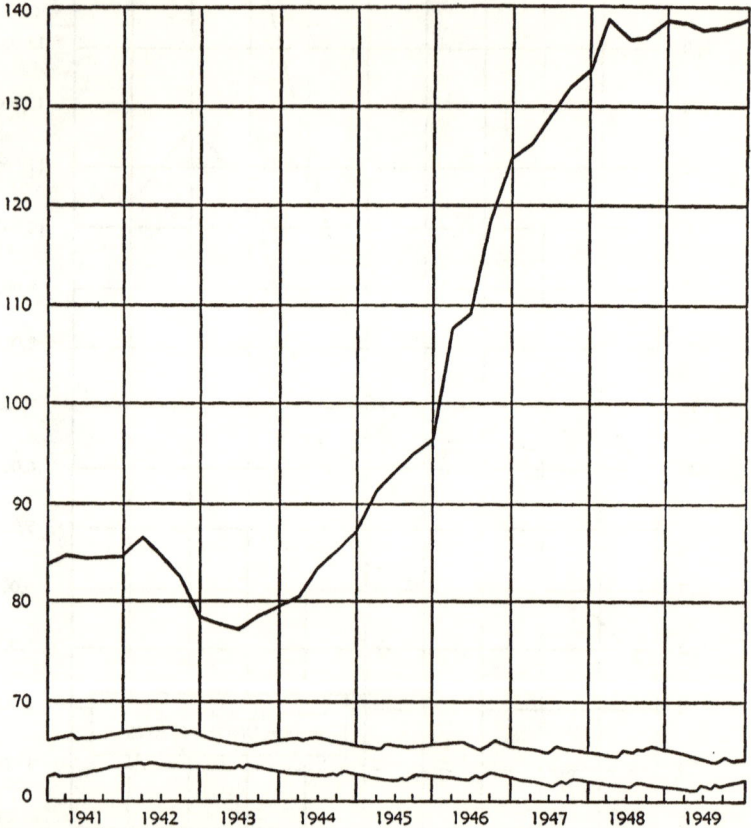

Fig. 18. Number of business enterprises, southern California, December 31, 1940–
December 31, 1949. *Note:* Figures represent number of employers to whom tax returns
were mailed under the Federal Insurance Contributions Act. 1949 figures are estimates.
Counties included: Imperial, Kern, Los Angeles, Orange, Riverside, San Bernardino,
San Diego, San Luis Obispo, Santa Barbara, and Ventura.
Source: Research Department, Security–First National Bank of Los Angeles.

1948 and fell only slightly in 1949. The facts show that private investment rose more rapidly, fell more rapidly, and fell sooner in Los Angeles
than in the rest of the country.[7] It was during this period, it will be

───────

[7] Compare chart 11 in *The Economic Report of the President, January, 1951*
(Washington: Government Printing Office, 1951), p. 58.

recalled, that manufacturing wages rose more rapidly nationally than locally.

Two other business series, business loans held by banks and number of business enterprises, show a somewhat similar pattern (figs. 17 and 18). Both of these series reflect developments in nonmanufacturing as well as manufacturing, so that we would not expect to see a direct parallelism with new capital outlays. However, both series show a rapid rise in 1946 and 1947, followed by a leveling off and/or a decline in 1948 and 1949. It is also interesting to note that business loans rose somewhat more rapidly locally than nationally in the former period and fell off more rapidly in the latter period. Wages in consumer services, locally and nationally, followed this same pattern.

Data which directly measure the changing fortunes of consumer service industries confirm these findings. Per capita retail sales in Los Angeles, when expressed in absolute terms, rose somewhat more rapidly than in the rest of the country in 1946 and 1947, rose less rapidly in 1948, and declined more rapidly in 1949 (fig. 19). Comparisons of local and national trends in per capita dollar buying power, however, show a somewhat different pattern. Thus, the turning point in both the series on bank deposits per capita and savings per capita came earlier, and the "advantage" enjoyed by Los Angeles during 1946 and 1947 is not evident in the data (figs. 20 and 21). These findings suggest that the curtailment of war production, the continued rapid rise in the area's population, and the rise in consumer spending which occurred after the war had a more pronounced effect on deposits and savings per capita in Los Angeles than elsewhere.

These forces, which played a vital role in the internal and external wage relations of the Los Angeles area at this time, were paralleled by changes in the amount of local unemployment. So long as the labor requirements of the community rose very rapidly, as in the early postwar period, the expansion in its population and labor force did not exert any depressing effect on wage levels. Indeed, so long as market conditions were highly favorable, the rise in population simply added to the upward pressures on the level of spending and wages. But with the slowing down of the business expansion in late 1947 and the contraction in 1948–1949, what had been a stimulating factor quickly turned into a depressive influence. Unemployment rose sharply; certain branches of the metal trades and consumer durables were particularly hard hit. Unemployment in Los Angeles County in September, 1947, stood at about 7 per cent of the total civilian labor force (127,000 against 1,714,000); by September, 1949, it had risen to 10 per cent. In the United States, unemployment rose from 3 per cent to 5 per cent over this same period (fig. 22). This difference in unemployment was quickly reflected in the comparative wage data summarized above.

In light of this, one wonders why wage levels in the Los Angeles area kept as closely in line with wages elsewhere as they did. It should be

SALES PER CAPITA

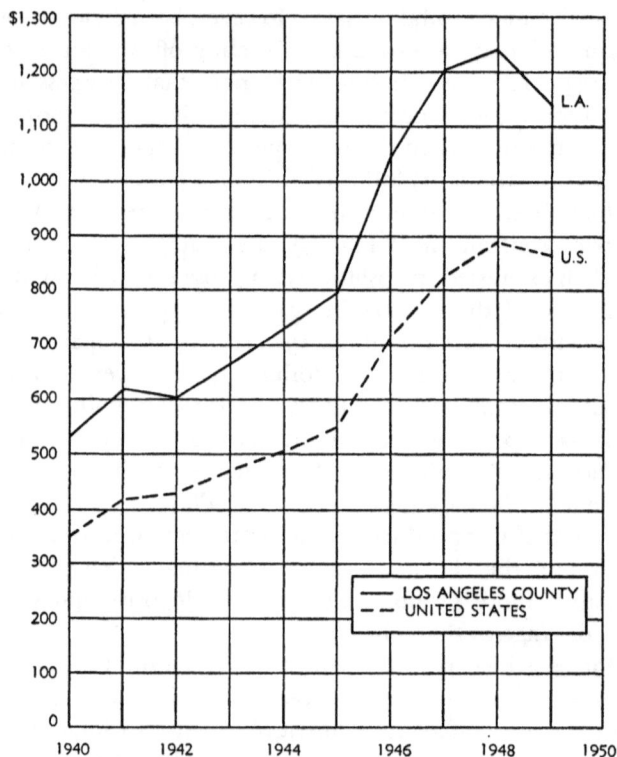

Fig. 19. Retail sales per capita, Los Angeles County and United States, 1940–1949. SOURCE: Research Department, Security–First National Bank of Los Angeles.

remembered in this connection that the decline in general business activity in late 1948 was brief, if sharp. By early 1949, the decline had been checked (fig. 15). In fact, the decline in total employment was slight even in the fall of 1948, the rise in unemployment being almost wholly the result of an enlarged labor force due to heavy inmigration. If business activity had continued to fall through 1949 and if the absolute level of employment had begun to decline, the behavior of wages doubtless would have been markedly different.

Another influence curbing any tendency toward a lowering in wages at this time was the organized labor movement. The 1948 decline was of a type particularly amenable to union control. Wage rates were generally stabilized in most fields, and in a number of industries the unions were even able to secure somewhat higher wages at this time.

DEPOSITS PER CAPITA

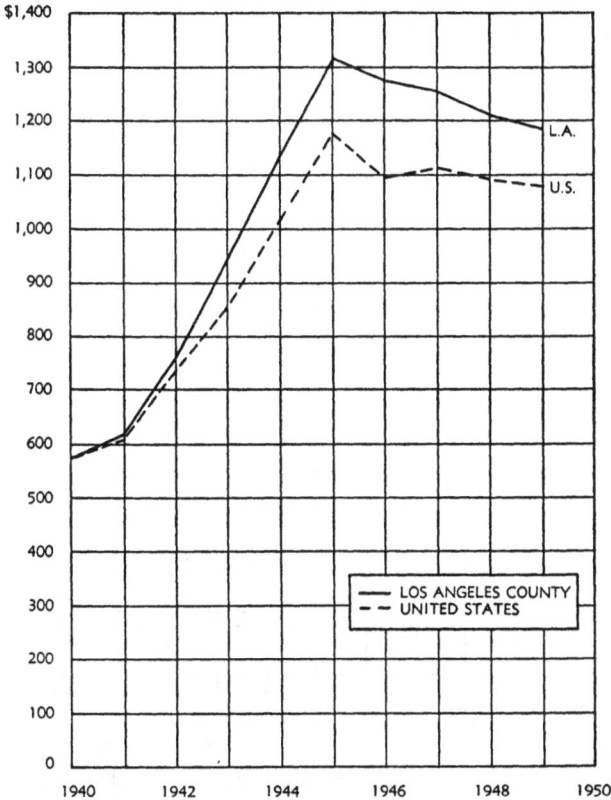

Fig. 20. Total bank deposits per capita, Los Angeles County and United States, 1940–1949. *Note:* Annually, as of December 31.
Source: Research Department, Security–First National Bank of Los Angeles.

The amount of the increases, however, were typically less than in earlier years. These matters raise questions about the course of union wage rates in individual industries and therefore call for more detailed treatment in a later chapter. Here it is enough to point out that organized labor exerted its principal effect on the local wage structure during a period when the volume of business was no longer expanding rapidly and when prices were generally falling.

CONCLUSION

In contrast to the discussion of long-term wage trends before 1940, this review of wage developments in Los Angeles during the 'forties has highlighted the short-term influences which control local area wage levels. The rise in the level of Los Angeles wage rates during this period, relative to other heavily industrialized communities and to the country as a whole, can be attributed almost entirely to the comparatively high

SAVINGS PER CAPITA

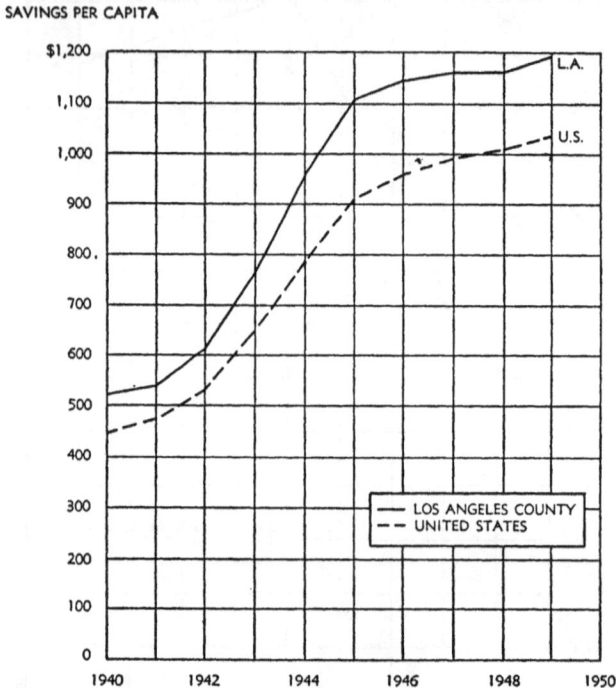

Fig. 21. Savings per capita, Los Angeles County and United States, 1940–1949.
SOURCE: Research Department, Security–First National Bank of Los Angeles.

rate of armament spending in the area early in the decade. The effect of these expenditures on the demand for labor, and hence on the community's general level of wage rates, was especially marked since they necessitated heavy capital outlays in a number of manufacturing industries which had languished or were practically nonexistent before the war. These outlays were concentrated in the period 1940–1943, the same period when the relative gains in hourly earnings and hourly rates of this area were also greatest. As a result, after many years of little or no change, the upheaval of war suddenly pushed Los Angeles well up among the high-wage centers of the nation.

Events after 1943 soon brought the movement of wage rates in this area into line with wage changes in the country as a whole. Locally, the peak in armament spending came in late 1943. During the period of wage-price control (1943–1945), wage rates rose locally at almost the same pace as in the rest of the country, whereas wages in some of the low-wage centers in the South and Southwest rose a good deal faster. Between 1945 and 1949, the expansion in manufacturing as measured by output, capital outlays, and employment was somewhat less locally than nationally, a relationship which was quickly reflected in comparative wage movements. On the other hand, the growth of nonmanufacturing fields in Los Angeles kept fully abreast of gains nationally during this four-year period, and the facts show that wages in these industries rose as much locally as nationally.

Study of the year-to-year and month-to-month movement of wages in Los Angeles during the war period reveals a close association between changes in the community's wage level and in its economic activity. Weekly earnings in manufacturing reflected changes in the index of Los Angeles business activity more accurately than did gross hourly earnings, but both paralleled the index quite closely. Although less consistent, the level of hourly rates also changed in general conformity with fluctuations in local business activity during this period. After the war, with the elimination of overtime and other special wartime influences, weekly earnings, hourly earnings, and hourly rates in local manufacturing, all behaved much the same way, rising at a steady rate through 1948 and then slackening in 1949. The index of business activity, however, followed a much more erratic course, slowing up noticeably in late 1946 and declining sharply in late 1948.

Over the postwar period as a whole, local economic conditions provided a favorable setting in which to raise wage rates, especially when account is taken of the rapid rise in prices between 1946 and 1948. But the *steadiness* of the gains in wages at this time, speaking particularly of manufacturing, can properly be attributed to the spread of trade unionism in this area and the development of so-called national wage patterns. In consumer services, the rise in wage rates was closely paralleled by the expansion in the volume of business in these fields throughout the postwar period.

Although many of the influences impinging on the relative wage rate position of the community were only transitory, two developments during this period had more lasting effects. The first was the increase in heavy industry already discussed. This development acted as a lever pushing up the community's whole level of wages, and at the same time laying the basis for still further gains. The second was the continued

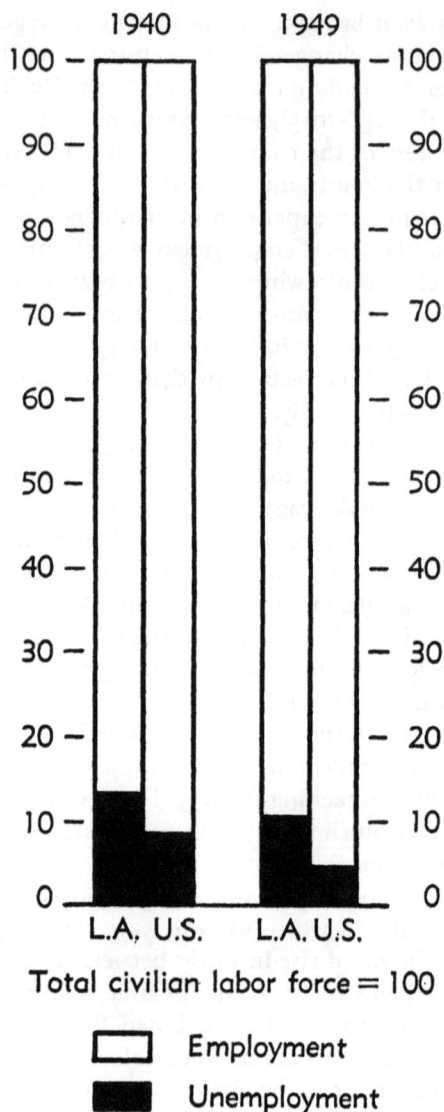

Fig. 22. Employment and unemployment, Los Angeles County and United States, 1940 and 1949.

SOURCE: Appendix table 8.

rise in population at a rate well in excess of the country as a whole. This made the community more vulnerable to a decline in business, but it also served to accelerate the rate of business expansion so long as economic conditions were generally favorable. The rapid rise in popu-

THOUSANDS OF PERSONS

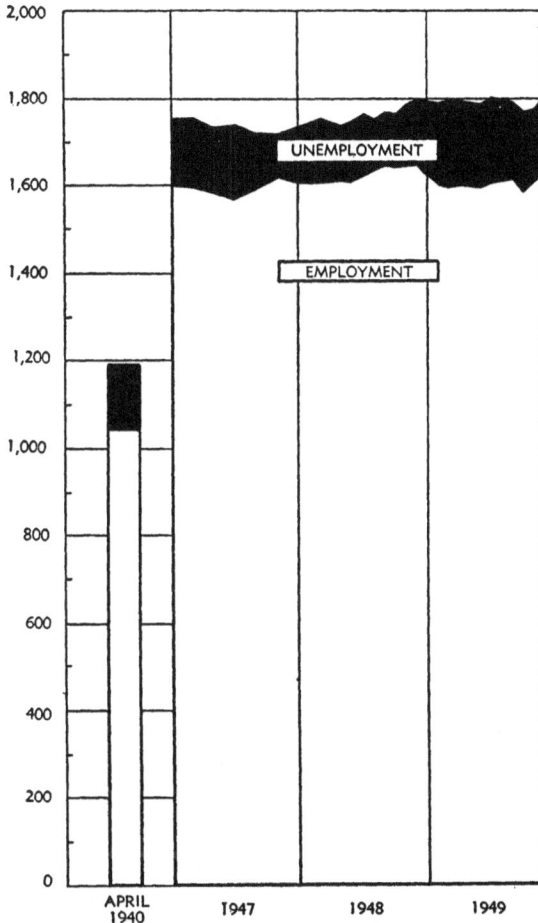

Fig. 23. Total civilian labor force, employment, and unemployment, Los Angeles County, April, 1940, and 1947–1949. *Note:* Figures charted monthly, May, 1948, through December, 1949; before May, 1948, bimonthly.
SOURCE: Appendix table 9.

lation was especially important to consumer services and other non-manufacturing fields in this area. It is significant that even though Los Angeles wage rates were relatively high in these fields in 1940, they rose somewhat more in relation to the rest of the country in the following decade than did manufacturing wage rates.

If one views the decade of the 'forties as a whole, the gain in the relative wage position of Los Angeles was surprisingly small. True, the data on rates showed that this community gained on higher-wage centers like San Francisco, but even sharper percentage increases occurred in lower-wage communities, so that the rise in the wage position of this area in relation to the country as a whole was not more than 3 or 4 per cent (in absolute terms, not more than 10 cents per hour). In manufacturing, average hourly earnings in Los Angeles rose 84½ cents per hour over the nine-year period, and earnings in the rest of the country rose 10 cents per hour less; in consumer services, the rise locally came to 70½ cents per hour, which was also 10 cents per hour above the gain in wages nationally. Viewed either in terms of interarea or intra-area relationships, the two patterns of wage behavior show a striking similarity.

The greater parallelism shown over the longer period, as opposed to the shorter subperiods, raises some interesting questions which can only be touched on briefly here. One of the major conclusions to emerge from the pre-1940 analysis was the marked stability evidenced by the data on interarea wage relationships over long periods of time. Even though we are dealing with only a nine-year span in this case, it is interesting to note that the 1940–1949 period shows marked stability as well. To a significant degree this finding is based on a comparison between wage movements in Los Angeles and the country as a whole. Comparisons among individual cities reveal more variation, with communities like Los Angeles registering definite gains on traditionally high-wage centers to the north and east. But in the postwar period, the Los Angeles area did not experience any marked change even on the basis of intercity wage comparisons. It seems, then, that only the upheaval of war was powerful enough to cause major shifts in the interarea wage position of this community.

This analysis of changes in the Los Angeles wage level has necessarily been couched in general terms. The very concept of a community wage level lacks specific content, made up as it is of a wide variety of individual job rates and individual industry wage levels. To discover what forces shape a community's wage structure and control its relative wage position, it is necessary to break down the data into more nearly homogeneous categories. Limitations imposed by the sources make it necessary to confine this statistical investigation to industry wage levels, and these are the data on which the rest of the study is largely based.

V. INTERINDUSTRY WAGE LEVELS

IN SPITE of the area's phenomenal growth and unusual economic and social environment, long-term trends in the Los Angeles wage level have been found to follow much the same course as in the rest of the country. If any observable differences in wage behavior have occurred, they would be most likely to show up in comparisons of individual industries or industry groups. Similarly, if developments in the local economy diverged markedly from developments nationally, the differences would presumably be reflected in changes in the distribution of employment within the two jurisdictions. Before analyzing the comparative structure and behavior of industry wage levels in Los Angeles in recent years, therefore, it seems appropriate to consider first what shifts in employment have occurred, locally and nationally, during the decade of the 'forties. The data, as of 1940 and 1949, are summarized in figures 24 and 25. The first figure contrasts the shifts in the patterns of employment in rather broad terms; the second, in somewhat greater detail.

The data summarized in these two figures reveal that the share of total employment accounted for by manufacturing increased in Los Angeles between 1940 and 1949, but remained about the same in the country as a whole. The share in trade rose in both jurisdictions, though more so nationally than locally, whereas the share in services fell perceptibly in both the Los Angeles area and the country at large. If the last two categories are considered together, it appears that there was a slight decline in the share represented by the service trade group in both areas. On the other hand, as shown in figure 24, nonmanufacturing industries as a whole declined in importance locally but gained in importance nationally. Thus, though there was a definite shift toward manufacturing employment in Los Angeles, employment in nonmanufacturing, though not in services and trade, became somewhat more important in the country at large.

This contrast in employment patterns reflects certain differences in the economic environment which surrounded the determination of wages in the two jurisdictions. Were they important enough to have any observable effects on relative wage movements? Judging from the evidence presented thus far, apparently not. It is true that between 1940 and 1949 wages in manufacturing rose more in Los Angeles than in the United States, but so did they in nonmanufacturing fields. Indeed, in percentage terms the gains in the latter fields (for example, wholesale and retail trade) tended to be larger in the Los Angeles area than in the country as a whole. Judged in this light, the data on wage movements suggest that such general influences as the extent of unemployment, the rate at which a community is growing economically, and the original level from which wage increases are calculated, are more important than relative changes in the distribution of employment in determining wage behavior. Thus far, however, the discussion has been concerned only with general industry groupings. Whether these conclusions hold for differences in the wage behavior of individual industries calls for more detailed analysis.

PER CENT OF TOTAL

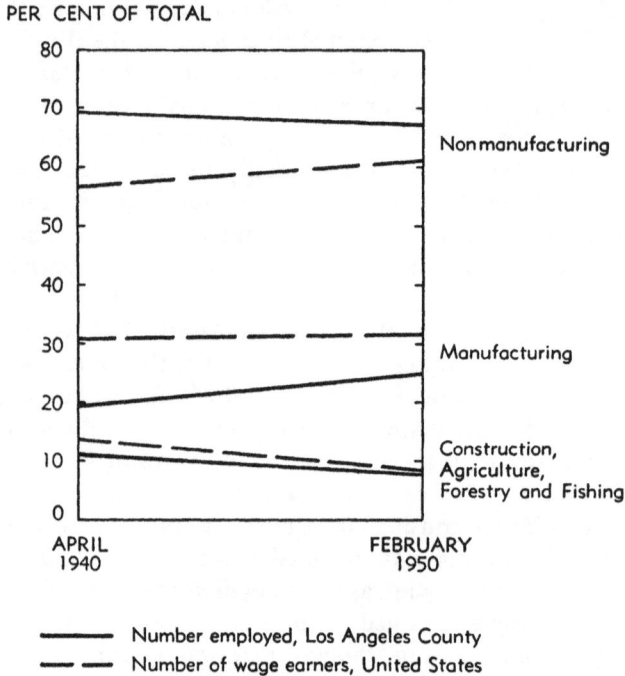

Fig. 24. Distribution of employment, Los Angeles County and United States, April, 1940, and February, 1950. *Note:* The lines on the chart are independent. They are put on the same scale only to facilitate comparisons of the changes.

SOURCE: Appendix table 10-A.

LOCAL INDUSTRY WAGE PATTERNS

Since adequate data by industry are not available for Los Angeles in fields outside manufacturing, attention is necessarily confined to the latter field. Figures 26 and 27 show the average hourly earnings of different manufacturing industries in Los Angeles and the United States for 1940 and 1949, the industries being ranked by their relative wage level in the local area.

The ranking of Los Angeles manufacturing industries by relative

LOS ANGELES COUNTY, APRIL 1940

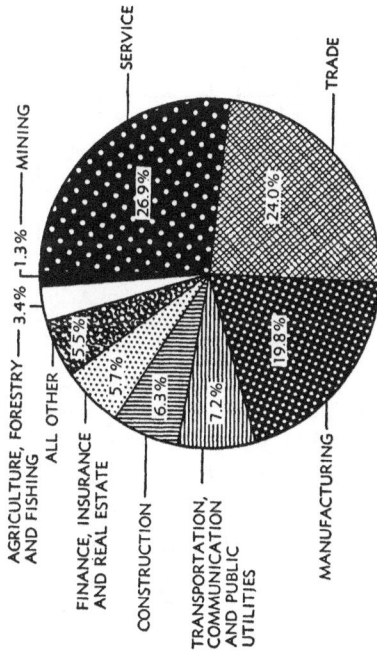

UNITED STATES, APRIL 1940

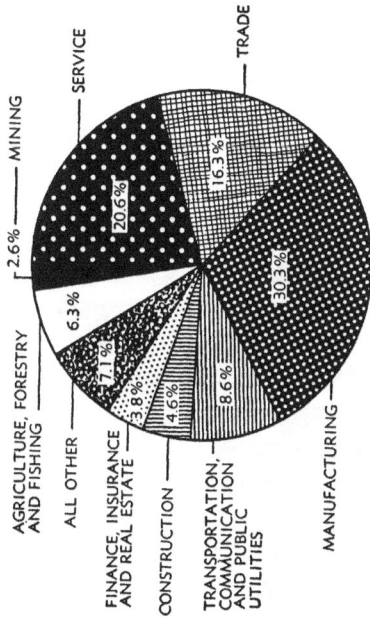

LOS ANGELES COUNTY, FEB. 1950

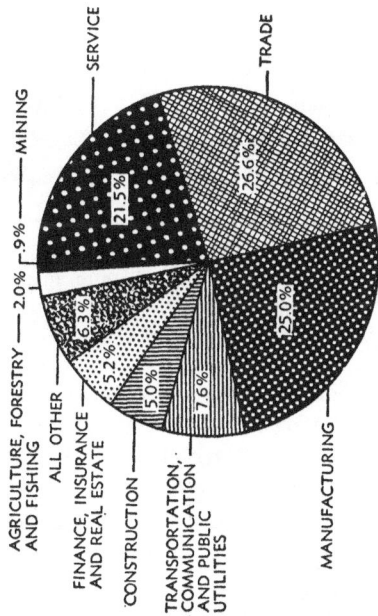

UNITED STATES, FEB. 1950

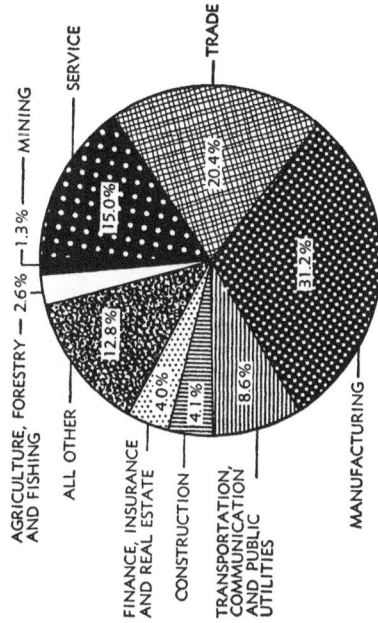

Fig. 25. Distribution of employment by major industry, Los Angeles County and United States, April, 1940, and February, 1950.
SOURCE: Appendix table 10-B.

wage level reveals a roughly similar pattern in both years. In 1949, average hourly earnings in local factories ranged from a top of $2.14 per hour in printing, publishing, and allied industries to a low of $0.94 per hour in textile mill products. In 1940, the range was from $0.98 to $0.55 per hour, with apparel at the bottom of the list. In both years, the

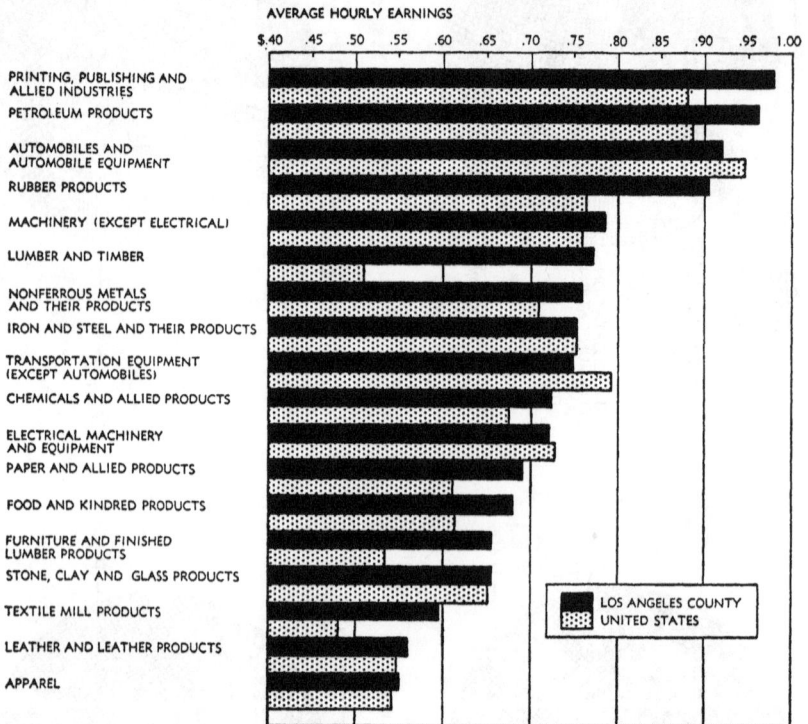

Fig. 26. Ranking of manufacturing industries by average hourly earnings, Los Angeles County and United States, 1940. *Note:* Industry order determined by Los Angeles ranking.
SOURCE: Appendix table 11.

wage levels in Los Angeles manufacturing industries exhibited a well-defined central tendency, though less in 1949 than in 1940. This is shown in figure 28, which gives the number of industries falling in each wage interval for 1940 and 1949 (the figure is based on twenty-three manufacturing industries instead of eighteen as in the two preceding listings). In 1940, the largest number of industries fell in the wage interval between $0.649 and $0.749 per hour, and in 1949, between $1.549 and $1.649, with seven industries involved in each case. But the number in the intervals immediately above and below this category was greater in the former year than in the latter, with the spread in the remaining intervals correspondingly reduced.

Groupings of these same industries in the United States, shown in figures 26 and 27 for the same two years, show roughly similar results. In fact, the contrast between the two dates is somewhat greater in the

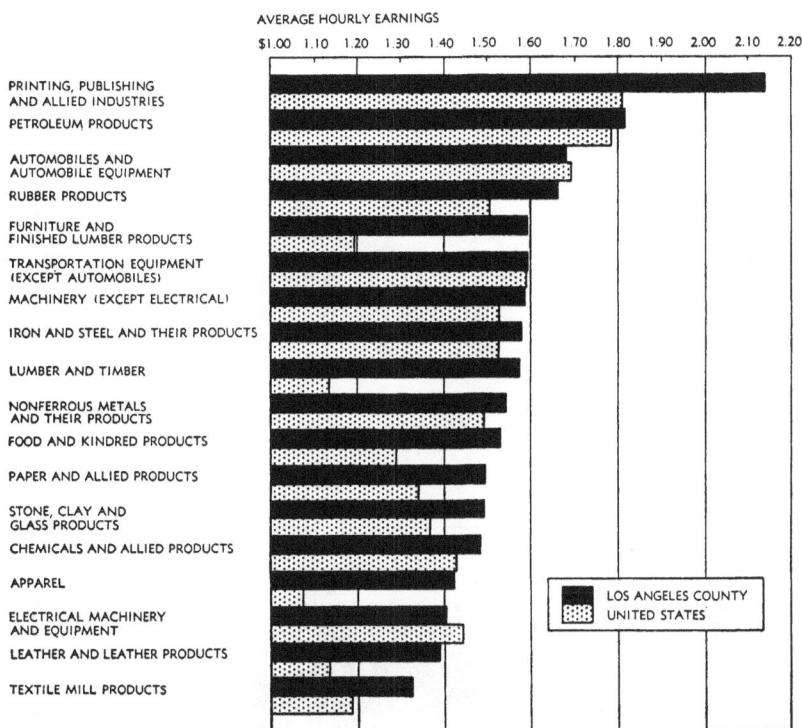

AVERAGE HOURLY EARNINGS

$1.00 1.10 1.20 1.30 1.40 1.50 1.60 1.70 1.80 1.90 2.00 2.10 2.20

PRINTING, PUBLISHING
AND ALLIED INDUSTRIES

PETROLEUM PRODUCTS

AUTOMOBILES AND
AUTOMOBILE EQUIPMENT

RUBBER PRODUCTS

FURNITURE AND
FINISHED LUMBER PRODUCTS

TRANSPORTATION EQUIPMENT
(EXCEPT AUTOMOBILES)

MACHINERY (EXCEPT ELECTRICAL)

IRON AND STEEL AND THEIR PRODUCTS

LUMBER AND TIMBER

NONFERROUS METALS
AND THEIR PRODUCTS

FOOD AND KINDRED PRODUCTS

PAPER AND ALLIED PRODUCTS

STONE, CLAY AND
GLASS PRODUCTS

CHEMICALS AND ALLIED PRODUCTS

APPAREL

ELECTRICAL MACHINERY
AND EQUIPMENT

LEATHER AND LEATHER PRODUCTS

TEXTILE MILL PRODUCTS

LOS ANGELES COUNTY
UNITED STATES

Fig. 27. Ranking of manufacturing industries by average hourly earnings, Los Angeles County and United States, 1949. *Note:* Industry order determined by Los Angeles ranking.

SOURCE: Appendix table 11.

country as a whole than in the Los Angeles area. Viewed in this light, it appears that the internal wage structures of both the local and national economies were controlled by similar influences during this period.

Examination of the rankings of individual industries in Los Angeles and the United States (figs. 26 and 27) also reveals some parallelism in both 1940 and 1949. Thus, the three highest industries locally were also highest nationally in both years. The lowest rankings show greater dissimilarity, though in 1940 the three lowest-wage industries in Los Angeles were among the five lowest nationally. By 1949, the differences in the rankings of the lowest-wage industries had increased somewhat. More intensive analysis, however, reveals that some industries, like furniture and finished lumber products, rose much more locally than nationally; others, like electrical machinery and equipment, fell much more. A few (for example, nonferrous metals) actually moved in opposite directions in the rankings.

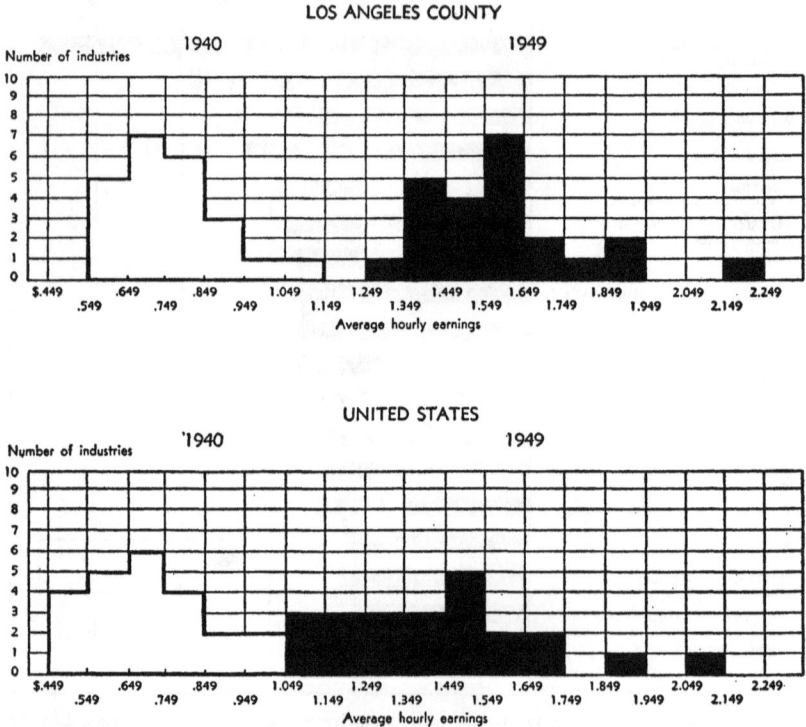

Fig. 28. Number of industries per wage interval, Los Angeles County and United States, 1940 and 1949.

SOURCES: Calif. State Dept. of Indus. Relations, *Labor in California, 1943–1944,* pp. 68–69; *California Labor Statistics Bulletin,* table 2 in nos. 295–305; and letter from M. I. Gershenson to the author, May 25, 1950. U. S. Bureau of Labor Statistics, *Handbook of Labor Statistics, 1947 Edition,* pp. 54–79; *Employment, Hours and Earnings,* special release, September, 1949; and *Monthly Labor Review,* 71 (July, 1950), 163–175.

LOCAL AND NATIONAL WAGE-EMPLOYMENT RELATIONSHIPS

In the foregoing discussion the interindustry wage structures of Los Angeles and the country as a whole have been considered as separate entities, with emphasis on the characteristics of each structure as of two moments of time, 1940 and 1949. To bring out the relationship *between* the two structures, it is helpful to compare the wage levels of Los Angeles industries with the wage levels of the same industries nationally. Figure 29 sets forth this comparison for 1940 and 1949, with the industries listed in terms of the ratio of Los Angeles to United States average hourly earnings which obtained in 1949. Thus, lumber and timber heads the list because the ratio of Los Angeles to United States earnings in 1949 was highest in this industry, whereas electrical machinery and equipment stands at the bottom of the list for the opposite reason. The right-hand section of the figure gives the percentage gains in the hourly earnings of each industry between 1940 and 1949.

Inspection of the figure suggests that the Los Angeles industries with the highest ratios to national wage levels tend to concentrate in light manufacturing—industries in which firms are small and highly competitive, in which labor constitutes a high proportion of total costs, and in which product markets are more highly localized than in so-called heavy manufacturing fields. It should be noted that these industries include a number which are considered to be traditionally low-paying fields. By the same token, the Los Angeles industries with the lowest ratios to national wage levels tend to concentrate in iron and steel, transportation equipment, and other heavy industries. These findings appear to hold for both 1949 and 1940, although the data on percentage wage increases between these two years indicate that somewhat bigger gains in Los Angeles industries relative to the rest of the country occurred in the so-called light manufacturing group.

What would a similar comparison based on percentage changes in employment show? This question is answered in a preliminary fashion by figure 30, which sets forth the percentage gains in employment of Los Angeles and United States industries between 1940 and 1949, listed on the basis of the industries which gained most in the Los Angeles area. Inspection of the results reveals no clearly discernible pattern—certainly not one that conforms to the relationships suggested by the preceding wage data chart. The employment figures reflect to some degree the growth of heavy industry in the Los Angeles area which occurred during this period, but there was little or no tendency for the same industries to gain the most employment (or the least employment) locally and nationally. It should be noted that the data on employment covered both manufacturing and nonmanufacturing, so that direct comparisons with the wage data chart are not possible.

PRODUCTS, MARKETS, AND LOCAL INDUSTRY WAGES

The preceding discussion has raised a number of questions which could only be answered in tentative terms. Passing reference has been made to

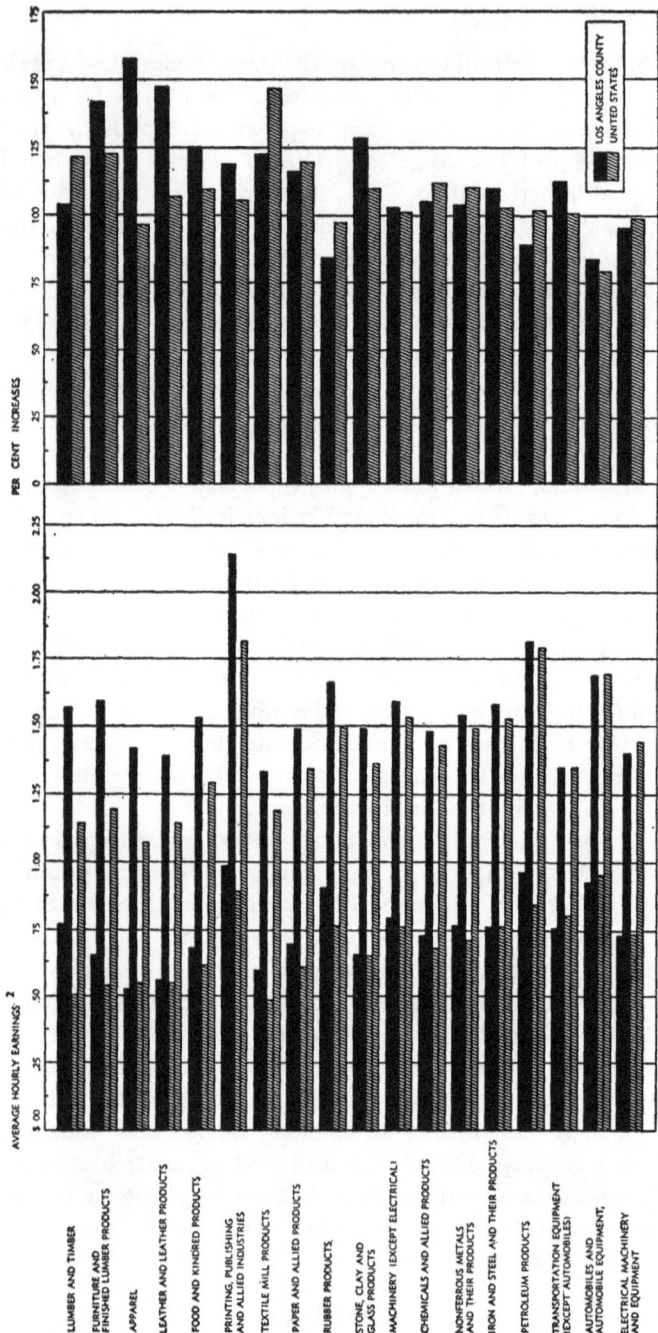

Fig. 29. Average hourly earnings in manufacturing, Los Angeles County and United States, 1940 and 1949, and per cent increases, 1940–1949. *Note:* Industries ranked by 1949 ratio of Los Angeles to United States average hourly earnings. The first and third bars of each group represent 1940; the second and fourth bars represent 1949.

SOURCE: Appendix table 11.

PER CENT CHANGES

100 | 400 | 250 | 225 | 200 | 175 | 150 | 125 | 100 | 75 | 50 | 25 | 0 | -25 | -50 | -75 | -100

Los Angeles County
United States

+ NO CHANGE

Shipbuilding and repairing
Rubber products
Electrical machinery
Lumber and timber
Aircraft and parts
Wholesale trade
Machinery (except electrical)
Apparel
Stone, clay and glass products
Communication
Government
Leather and leather products
Primary and fabricated metal products
Automobiles and automobile equipment
Food and kindred products
Chemicals and allied products
Petroleum products
Retail trade
Utilities
Finance, insurance and real estate
Furniture and fixtures
Printing, publishing and allied industries
Textile mill products
Construction
Mining
Paper and allied products
Agriculture
Domestic service
Other transportation equipment

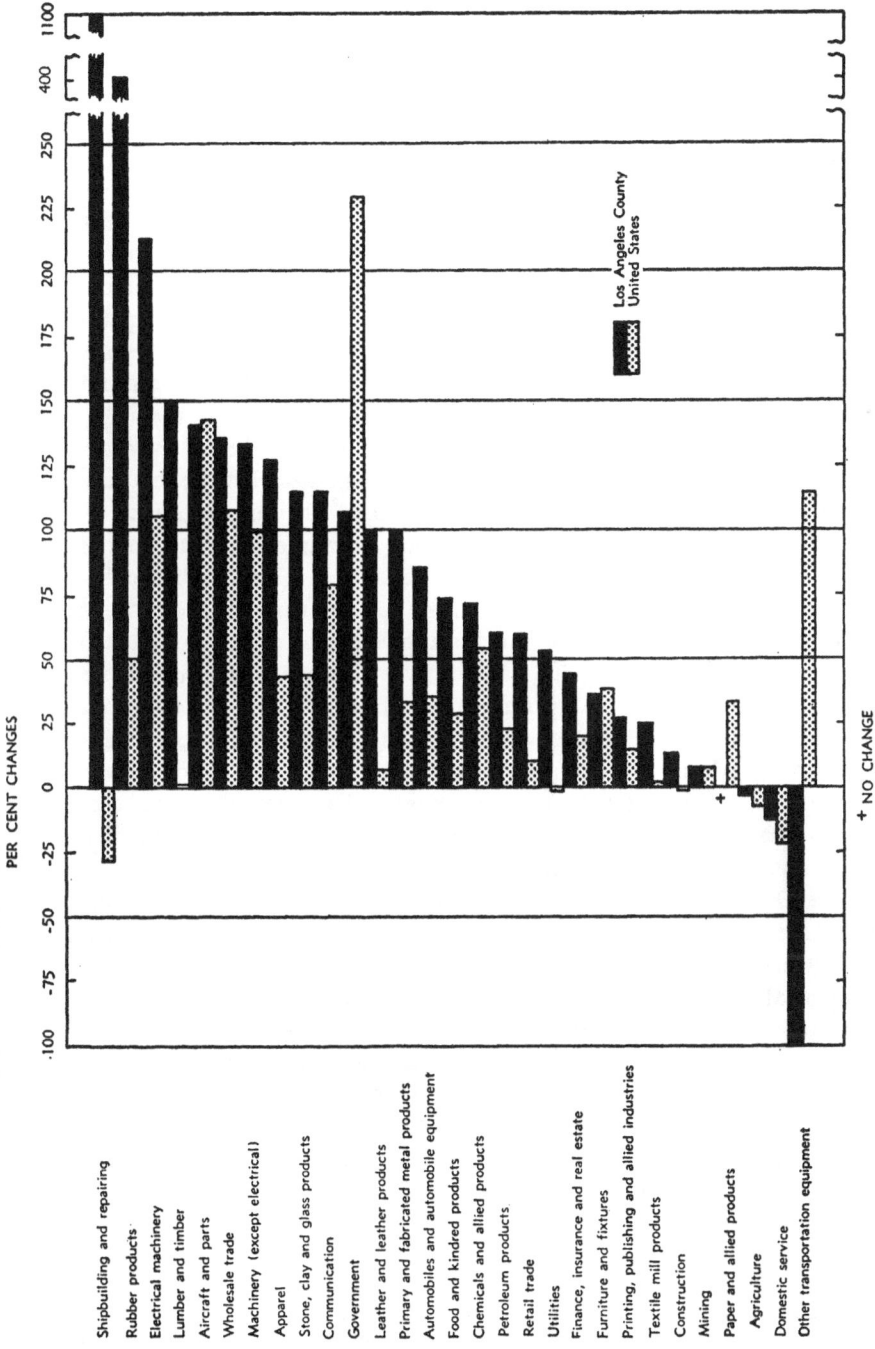

Fig. 30. Ranking of per cent changes in employment, Los Angeles County and United States, April, 1940–April, 1949. *Note:* Industry order determined by Los Angeles ranking.

SOURCE: Appendix table 12.

groupings of industries by type of product or type of product market as they may relate to differences in industry wage levels and industry wage behavior, but no attempt has been made to deal with these issues in any detailed or direct manner.

Students of wage economics have long stressed the important influence exerted by different types of products and product markets on company and industry wage levels. The common view is that there is a fairly close tie between product markets and wages and that this holds true for local market areas as well as for the national economy.[1] The following discussion is an attempt to appraise this viewpoint in terms of the Los Angeles experience, judged so far as possible against the background of the United States as a whole.

To examine this matter under ideal conditions a number of hypotheses should be constructed, in each case care being taken that the relationship under consideration is uninfluenced by any "outside" circumstance. Unfortunately, such a series of laboratory experiments is out of the question. All that can be done is to establish a few, rather broad hypotheses, and then to proceed to examine each in turn on the basis of the available evidence. Not too much reliance can be placed on the testing of any one hypothesis, either in the way of proof or disproof, since more than one environmental condition is always present. On the other hand, if a series of such testings, when taken together, yields consistent results, the findings would warrant more attention. Even so, of course, it should be remembered that in the present discussion the data refer to one locality only and that the picture might be very different if a number of communities could have been included.

Three kinds of product influence are examined in this connection: (1) degree of product durability, (2) type of product use, and (3) extent of product market area. Los Angeles manufacturing industries are grouped along these three lines and then ranked on the basis of comparative hourly wage data for two years, 1940 and 1949. In addition, the ratios to the corresponding wage levels in the United States are also shown in rank form for these two years. The rankings make it possible to determine if any association exists between these three types of product classification, on the one hand, and the local interindustry wage structure, on the other, viewing the relationship at instants of time, over a period of time, and in relation to wage levels in the rest of the country.

[1] See, for example, W. Rupert Maclaurin and Charles A. Myers, "Wages and the Movement of Factory Labor," *Quarterly Journal of Economics*, LVII (February, 1943), 253–256. Speaking of the relation between product markets and union wage policies, Dunlop states: "A wealth of material exists to show that trade unions are very much interested in product markets and other supply markets and undertake elaborate programs to affect their pricing decisions." John T. Dunlop, *Wage Determination Under Trade Unions* (New York: Macmillan, 1944), p. 120.

DEGREE OF PRODUCT DURABILITY

In considering the association between product characteristics and wage levels, attention is first focused on differences in product durability. It is a reasonable presumption that industries in the durable goods category have a number of important characteristics in common and that a similar wage pattern can therefore be expected. Methods of production in such fields tend to be more fully mechanized than for nondurable goods. Average value per unit of output is, of course, much higher than in nondurable industries, and it is generally assumed that average value per unit of input is higher too. Production is more likely to be concentrated in a few large firms, and price competition is therefore thought to be less active. Because of the durability factor, demand is postponable and wider fluctuations in output and employment follow as a natural course. In the light of these circumstances, wage levels in durable goods industries are generally presumed to be higher than in nondurables and also more flexible over time.

What do the facts show? Table 3 gives the wage levels of eighteen Los Angeles manufacturing industries ranked on the basis of product durability. The data show that in both 1940 and 1949 one of the durable goods industries was close to the top and a few near the bottom, but a majority were in the middle third of the range. The semidurable and nondurable goods industries tended to fall, on the other hand, in the upper and lower thirds of the list. Thus, speaking of the Los Angeles area, industries producing durable goods exhibit somewhat greater wage homogeneity than the other two industry groups, especially when the latter are considered together. To this extent, it would appear that the characteristics of durable product industries noted above have an observable effect on this community's interindustry wage structure.

At the same time, wages in the durable goods industries were not as high in the Los Angeles area as might have been expected. The rank values averaged somewhat below the nondurable group in both years, though well above the semidurable group. The disparity in terms of actual hourly earnings proved even greater. At least in this area, it is clear that other characteristics of industries had a more important part in determining wage levels than those associated with product durability.

As for changes over the nine-year period, the wage levels of the three industry groups, expressed either in terms of average rankings or of average earnings, shifted hardly at all. This seems all the more noteworthy since wage levels were rising so rapidly during this nine-year period. It is evident that the forces pushing up wages in this community

TABLE 3

RANKING OF MANUFACTURING INDUSTRY WAGE LEVELS, AND RANKING OF RATIOS TO
UNITED STATES, BY DEGREE OF PRODUCT DURABILITY, LOS ANGELES COUNTY,
1940 AND 1949

	Average hourly earnings			
Industry[a]	Los Angeles County		LA/US ratio	
	1940	1949	1940	1949
Group I				
Durable				
Automobiles and automobile equipment.........................	3	3	17	17
Furniture and finished lumber products......................	14	5.5	3	2
Transportation equipment (except automobiles).....................	9	5.5	18	16
Machinery (except electrical)........	5	7	11	11
Iron and steel and their products.....	8	8	15	13.5
Lumber and timber................	6	9	1	1
Nonferrous metals and their products.	7	10	10	13.5
Stone, clay, and glass products.......	15	13	14	10
Electrical machinery and equipment..	11	16	16	18
Group II				
Semidurable				
Rubber products..................	4	4	4	9
Apparel..........................	18	15	13	3
Leather and leather products........	17	17	12	4
Textile mill products...............	16	18	2	7
Group III				
Nondurable				
Printing, publishing, and allied industries.......................	1	1	6	6
Petroleum products................	2	2	8	15
Food and kindred products..........	13	11	7	5
Paper and allied products...........	12	12	5	8
Chemicals and allied products........	10	14	9	12

Industry category	Unweighted averages of average hourly earnings		Averages of rank values	
	1940	1949	1940	1949
Durable............................	$.754	$1.564	8.7	8.6
Semidurable........................	.654	1.453	13.8	13.5
Nondurable........................	.808	1.694	7.6	8.0

SOURCE: Appendix table 11.
[a] Industries listed according to wage ranking in 1949 in Los Angeles County.

affected all three of these industry groups to about the same degree. As a matter of fact, the only striking differences in rankings occurred within a single group, the durable goods industries. In this category a few fields, such as furniture and finished lumber products, rose sharply in the rankings and a few, like electrical machines and equipment, fell noticeably. In other words, in the few examples in which marked changes in the rankings occurred, degree of product durability was obviously of little importance.[2]

In large measure these relationships reflect conditions peculiar to the Los Angeles market. This becomes apparent when the hourly earnings data are expressed as ratios to the corresponding United States figures and ranked from high to low. In 1940, with two exceptions, the highest ratios were clustered in the nondurable and semidurable goods fields. The durable goods industries, on the other hand, proved to be relatively low in the local economy and relatively high in the national economy, with the result that almost all the durable goods ratios (Los Angeles to United States) were on the low side. Moreover, the latter industries were still low compared to the rest of the country in 1949. The most marked gains occurred in the semidurable group, whereas the sharpest declines occurred in nondurables. Within each of the three categories, however, certain industry ratios behaved quite differently from the others.

The principal conclusion to emerge from the data is that product durability has a limited bearing on intra-area and interarea wage relationships, but, at least with respect to Los Angeles, not of the type that might have been expected. In this market, perhaps because of the rise in population and other developments associated with a rapidly growing community, nondurable goods industries have come to rank higher in terms of wages than in the rest of the country. As to shifts in the rankings, viewed either in local or national terms, product durability exerted little or no consistent influence over the period 1940–1949, intragroup changes being more marked than those of an intergroup nature.

---

[2] To ascertain whether the results would have been materially different if a more detailed classification of industries had been used, the 1949 wage figures were broken down into thirty-seven instead of eighteen industry categories. The resulting averages, which are summarized below, reveal a somewhat different picture but the comparative levels are in the same order of ranking as before.

AVERAGE HOURLY EARNINGS AND RANKS OF THIRTY-SEVEN MANUFACTURING INDUSTRIES, BY DEGREE OF PRODUCT DURABILITY, LOS ANGELES COUNTY, 1949

Industry category	Unweighted averages of average hourly earnings	Averages of rank values
Durable	$1.557	18.6
Semidurable	1.425	24.4
Nondurable	1.842	16.4

Capital and Consumers' Goods

In view of these findings, wages in Los Angeles manufacturing, if divided between capital goods and consumption goods industries, may be expected to show a more clearly defined pattern than the classification based on degree of durability. Industries making capital equipment and producers' supplies form a more nearly homogeneous group than any of those contained in the previous listing. Their operations are marked by extensive use of machinery, the bulk of their labor is semi- or unskilled, and their output depends on the needs of other industries for capital equipment and supplies. Demand for capital goods, partly because of the element of postponability, is subject to wide fluctuations. Finally, the bulk of the firms supplying capital needs are in the metal, machinery, and allied trades, a rather closely knit group of manufactures. The consumption goods industries, on the other hand, though more diversified, tend to fall into two rather distinctive wage categories. The first category is made up of consumption goods fields in which the amount of skilled labor required is unusually large or in which a high degree of mechanization has been attained. The second comprises consumption goods fields in which quite opposite conditions obtain. Consequently, we may expect to find a definite break between the wage levels of these two groups of consumers' goods industries.

Table 4, which gives the wage rankings of Los Angeles manufacturing industries classified as capital goods and consumers' goods, supports this hypothesis. The highest and lowest wage levels, both in 1940 and 1949, appear in the consumers' goods group, whereas the capital goods fields tend to be grouped together in the middle of the range. This same pattern was reflected in the classification of industries by degree of product durability, a result which is, of course, attributable to the fact that the two classifications tend to overlap. All but one of the industries in the semidurable and nondurable groups are in the consumption use category, whereas five of the nine durable goods industries are in the capital goods group. It is interesting to note that the wage rankings of the latter five industries are widely scattered, whereas the four durable goods industries which fall in the consumption use category are more closely bunched. This is probably due in part to the fact that durable capital goods are sold to a wide variety of industries, whereas the market for durable consumers' goods is more homogeneous. Diversity of markets also helps explain why differences in the wage levels of capital goods industries are about as great as in the durable group as a whole, even though the latter are almost evenly divided between the consumers' goods and capital goods categories.

TABLE 4

Ranking of Manufacturing Industry Wage Levels, and Ranking of Ratios to United States, by Type of Product Use, Los Angeles County, 1940 and 1949

Industry[a]	Average hourly earnings			
	Los Angeles County		LA/US ratio	
	1940	1949	1940	1949
Group I				
Consumption use				
Printing, publishing, and allied industries....................	1	1	6	6
Petroleum products.................	2	2	8	15
Automobiles and automobile equipment..........................	3	3	17	17
Rubber products...................	4	4	4	9
Furniture and finished lumber products......................	14	5.5	3	2
Lumber and timber................	6	9	1	1
Nonferrous metals and their products.	7	10	10	13.5
Food and kindred products	13	11	7	5
Chemicals and allied products........	10	14	9	12
Apparel...........................	18	15	13	3
Leather and leather products........	17	17	12	4
Textile mill products...............	16	18	2	7
Group II				
Capital equipment and producers' supplies				
Transportation equipment (except automobiles)....................	9	5.5	18	16
Machinery (except electrical)........	5	7	11	11
Iron and steel and their products.....	8	8	15	13.5
Paper and allied products...........	12	12	5	8
Stone, clay, and glass products.......	15	13	14	10
Electrical machinery and equipment..	11	16	16	18

Industry category	Unweighted averages of average hourly earnings		Averages of rank values	
	1940	1949	1940	1949
Consumption use.....................	$.756	$1.599	9.3	9.1
Capital equipment and producers' supplies..........................	.727	1.528	10.0	10.1

Source: Appendix table 11.
[a] Industries listed according to wage ranking in 1949 in Los Angeles County.

A review of changes in the wage levels of consumers' and capital goods industries over the nine-year period, 1940–1949, yields much the same results as those based on degree of durability. Average earnings of the two categories taken as a whole stood in the same relationship to one another at the end of the period as at the beginning, with consumers' goods earnings slightly higher in both instances. Among individual industries, the greatest gain in ranking between 1940 and 1949 occurred in a consumers' goods field (furniture and finished lumber products), and the greatest loss, in a capital goods field (electrical machinery and equipment). On the other hand, there were offsetting changes within each of the two general categories, so that the adjustments, over-all, just about canceled out.[8]

Comparisons with wages in the United States show that consumers' goods industries in Los Angeles paid higher wages relative to the rest of the country than did capital goods industries. Of the rankings of Los Angeles to United States wage ratios, all but four of the consumers' goods industries fell in the upper half, and all but one of the capital goods industries fell in the lower half of the listings. This pattern held for both 1940 and 1949, though the gains in the rankings of capital goods industries were more marked than those of consumers' goods industries. Thus, as in the groupings based on degree of durability, the special opportunities afforded consumers' goods industries in the Los Angeles area are reflected in interarea wage comparisons. Nonetheless, in recent years, greater industrialization has served to bring the community's interindustry wage structure more in line with the rest of the country.

GEOGRAPHICAL MARKET AREAS

Still another influence bearing on industry wage levels stems from the geographical scope of product markets. Presumably, industries serving broad national markets tend to pay higher wages than those whose sales

---

[8] As in the preceding section, the 1949 figures were analyzed on the basis of thirty-seven instead of eighteen industry categories and, again, though the absolute averages were different, the rankings were in the same order. The results of the more detailed industry breakdown are summarized below.

AVERAGE HOURLY EARNINGS AND RANKS OF THIRTY-SEVEN MANUFACTURING INDUSTRIES, BY TYPE OF PRODUCT USE, LOS ANGELES COUNTY, 1949

Industry category	Unweighted averages of average hourly earnings	Averages of rank values
Consumption use	$1.663	18.9
Capital equipment and producers' supplies	1.560	19.1

are confined to a very limited geographical area. On the other hand, if local demand conditions are favorable, we may expect to find certain local market industries with comparatively high wages since they are sheltered from low-wage competition in other communities. In short, if the product market area is an important influence, we should expect to find some local market industries at the top of the list and others at the bottom, with wages in industries serving broad markets falling in between.

To test these relationships, Los Angeles manufacturing industries were grouped into three categories: (1) local, (2) regional or national, and (3) local and regional or national (i.e., sales about equally divided between local and nonlocal markets). An attempt was made to divide industries into just two categories, local and nonlocal, but a number of industries were found to sell about half of their product locally and the other half regionally or nationally. Hence, a third grouping midway between the other two was felt to be necessary.

The method of classification was based on the "location quotient" technique. According to this method, the market classification of an industry depends on the proportion of the community's total employment in the industry relative to the proportion of the region's or nation's total employment in the same industry. An industry in which there is a relatively high degree of employment concentration can be assumed to enjoy a comparative cost advantage with reference to the larger market area, and hence to "export" out of the local area.[4] In a few instances the market classifications were shifted in the light of other data, but the groupings based on location quotients were found in almost all cases to square with other tests and "expert opinion." The three market groupings, together with the wage ranking data for 1940 and 1949, are shown in table 5.

Viewed broadly, the data support the thesis that differences in product market areas exert an important influence on interindustry wage levels within local communities. The results, moreover, coincide quite closely with those anticipated above. Generally speaking, wages in industries serving regional or national markets (Group II) stood higher in the rankings, both in 1940 and 1949, than wages in the other two narrower market groups. This result lends support to the proposition that industries which have broad product markets pay relatively high wages.

---

[4] A detailed explanation of the use of location quotients in determining the geographical areas of product markets is given in George H. Hildebrand and Arthur Mace, Jr., "The Employment Relation in an Expanding Industrial Market: Los Angeles County, 1940–1947," *Review of Economics and Statistics*, XXXII (August, 1950), 241–249. See also Frank L. Kidner and Philip Neff, *An Economic Survey of the Los Angeles Area* (Los Angeles: The Haynes Foundation, 1945), pp. 15–16.

TABLE 5
RANKING OF MANUFACTURING INDUSTRY WAGE LEVELS, AND RANKING OF RATIOS TO UNITED STATES, BY PRODUCT MARKET AREA, LOS ANGELES COUNTY, 1940 AND 1949

Industry[a]	Average hourly earnings			
	Los Angeles County		LA/US ratio	
	1940	1949	1940	1949
Group I				
Local (Los Angeles County and 10 southern California counties)				
Printing, publishing, and allied industries	1	1	6	6
Lumber and timber	6	9	1	1
Food and kindred products	13	11	7	5
Textile mill products	16	18	2	7
Group II				
Regional or national (Southwest, 11 western states, or the United States)				
Petroleum products	2	2	8	15
Automobiles and automobile equipment	3	3	17	17
Rubber products	4	4	4	9
Transportation equipment (except automobiles)	9	5.5	18	16
Leather and leather products	17	17	12	4
Group III				
Local and regional or national				
Furniture and finished lumber products	14	5.5	3	2
Machinery (except electrical)	5	7	11	11
Iron and steel and their products	8	8	15	13.5
Nonferrous metals and their products	7	10	10	13.5
Paper and allied products	12	12	5	8
Stone, clay, and glass products	15	13	14	10
Chemicals and allied products	10	14	9	12
Apparel	18	15	13	3
Electrical machinery and equipment	11	16	16	18

Industry category	Unweighted averages of average hourly earnings		Averages of rank values	
	1940	1949	1940	1949
Local	$.758	$1.644	9.0	9.3
Regional or national	.820	1.631	7.0	6.3
Local and regional or national	.701	1.514	11.1	11.2

SOURCE: Appendix table 11.
[a] Industries listed according to wage ranking in 1949 in Los Angeles County.

In 1949, both the highest ranking industry, printing and publishing, and the lowest ranking industry, textile mill products, were in the group serving the local market area. The wage rankings of this group of industries diverged almost as much in 1940. This suggests, as indicated earlier, that industries of this type fall into two distinct categories: (1) those in which the product market, by protecting local employers from outside competition, results in especially high wages, and (2) those in which the product market is so narrow that it prevents an efficient type of operation and hence results in extremely low wages. On the other hand, industries in which sales were about evenly divided between local and nonlocal markets (Group III) tended to cluster somewhat below the mid-point of the rankings. None of the industries near the top of the list fell in this group, either in 1940 or 1949, but a few of the low-wage fields such as apparel did so.

As for changes over the nine-year period, the three market groups stood in about the same relationship to one another in 1949 as in 1940. The average hourly earnings of the local market group, however, rose more sharply both in percentage and absolute terms than those of the other two. This squares with the view that wages in locally oriented industries are more flexible in periods of general labor scarcity than wages in industries selling in broader markets. Over the nine-year period, shifts in rankings within the local market and regional or national market groups (Groups I and II) were relatively small, particularly in view of general business and labor conditions prevailing at this time. Substantial changes, however, took place within the group serving both local and nonlocal markets (Group III), a sharp rise in the rankings occurring in such industries as furniture and finished lumber products and a sharp fall in industries like electrical machinery and equipment. Apparently, this group of industries included certain fields in which market territories were in the process of expansion but which had not yet, at least, become predominantly nonlocal in character. Included also are certain industries that experienced adverse product market conditions or other developments during this period which resulted in a lowering of their relative wage level. In any event, it is clear that this is the category of industries in which the widest changes in the rankings occurred.[5]

When the industries are ranked in relation to average hourly earnings in the United States, the results are almost entirely opposite to those just reviewed. Thus, the ratios of local to national wages in the industries serving regional or national markets (Group II) are grouped

---

[5] Analysis of the data for 1949 on the basis of thirty-seven instead of eighteen manufacturing industries reveals an even lower average ranking for industries in the local

toward the bottom, rather than the top, of the list. The local market group (Group I), on the other hand, stands a good deal higher in the listing, whereas the industries selling in both local and nonlocal markets (Group III) include some of the highest and lowest ratio values. Interestingly enough, the greatest changes over the nine-year period occurred, not among this latter group, but among industries serving regional or national markets; for example, petroleum and rubber both fell sharply but leather products rose markedly in the ranking of Los Angeles and United States ratios. Another big gainer in terms of ratio rankings, however, was apparel, which was included in Group III.

The rankings of Los Angeles/United States wage levels clearly demonstrate that, compared to the rest of the country, conditions in this community have generally favored the growth of industries serving the local area, whereas industries selling in very broad markets have lagged behind other parts of the country. Moreover, between 1940 and 1949, there were more divergent economic developments in industries in the regional or national market category than in the other two. The data on wage ratios accurately reflect these developments.

EMPLOYMENT AND WAGE LEVELS

All three of the environmental factors just discussed were found to have some bearing on the structure of industry wages in this area, but comparisons based on product market areas yielded the most consistent and most clear-cut results. As to changes in the interindustry wage structure over time, however, no one of these factors proved controlling, shifts within the various industry groupings being hardly less marked than shifts between the groupings. Another approach is to study changes in industry wage levels from the viewpoint of broader product market influences, on the assumption that changes in interindustry wage levels are related to differences in rates of business expansion. Thus, other things being equal, wages in an industry which is growing rapidly will

---

and regional or national category (Group III) than was obtained before, but the order of ranking remains the same. The results of the more detailed industry breakdown are summarized below.

AVERAGE HOURLY EARNINGS AND RANKS OF THIRTY-SEVEN MANUFACTURING INDUSTRIES,
BY PRODUCT MARKET AREA, LOS ANGELES COUNTY, 1949

Industry category	Unweighted averages of average hourly earnings	Averages of rank values
Local	$1.827	16.5
Regional or national	1.661	12.6
Local and regional or national	1.464	23.7

presumably increase more than in an industry which is growing slowly. Because of the comparability of the data, changes in employment in individual industries afford the best measure of differences in rates of expansion. If a close association is found between the comparative behavior of employment and industry wage levels, it would indicate that

TABLE 6

RANK ORDER OF PER CENT CHANGES IN WAGES AND EMPLOYMENT, LOS ANGELES MANUFACTURING INDUSTRIES, 1940–1949

Industry	Ranking by level of average hourly earnings 1940	Ranking by per cent change in average hourly earnings 1940–1949	Ranking by per cent change in employment 1940–1949
Apparel	18	1	10
Leather and leather products	17	2	5
Furniture and finished lumber products	14	3	11
Stone, clay, and glass products	15	4	3
Food and kindred products	13	5	18
Textile mill products	16	6	13
Printing, publishing, and allied industries	1	7	14
Paper and allied products	12	8	9
Transportation equipment (except automobiles)	9	9	12
Iron and steel and their products	8	10	15
Chemicals and allied products	10	11	7
Lumber and timber	6	12	17
Nonferrous metals and their products	7	13	16
Machinery (except electrical)	5	14	8
Electrical machinery and equipment	11	15	1
Petroleum products	2	16	6
Rubber products	4	17	4
Automobiles and automobile equipment	3	18	2

SOURCE: Calif. State Dept. of Indus. Relations, Div. of Labor Statistics and Research, *Estimated Employment, Total Wages, and Average Earnings and Hours Worked, Production and Related Workers, Manufacturing Industries, California and Los Angeles and San Francisco Bay Industrial Areas, 1940–1948* (May, 1949), pp. 26–32; and special release, July 5, 1950.

changes in product demand have important wage effects in local markets. If a close association is not found, the opposite position would be supported.[8]

The data on percentage changes in hourly earnings and employment

[8] Ross and Goldner, in their analysis of interindustry wage movements in the country as a whole, concluded that changes in earnings have been associated with differential changes in employment. At the same time they found that unionization and oligopolistic market structure were also factors affecting industry earnings levels and that all three circumstances "went along together in large sectors of the economy." Arthur M. Ross and William Goldner, "Forces Affecting the Interindustry Wage Structure," *Quarterly Journal of Economics*, LXIV (May, 1950), 272–276.

of eighteen Los Angeles manufacturing industries between 1940 and 1949 are summarized in rank form in table 6. The figures show no positive association. In fact, speaking in percentage terms, industries in which hourly earnings rose most were those in which employment gains tended to be least! Thus, an analysis of industry ranks based on per cent changes in hourly earnings and in employment resulted in a negative coefficient value of – 0.304.

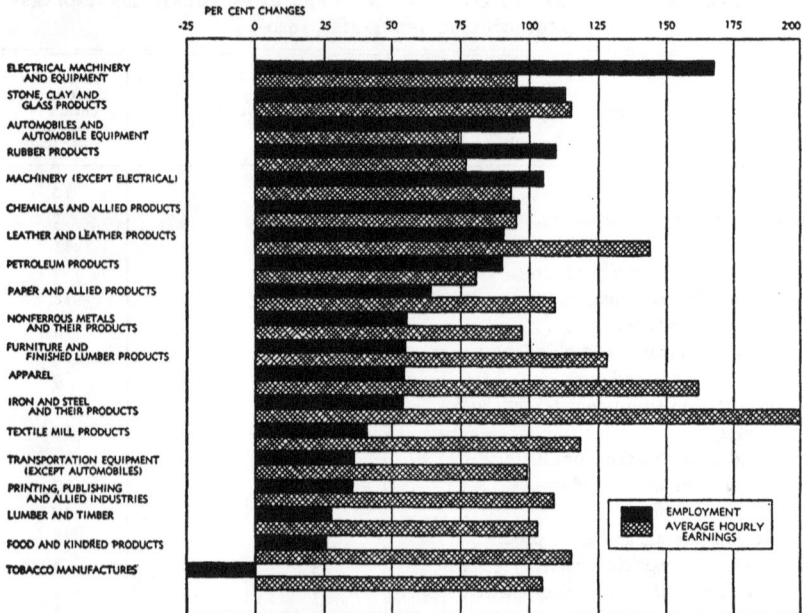

Fig. 31. Ranking of per cent changes in employment and average hourly earnings by major industry, Los Angeles County, 1940–1948. *Note:* Industries ranked by employment changes.

SOURCE: Appendix table 13.

A more complete picture of these relationships is afforded by comparing the actual percentage figures rather than the rank values. These results, together with similar data for the United States, are set forth in figures 31 and 32. These data show even more clearly the lack of a positive association between the two variables. In Los Angeles during this period, forces associated with differences in employment had no observable effects on the community's interindustry wage structure; apparently this also was true of the national economy.

The reasons for this negative result warrant consideration. The most striking association exhibited by the data is the inverse correlation between wage levels at the beginning of this period and per cent changes in industry wage levels in the subsequent period. The figures show a rank correlation of − 0.792 between initial wage levels and percentage wage changes in the subsequent period. The most plausible explanation of this negative relationship is that the general scarcity of labor, combined with a high level of product demand for all types of goods, placed employers in low-wage industries under particularly heavy pressure to bring their pay levels more in line with those prevailing elsewhere.

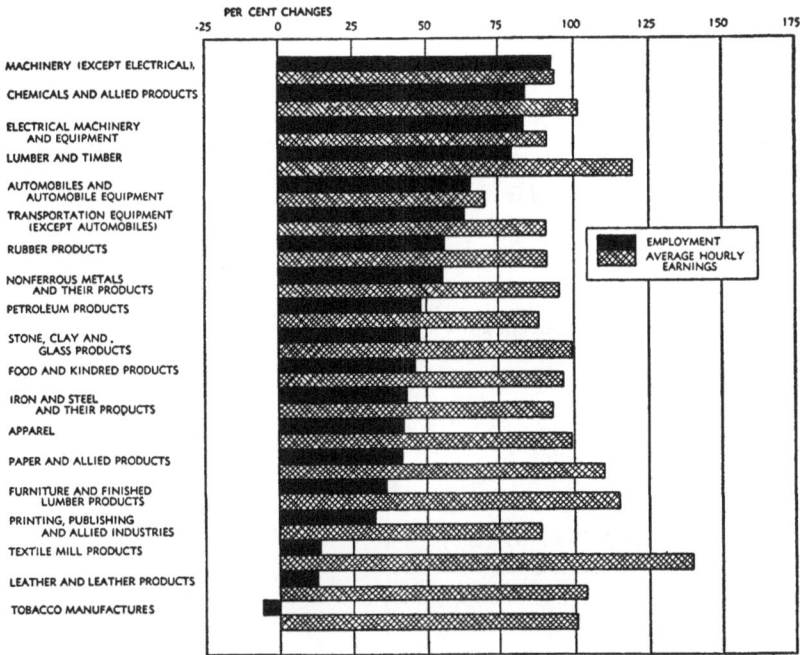

Fig. 32. Ranking of per cent changes in employment and average hourly earnings by major industry, United States, 1940–1948. *Note:* Industries ranked by employment changes.
SOURCE: Appendix table 14.

These employers were not typically in fields in which employment rose most rapidly. Indeed, with few exceptions, they were in industries like apparel and food and kindred products, in which wages at the beginning of the period were relatively low but in which subsequent employment gains were relatively slight.

Another aspect of the relationship between interindustry wage and employment levels is brought to light when the data contained in table 6 are ranked, not in percentage terms, but in absolute terms. The results, set forth in table 7, show a correlation of + 0.276 instead of the value of − 0.304 obtained earlier. In other words, there was some tendency for

industries which experienced the greatest absolute gains in employment
to experience the greatest absolute gains in average hourly earnings as
well. The lack of a positive association which characterized the percentage data was in large measure simply the result of figuring the changes
from different original levels. In measuring changes from a given date,

TABLE 7

RANK ORDER OF ABSOLUTE CHANGES IN WAGES AND EMPLOYMENT,
LOS ANGELES MANUFACTURING INDUSTRIES, 1940–1949

Industry	Ranking by level of average hourly earnings 1940	Ranking by absolute change in average hourly earnings 1940–1949	Ranking by absolute change in employment 1940–1949
Printing, publishing, and allied industries....	1	1	12
Furniture and finished lumber products......	14	2	11
Apparel.................................	18	3	2
Petroleum products......................	2	4	10
Food and kindred products................	13	5	7
Transportation equipment (except auto-			
mobiles)	9	6	1
Stone, clay, and glass products.............	15	7	5
Leather and leather products...............	17	8	16
Iron and steel and their products...........	8	9	6
Machinery (except electrical)..............	5	10.5	4
Paper and allied products.................	12	10.5	14
Lumber and timber......................	6	12	18
Nonferrous metals and their products........	7	13	15
Automobiles and automobile equipment......	3	14	3
Rubber products.........................	4	15	8.5
Chemicals and allied products..............	10	16	13
Textile mill products.....................	16	17	17
Electrical machinery and equipment.........	11	18	8.5

SOURCE: The same as for table 6.

the per cent calculations are perhaps preferable as a means of showing
comparative employment and wage trends among industries. To show
how changes in conditions within a particular market affect the community's wage structure, however, interindustry comparisons based on
absolute changes in wages and employment are more appropriate, because in a given situation it is the absolute changes which directly affect
supply-and-demand relationships.

At the same time, the rank correlation value of + 0.276 secured on the
basis of absolute changes is well below the 5 per cent level of significance
(+ 0.468), so that, even when figured in this way, the association is not so
close as one might expect. A still broader explanation for the lack of a

close association between industry wage and employment changes is therefore called for. If one judges from the evidence presented thus far, the circumstances governing differential wage behavior in local markets are markedly different, depending on the existence or nonexistence of full employment. In periods of extreme labor shortage, all employers face the problem of recruiting and holding man power. Even in fields in which employment remains unchanged, the necessity to raise wage rates, as mobility of labor and competition for labor increase, is ever present. The controlling circumstance, therefore, is not differences in employment requirements but comparative wage levels among various industry groups.

The existence of governmental wage and man-power controls during part of this period contributed to this result. The policy of the National War Labor Board permitting wage increases on the basis of cost of living, substandards, and interplant inequities had the effect of limiting wage differences between war and nonwar industries. If these controls had not been in existence, wages would doubtless have reflected differences in employment requirements more closely. Not much weight should be given this factor, however, since controls were in effect for a comparatively brief part of the period under examination, the effects of controls were by no means all in one direction, and enforcement was far from complete.

Since this discussion has been confined to a single community and period, it has not been possible to deal with the more general aspects of these problems. The data on different types of product markets, even though severely limited in scope, show well enough defined patterns to justify the conclusion that product markets have an important bearing on the structure of local industry wage levels. But the critical question, whether variations in product market demand, as reflected in differences in employment, determine *changes* in the structure, remains unanswered. Indeed, little light has been thrown on the whole issue of changes in the wage levels of local industries. This calls for an analysis of wage movements in a number of communities over longer and more diversified periods of time. Attention is now turned to this broader view of the problem, first, in terms of shifts in demand and, second, in terms of shifts in comparative cost levels in different industries.

VI. EMPLOYMENT AND WAGES

PREVIOUS CHAPTERS have dealt with long-term and short-term changes in the general wage level of Los Angeles, and with this community's industry wage structure considered both at particular moments of time and over a period of time. The latter analysis, at least with respect to influences on the side of labor demand, yielded no consistent pattern of behavior, and therefore a broader investigation, including more than this one community, seems called for.

To the extent variations in the demand for labor control industry wage levels, we would expect to find a close association between changes in wages and employment, since industries in which employment is rising most rapidly are presumably the fields in which the demand for labor, for whatever reason, is also rising most rapidly. Hence a comparison of employment and wage series for individual industries in different communities provides an objective basis for measuring the importance of the demand influence on industry wage changes. Such a comparison, however, does not tell us which of the many influences impinging on employment (demand for labor) is most important in explaining industry wage behavior. It simply indicates whether inter-industry shifts in demand for labor are or are not closely associated with shifts in industry wage levels.

Unfortunately, because of limitations imposed by the data, a comparison of industry employment and wage behavior in a large number of communities is not possible. For the 'forties, San Francisco and Los Angeles are the only two communities for which comparable statistics are obtainable, the data in these localities being confined to changes in average hourly earnings and in employment of nineteen manufacturing industries between 1940 and 1948. For earlier periods, strictly comparable data are available for six large industrial areas, including Los Angeles, the wage data being in the form of yearly, as opposed to hourly, earnings, and on a biennial, as opposed to an annual, basis.[1] The figures for six areas cover the period 1929–1939. Because annual and hourly earnings are subject to different influences, the two sets of data are analyzed separately below. Certain comparisons can be made between

---

[1] The Census of Manufactures, from which the original data were drawn, occasionally changes its industry definitions so that it is extremely difficult to get data on a strictly comparable basis for any extended period of time. Since the staff of the Haynes Foundation (Los Angeles) had already performed the laborious task of making the series comparable for six industrial areas covering the period 1929–1939, it was decided to use their results in this investigation. Philip Neff, Lisette C. Baum, and Grace E. Heilman, *Production Cost Trends in Selected Industrial Areas* (Berkeley and Los Angeles: University of California Press, 1948), pp. 196–204, 226–231.

the two periods, however, since the industry rankings on the basis of annual and hourly earnings appear to be much the same, and since, further, this investigation is primarily concerned with general or long-term aspects of wage phenomena.[2] The reader is forewarned that the data underlying the following analysis are not extensive, and the conclusions should be treated accordingly. At the same time, it should be noted that the various statistical measures used, such as the rank correlation calculations presented below, take account of the fewness of the observations covered.

RANK CORRELATION ANALYSIS

To test the issue empirically, the industries in each community were ranked on the basis of per cent changes in employment and wages between 1929 and 1939 and between 1940 and 1948. A correlation analysis was then made of the rankings to determine if there was any observable association between relatively large (small) percentage changes in industry employment levels and relatively large (small) percentage changes in industry wage levels.

Table 8 gives the per cent of change rankings for eleven manufacturing industries in six large industrial areas for the ten-year period 1929–1939. The data yielded plus r values in every community but one (Detroit), suggesting a positive relationship between degree of employment change and degree of wage change among the industries in these areas. In no instance, however, were the rank correlation coefficients statistically significant. Even the highest coefficient value, 0.545 in the case of Cleveland, was somewhat below the 5 per cent significance level of 0.632, and the others were substantially less. When the data were combined and an average r obtained for all six areas, however, the resulting coefficient value was much more significant, 0.261 as against the 5 per cent significance value of 0.273. In other words, the association between the rank of employment and wage changes was found to be much greater when the number of observations was increased, a result which reinforces the hypothesis of association.[3]

---

[2] As noted earlier, an analysis of manufacturing industries at different points in time yielded rank correlation values of more than 90 per cent between annual earnings and hourly earnings, both in the United States and in Los Angeles County. See chap. 2, n. 7.

[3] Since changes in average annual earnings are affected by changes in the number of workers employed, the question may be raised whether this does not introduce a spurious element into the correlation (i.e., changes in employment would affect both series). Actually, to the extent the latter may be true, changes in employment would *lessen* rather than *increase* the degree of positive association between the two series since average annual earnings are calculated by dividing employment into the total wage bill. In other words, the results tend to *understate* rather than *overstate* the degree of positive association between employment changes and wage changes.

TABLE 8

RANKINGS AND RANK CORRELATION COEFFICIENTS OF PER CENT CHANGES IN EMPLOYMENT AND AVERAGE ANNUAL EARNINGS FOR ELEVEN MANUFACTURING INDUSTRIES, SIX INDUSTRIAL AREAS, AND AVERAGE r, 1929–1939

Industry	Los Angeles County		Chicago		Cleveland		Detroit		Pittsburgh		San Francisco	
	E[a]	AAE[b]	E	AAE	E	AAE	E	AAE	E	AAE	E	AAE
Food and kindred products	6	1	6	2	8	5	7	4	6	2	8	3
Textiles and their products	4	9.5	3.5	7	6	9	1	11	3	10	2	8
Paper and allied products	3	2.5	5	4	3	2	3	5.5	2	1	1	1.5
Printing, publishing, and allied industries	8	7	9	3	9	8	10	9.5	8	7.5	9	6
Chemicals and allied products	2	2.5	2	1	4	4	2	1	5	7.5	5	4
Forest products	9	11	11	10	5	10	11	8	4	9	11	10
Stone, clay, and glass products	7	5	7	9	7	11	5	7	10	4.5	4	8
Iron and steel and their products, not including machinery	10	8	8	5	10	7	8	5.5	9	6	3	8
Transportation equipment—air, land, and water	11	6	10	8	11	6	6	3	11	11	6	11
Nonferrous metals and their products	5	9.5	1	6	1	3	9	2	1	4.5	7	5
Machinery, not including transportation equipment	1	4	3.5	11	2	1	4	9.5	7	3	10	1.5
Correlation coefficients	.404		.293		.545		−.018		.250		.025	
Significance levels $r_{.01}$	.765		.765		.765		.765		.765		.765	
$r_{.05}$	.632		.632		.632		.632		.632		.632	

Average r = .261

Significance levels $r_{.01}$ = .354
$r_{.05}$ = .273

SOURCE: Calculated from Philip Neff, Lisette C. Baum, and Grace E. Heilman, *Production Cost Trends in Selected Industrial Areas* (Berkeley and Los Angeles: 1948), pp. 196–201, 226–231.
[a] E = Employment.
[b] AAE = Average annual earnings.

TABLE 9

RANK CORRELATIONS OF PER CENT CHANGES IN EMPLOYMENT AND AVERAGE ANNUAL EARNINGS FOR ELEVEN MANUFACTURING INDUSTRIES, SIX INDUSTRIAL AREAS, 1929–1933, 1933–1937, AND 1937–1939

Period	Los Angeles County	Chicago	Cleveland	Detroit	Pittsburgh	San Francisco	Significant values of r	
							.01 level	.05 level
1929–1933	S[a].05 .693	.407	S.05 .705	.182	S .752	.435	.735	.602
1933–1937	S .825	S.05 .646	.443	.527	.427	S.05 .716	.735	.602
1937–1939	.225	−.061	.146	.184	.334	.071	.735	.602

Period	Computed average r[b]	Degrees of freedom	Significant values of r[c]	
			.01 level	.05 level
1929–1933	S .560	48[d]	.372	.288
1933–1937	S .621	48	.372	.288
1937–1939	S .152	48	.372	.288

[a] The symbol "S.05" before a correlation coefficient indicates that the coefficient is significant at the 0.05 level. The symbol "S" indicates significance at the 0.01 level.
[b] The concept of average r and the methods used are obtained from George W. Snedecor, *Statistical Methods Applied to Experiments in Agriculture and Biology* (4th ed.; Ames, Iowa: 1948), pp. 151–155. This source was also used as a guide in the computation of rank correlations and their significance tests, pp. 149, 164–167.
[c] Snedecor, *op. cit.*, p. 149. Since significant values of r are not given for 48 degrees of freedom, the higher values for 45 degrees of freedom have been used.
[d] On the advice of Dr. Armen Alchian, Economics Department, University of California, Los Angeles, 48 degrees of freedom have been used.

TABLE 10

RANKINGS AND RANK CORRELATION COEFFICIENTS OF PER CENT CHANGES IN EMPLOYMENT AND AVERAGE HOURLY EARNINGS FOR NINETEEN MANUFACTURING INDUSTRIES, LOS ANGELES COUNTY AND SAN FRANCISCO BAY INDUSTRIAL AREA, 1940–1948 AND SUBPERIODS

Industry group	Los Angeles 1940–1948 E^a	AHE^b	1940–1943 E	AHE	1943–1945 E	AHE	1945–1948 E	AHE	San Francisco 1940–1948 E	AHE	1940–1943 E	AHE	1943–1945 E	AHE	1945–1948 E	AHE
Food and kindred products	18	5.5	15.5	12	7	17	8	2	14	2	9	6.5	5	12.5	15.5	6
Tobacco manufactures	19	9	17	8.5	10	1	18	19	8	13	5	16	14.5	5	9	7.5
Textile mill products	14	4	12	4	17	10.5	3	9	18	18	15.5	18	17	16.5	10.5	2
Apparel	11.5	1	13	2	9	2	5	15	10.5	1	14	5	11	1	4.5	13
Paper and allied products	9	7	9	15	4.5	14	9	3	7	4.5	13	13	4	5	8	4
Printing, publishing, and allied industries	16	8	18	18	4.5	5.5	4	1	15.5	3	17	19	6	7.5	3	1
Chemicals and allied products	6	14	7	14	2	10.5	14	7	13	11	11	14	9.5	12.5	10.5	5
Petroleum products	8	17	11	17	1	19	12	5	10.5	15.5	10	15	2	16.5	15.5	3
Rubber products	4	18	8	19	15	5.5	16	6	19	6	15.5	9	3	2	18	15
Leather and leather products	7	2	8	1	3	3	10	16	15.5	9	12	12	7.5	7.5	12.5	11
Lumber and timber	17	10	15.5	10.5	12	14	6	9	17	4.5	18	4	12	12.5	2	10
Furniture and finished lumber	11.5	3	10	7	7	4	7	4	4	15.5	8	17	9.5	3	6	9
Stone, clay, and glass	2	5.5	14	5	7	7.5	2	9	3	8	8	10.5	7.5	12.5	4.5	7.5
Iron, steel and their products	13	11.5	6	6	16	16	11	14	6	13	6.5	6.5	13	15	7	13
Transportation equipment	15	11.5	1	3	19	10.5	19	18	5	13	1	2.5	19	10	19	19
Nonferrous metals	10	13	4	10.5	18	14	15	13	12	10	4	2.5	16	9	14	17
Electrical machinery	1	15	2	13	11	7.5	17	12	1	7	2	8	18	5	17	13
Machinery (except electrical)	5	16	5	8.5	13	10.5	17	17	2	17	3	1	14.5	18.5	12.5	17
Automobiles and automobile equipment	3	19	19	16	14	18	1	11	9	19	19	10.5	1	18.5	1	17
Rank correlation coefficient	$r = -.430$		$r = .124$		$r = .135$		$r = .409$		$r = -.275$		$r = .382$		$r = -.020$		$r = .233$	

Significance levels $r_{.01} = .575$
$r_{.05} = .456$

SOURCE: Computed from Calif. State Dept. of Indus. Relations, Div. of Labor Statistics and Research, *Estimated Employment, Total Wages, and Average Earnings and Hours Worked, Production and Related Workers, Manufacturing Industries, California and Los Angeles and San Francisco Bay Industrial Areas, 1940–1948* (May, 1949), pp. 27–32, 34–39.
a E = Employment.
b AHE = Average hourly earnings.

To test the comparative behavior of the two series over shorter intervals of time, the data on ranked per cent changes were broken down into three subperiods which roughly coincided with phases of the cycle. The results are summarized in table 9. Although the *r* values did not prove to be significant in a majority of cases, they were well above the significance level in a number of instances. This was particularly true of the two well-defined cycle phases, 1929–1933 and 1933–1937. Indeed, when the results for the six areas were combined and average correlation coefficients were obtained, the values proved to be well above even the 1 per cent level of significance for these two periods.

Data for the period 1940–1948, covering the Los Angeles and San Francisco areas, yielded more diverse results. The rankings of industries in terms of per cent changes in employment and average hourly earnings for this period and for certain subperiods are given in table 10. For 1940–1948, negative coefficient values were obtained in both communities, that is, industries which had low rankings in percentage employment changes tended to have high rankings in percentage wage changes. When the eight-year period was broken down into three shorter periods, the resulting *r* values, though positive in all but one instance, did not exceed the 5 per cent level of significance in a single case.[4] It should be observed that these results square with the findings for Los Angeles during the 'forties, set forth in the preceding chapter.

Significance of Findings

The rank correlation analysis of the 1929–1939 period indicates a fairly close, though by no means consistent, association between changes in employment and wages at the local area level. The analysis of the 1940–1948 period points to the opposite conclusion. The difference is perhaps due to the fact that annual earnings had to be used in the former period but hourly earnings were used in the latter. Also the communities covered by the two sets of data were not the same. But it seems unlikely that the entire difference is attributable to lack of homogeneity in the data. The economic and social environment was also markedly different in the two periods. During the years 1940–1948, labor was generally scarce and even employers who were not seeking to expand their labor force found it necessary to raise wages. Indeed, it was in the low-wage firms, most of which were not in defense industries, that hourly earnings rose by the greatest percentage amounts during this period. As indicated

---

[4] In an attempt to compare employment and wage changes among "similar" industries only, the nineteen manufacturing fields were classified into three roughly homogeneous groups as indicated by type of product and/or method of production, a rank correlation analysis being made of each group. In no case, however, was a consistent pattern found either in the long or short periods.

elsewhere, the government's wage control program during the war years contributed somewhat to this result.[5] Between 1929 and 1939, there was a substantial amount of unemployment and the labor market conditions which confronted employers were more diversified. Firms in which employment was not increasing were able to hold wages at reduced levels and still retain enough personnel. Firms which were experiencing an expansion in business and hence in employment found some increases in wages advisable in order to attract more workers. Even if they could have secured the additional workers without a rise in pay levels, union pressure in the organized industries brought about the same result, as the wage-paying ability of employers in these fields increased. Under these circumstances a closer association between changes in employment and wage levels was to be expected.

Specific examples throw a clearer light on the difference between the two periods. In 1929–1939, industries like paper and allied products and chemicals and allied products, which ranked consistently high in per cent changes in employment, also ranked high in per cent changes in average annual earnings. Industries like iron and steel and their products and transportation equipment, on the other hand, ranked consistently quite low in both series. But in the 1940–1948 period, industries such as electrical machinery and automobiles and automobile equipment, which ranked high in gains in employment, ranked low in gains in hourly earnings. In industries like apparel and food and kindred products, the reverse relationship obtained. Of course the data are far from complete, but the evidence definitely indicates that there is a closer association between interindustry changes in employment and wages in periods of extensive unemployment than in periods of labor scarcity.

Does the contrast between the two periods become less marked when they are broken down into shorter time periods? If one judges from the evidence summarized above, the answer is in the negative. Indeed, if anything, the difference is sharper. During the downswing between 1929 and 1933 and the upswing between 1933 and 1937, industries in which employment rose most (fell least) were the fields in which wages as measured by average annual earnings also tended to rise most (fall least). No such consistent pattern was found in the shorter periods between 1940 and 1948. Again, this suggests that under conditions of abundant labor supply, differential changes in employment have an important bearing on local industry wage levels even over short periods of time. Under such conditions wages appear to be so closely tied to shifts in relative demand, as measured by differences in employment, that the association even holds for three- or four-year periods. No such

---

[5] See p. 59 of this study.

conclusion is suggested, however, by the data on the different subperiods between 1940 and 1948 when the supply of labor was generally scarce.

VARIANCE OF EMPLOYMENT AND OF WAGES

The preceding analysis was directed only to the question whether local industries which experienced the greatest gains in employment also experienced the greatest gains in wages. It is, of course, possible that the two series could have behaved quite differently in other respects and still have shown a high correlation when analyzed on the basis of rankings alone. A quite different picture would emerge, for example, if it turned out that there was much greater diversity among industries with respect to changes in employment than with respect to changes in wages. Even though the respective rankings moved together, this would suggest that the forces controlling interindustry changes in employment levels in local areas were essentially different from those controlling interindustry changes in wage levels. On the other hand, if differences among industries proved to be small with respect to changes in both employment and wages, it would appear that the forces determining changes in both employment and wages affect all industries in local areas in a uniform manner.

Another dimension of the problem concerns the differential behavior of employment and wages, not among industries, but among areas. As noted earlier, changes in general levels of economic activity occur at different rates in different communities, the comparatively rapid economic expansion of the Los Angeles area in recent years being a striking case in point. This raises the question whether changes in the general levels of employment and wages of different communities show much variation, or whether the changes in the two series are in fact much the same in all areas. A priori, it would seem reasonable to suppose that rates of change among communities would vary more in employment levels than in wage levels. If the facts show this to be true, the results of the correlation analysis would again be modified. If, on the other hand, the facts show that, despite varying rates of economic growth, intercommunity differences in employment and wages are negligible, we would conclude that the influences determining general employment and wage levels affect all communities in much the same manner.

Still another dimension of the problem concerns changes in local employment and wage levels studied, in this instance, not from an interindustry or interarea, but from an interyear point of view. In this connection we are interested in finding out whether year-to-year variations in community employment and wage levels occur at uniform or diverse rates of change. If the former, the conclusion follows that the forces controlling community employment and wage levels yield substantially the same results in any given year; if the latter, the opposite conclusion follows. During periods of marked cyclical variation or other types of general economic change, year-to-year changes in employment and wages would be more likely, of course, to exhibit wide variations than during periods of general stability or uniform growth. Whatever the surrounding circumstances, however, we are interested in determining whether the forces which control interyear employment and wage changes in local areas behave in the same manner or in a different manner over a period of time.

Analysis of the data on the basis of interindustry, interarea, and interyear variation yields a more detailed, and hence more meaningful, picture of local employment-wage relationships than is possible under the method of rank correlation used earlier. The latter approach is concerned only with the over-all relationship between the two series, whereas the former breaks it down into its industry, area, and time aspects. This makes it possible to determine more precisely wherein the similarity and diversity in the behavior of employment and wages lie. Considering each of the two series alone, it also provides a means for measuring the relative importance of different influences which bear on each of the two variables. If, for example, interindustry differences in employment and wage changes were to prove of no statistical significance, whereas the reverse held true for interarea or interyear comparisons, we would conclude that the interindustry factor is relatively unimportant when compared to influences operating on an interarea or interyear basis. In other words, if employment and wages in every industry within a given area rose or fell by the same proportion, the effects attributable to differences in industry characteristics as such would be nil, but if they rose or fell by widely varying proportions the opposite conclusion would follow.

As is well known, the forces controlling changes in employment or wages are closely intertwined with one another, so that it becomes most difficult to separate them and to evaluate the respective importance of each. Study of the extent to which each series varies on an interindustry, interarea, and interyear basis provides a means for tackling this problem. Of course, as will be illustrated later, the data can be grouped in any number of ways, so that the effects of still other influences can be singled out and measured by this procedure as well.

The technique best adapted to this approach to the problem is multisample statistical analysis. By use of this technique it is possible to measure the comparative behavior of employment and wages with respect to each of the three categories referred to above. Specifically, this analysis tells us whether differences in a particular series are so small as to be attributable to chance sampling variation or so large as to indicate the data are drawn from different populations. Thus, if the data show that differences among industries with respect to changes in employment and in wages are so small as to fall within the range of chance sampling variation, we conclude that the influences controlling employment and wages affect all industries in a uniform manner. If the differences are so large as to fall outside this range, however, we conclude that industry employment and wage levels are subject to essentially different influences. The same would follow, of course, if the comparison is made on an interarea or interyear, as opposed to an interindustry, basis.

The data which are analyzed in this manner cover the same industries, areas, and years as in the rank correlation analysis already discussed. These figures, it will be remembered, pertain to eleven manufacturing industries in six large industrial centers during the period 1929–1939 and to nineteen manufacturing industries in Los Angeles County and the San Francisco Bay area during the period 1940–1948. Wage figures on an hourly earnings basis were not available by industry and area for the earlier period, so that for these years average annual earnings had to be employed. Because of the limitations of the data, a detailed discussion of the results hardly seems necessary; accordingly, the principal conclusions, together with supporting tables, are presented in summary form only.

The data for the 'forties covered but two cities; hence, the analysis of employment and wage changes in this period was limited to interindustry and interyear comparisons alone. The data for the 'thirties, on the other hand, permitted interarea comparisons as well. All the calculations were based on yearly per cent changes in the level of employment and wages, as shown in Appendix tables 15 and 16. The interindustry influence on local employment-wage levels was measured by comparing each industry's sum of per cent changes in employment and wages with the sum of per cent changes for all industries included in the study. The interarea influence was determined by comparing each community's sum of per cent changes with the sum of per cent changes for all communities included in the study. Finally, the interyear influence was measured by comparing each year's per cent change with the average per cent change for all years studied.[6] Where the comparisons showed greater deviations from the general average of changes than could reasonably be attributed to chance, the differences were held to be

---

[6] For the years between 1929 and 1939, since only Census of Manufactures data were available, the figures refer to biennial, not annual, periods.

TABLE 11

SUMMARY OF RESULTS, ANALYSIS OF VARIANCE F TESTS, PER CENT CHANGES IN EM-
PLOYMENT AND AVERAGE ANNUAL EARNINGS, ELEVEN MANUFACTURING INDUSTRIES,
SIX INDUSTRIAL AREAS, 1929–1939[a]

Period	Source of variation	Employment (a)	Average annual earnings (b)	F required for significance $F_{.01}$	$F_{.05}$
1929–1939	Industries....	.61	.45	(a) 2.80 (b) 2.80	2.07 2.07
	Areas........	1.46	.38	(a) 3.11 (b) 4.10	2.26 2.71
	Years........	S 8.60	S 95.60	(a) 3.83 (b) 4.43	2.61 2.87

Phases of the business cycle

Period	Source of variation	Employment (a)	Average annual earnings (b)	F required for significance $F_{.01}$	$F_{.05}$
1929–1933	Industries....	.72	S 5.70	(a) 2.49 (b) 2.49	1.91 1.91
	Areas........	.83	S 5.04	(a) 3.18 (b) 3.18	2.29 2.29
	Years........	2.94	S 51.50	(a) 6.87 (b) 6.87	3.93 3.93
1933–1937	Industries....	1.36	S 3.34	(a) 4.85 (b) 2.70	2.97 2.02
	Areas........	S.05 2.47	1.17	(a) 3.41 (b) 5.64	2.40 3.33
	Years........	S 11.00	.49	(a) 10.04 (b) 10.04	4.96 4.96
1937–1939	Industries....	S 2.90	.41	2.70	2.02
	Areas........	1.19	.67	3.41	2.40
	Years........	....	....	....	....

SOURCE: Appendix table 15.
  [a] Each of the values in this table is a ratio of a variance attributed to industries, areas, or years to the variance of the interaction among these industries, areas, and years. The significant F values are different for each of the ratios in the table because they vary with number of degrees of freedom in the interaction term as well as the industry, area, and year variances; in a three-way analysis of variance, each ratio may have a different interaction term. The computations of these F ratios and their respective degrees of freedom are in Appendix table 18.

statistically significant, as indicated by the notation "S"; where the opposite was the case, the results were held to be without statistical significance. It should be noted that these calculations measured both the ranges of variation and the distributions within the ranges, with respect to each of these three influences; also, in addition to comparisons covering the years 1940–1948 and 1929–1939 as a whole, the behavior of employment and wages was analyzed for certain subyears and subgroups within the two longer periods.[7] The findings are summarized in tables 11 and 12.

RESULTS OF MULTISAMPLE ANALYSIS: LONG PERIODS

The rank correlation analysis of the 1929–1939 period already discussed revealed a fairly close association between interindustry changes in manufacturing employment and wages at the community level. The multisample analysis indicates, however, that interindustry differences in both employment and wage changes are relatively small. Over the ten-year period, differences among the eleven manufacturing industries in the six areas studied amounted to a value of 0.61 in employment changes and 0.45 in average annual earnings, far short of even the 5 per cent significance value of 2.07 as shown in table 11. The data for Los Angeles and San Francisco covering the period 1940–1948 (table 12) point to a similar conclusion. Thus, though it may be true that the largest gains in employment tend to be associated with the largest gains in wages, the more important consideration is that differences among manufacturing industries in these two series tend to be extremely limited.

Variations among areas in rates of change of manufacturing employment and wages also appear to be negligible. Table 11 shows that between 1929 and 1939 the differences among areas came only to 1.46 in changes in employment and to 0.38 in changes in average annual earnings, again well below even the 5 per cent significance level. (Data for the period 1940–1948 on an interarea basis were not available.) On the basis of this evidence, which is admittedly incomplete, it appears that the forces controlling employment and wages affect all manufacturing industries and areas in much the same manner.

The variance analysis based on interyear comparisons yielded quite different findings. In every instance but one (San Francisco between

---

[7] As already mentioned in connection with the rank correlation analysis, there is no autocorrelation in the employment and annual earnings series even though employment data are involved in both. (See footnote 3, above.) As to whether it is valid to apply multisample analysis to time series, any selectivity introduced by consecutive data does not invalidate the analysis so long as the results, as here, are applied only to the particular period under investigation.

1940 and 1948), year-to-year variations around the average annual rate of change proved to be statistically significant. In other words, interyear changes in employment and wages seem to occur at varying rates of speed, sometimes rapidly and sometimes slowly. Speaking of changes of this sort, then, it cannot be said, as with interindustry and interarea changes, that the controlling forces affect all years in the same manner.

TABLE 12

SUMMARY OF RESULTS, ANALYSIS OF VARIANCE F TESTS, PER CENT CHANGES IN EMPLOYMENT AND AVERAGE HOURLY EARNINGS, NINETEEN MANUFACTURING INDUSTRIES, LOS ANGELES COUNTY AND SAN FRANCISCO BAY INDUSTRIAL AREA, 1940–1948[a]

All industries	Source of variation	Los Angeles		San Francisco		F required for significance	
		Employment	Average hourly earnings	Employment	Average hourly earnings	$F_{.01}$	$F_{.05}$
1940–1948	Industries	.45	.65	1.00	.63	2.09	1.69
	Years.....	S 3.48	S 8.88	1.74	S 25.68	2.79	2.08
1940–1943	Industries	S 6.10	1.34	S 5.49	1.35	2.49	1.90
	Years.....	1.61	S 6.54	1.31	S 13.01	5.25	3.26
1943–1945	Industries	2.15	S 6.25	S 3.35	S 3.77	3.13	2.22
	Years.....	S 8.66	S 42.54	S 14.27	S 14.48	8.28	4.41
1945–1948	Industries	S.05 2.04	S 3.27	S.05 1.98	.95	2.49	1.90
	Years.....	.54	S 6.58	S.05 4.56	S.05 3.77	5.25	3.26

SOURCE: Appendix table 16.
[a] Each of the values in this table is a ratio of a variance attributed to industries or years to the variance of the interaction among these industries and years. For an explanation of the method of computing the F ratio term, see note to table 11.

Although final answers are not to be expected, it is appropriate to consider what were the circumstances underlying these relationships. The most plausible explanation is that in our economy variations in the general level of business activity are so important and so all-pervasive that changes in employment and in wages in individual manufacturing industries and areas tend to be dominated by this one influence, differences of an interindustry or interarea nature being correspondingly reduced.

Differences in the rate of change in general business activity over a period of time, however, are marked by no such consistent or uniform pattern, the differences in the data being too great to be explained by sampling variation alone. Over the period of the 'forties these differences in the general level of business activity were associated, first, with the defense and war production program; second, with the sharp drop in output immediately after World War II; and, third, with the rapid expansion of business activity to fill civilian needs during the last three years of the decade. Over the period of the 'thirties, differences in the rate of change in the general level of business activity were associated with the post-1929 depression, the limited expansion of 1933–1937, and the brief downswing and upswing of the period between 1937 and 1939.[8] The particular way this influence made itself felt, of course, changed from one phase or one period to the next. In the postwar expansion period, for example, the single most important factor was probably the general price inflation. In the depression period of the early 'thirties, the chief development was the contraction in the total volume of spending associated with the general decline in business and the rapid spread of unemployment. In spite of such differences in surrounding circumstances, however, the influences controlling employment and wage changes over the two long periods affected all manufacturing industries and areas in the same way.

Results of Multisample Analysis: Short Periods

A similar analysis of the different subperiods within the years 1929–1939 and 1940–1948 shows a quite different pattern of employment and wage behavior. This is evident from inspection of the findings set forth in tables 11 and 12 for the three subperiods between 1929 and 1939 which roughly coincided with phases of the business cycle, and for the three subperiods between 1940 and 1948 which coincided with turning points in wartime and postwar developments. The data for the shorter periods showed a greater degree of variation in interindustry and interarea employment and wage changes, and a smaller degree of variation in interyear changes, than the longer periods. These findings, however, did not hold for every period studied.

The analysis bears out again what would be expected on a priori grounds, that over short periods employment and wages exhibit a variety of behavior patterns in different industries and areas, but that over long periods these diversities tend to disappear. This is well illustrated by the variance data for interindustry employment changes in Los Angeles and San Francisco between 1940 and 1948. In the three subperiods the facts showed greater diversity among industries in every case but one than can be explained by sampling variation, but over the eight-year period as a whole the rates of change were not found to be significantly different. The explanation appears to be that in the subperiods, because of war and postwar conditions, employment rose much more rapidly

---

[8] It should be noted again that the data for the 'thirties used in this part of the study were on a biennial, not an annual, basis, so that a more precise analysis of the different periods was impossible.

in some industries than in others, but over the eight-year period as a whole these divergent tendencies in employment just about canceled out. Another striking illustration of this same contrast is afforded by the variance data on interindustry wage changes between 1929 and 1939. In this instance, rates of change among industries over the entire ten-year period were not found to be significantly different, but the opposite held true for two of the three subperiods. Again, the divergent tendencies which characterized wage changes among industries in the various shorter periods were ironed out over the longer period. The data on interarea changes in employment and wages likewise evinced much more dissimilarity of behavior in the shorter periods than in the longer periods.

The interyear comparisons of employment and wages, on the other hand, yielded opposite conclusions, a number of the shorter time intervals exhibiting differences of no statistical significance in contrast to the interyear pattern of the longer periods. Again, the result is in accord with expectations. Over short periods, the general levels of employment and wages are more likely to change at uniform rates than over long periods, since conditions in a single phase of the cycle tend to be more uniform than in a number of different phases.

To summarize this part of the discussion, it appears that the longer the period under examination, the more important are year-to-year effects, and the less important are interindustry and interarea effects, on employment and wage changes in local markets; whereas the shorter the period under examination, the less important are interyear influences and the more important are factors of an interindustry and inter-area character.

INDUSTRY VS. AREA INFLUENCES

Even in the relatively short periods, however, interyear influences were reflected in the data on local employment and wages, and to the extent this was true, the importance to be attached to the influence of industry, as against the influence of area alone, was difficult to measure. To eliminate the interyear factor to the greatest extent possible, the data for 1929–1939 were assembled on a biennial basis, with results as set forth in table 13.

Analysis of interindustry changes in manufacturing employment and wages on a biennial basis revealed significant differences in all but two of the ten employment and wage biennial periods, the exceptions being employment in the period 1931–1933, and wages in 1937–1939. The interarea comparisons on this basis yielded less consistent results, significant differences in employment and wages occurring in only two of the five periods. Between "industry" and "area," therefore, this limited body of data indicates that the former is a more important element in explaining variations in employment and in wages than the latter.

As already indicated, both series exhibited more diverse behavior among industries and areas in the biennial periods than in the longer period, 1929–1939. It should also be remembered that in almost every period in which differences in employment in the biennial analysis were significant, wage differences were also significant, the one exception

TABLE 13

Summary of Results, Analysis of Variance *F* Tests, Per Cent Changes in Employment and Average Annual Earnings, Eleven Manufacturing Industries, Six Industrial Areas, and Five Two-Year Periods, 1929–1939.

Biennial periods	Source of variation	Employment	Average annual earnings	F required for significance	
				$F_{.01}$	$F_{.05}$
1929–1931	Industries............	S 4.41	S 7.08	2.70	2.02
	Areas...............	S.₀₅ 2.69	S 6.98	3.41	2.40
1931–1933	Industries............	.83	S.₀₅ 2.35	2.70	2.02
	Areas...............	.85	.97	3.41	2.40
1933–1935	Industries............	S 4.39	S.₀₅ 2.13	2.70	2.02
	Areas...............	S.₀₅ 2.63	S 7.14	3.41	2.40
1935–1937	Industries............	S 4.76	S.₀₅ 2.36	2.70	2.02
	Areas...............	.82	.16	3.41	2.40
1937–1939	Industries............	S 2.90	.41	2.70	2.02
	Areas...............	1.19	.67	3.41	2.40

Source: Appendix table 15.

being the period 1937–1939. On the other hand, in a substantial majority of the cases where employment differences were not significant, this was true of wages as well. In this respect, the behavior of these two variables was found to be fairly uniform even in the short periods.

EMPLOYMENT AND WAGES IN SIMILAR INDUSTRIES

In the shorter periods it is clear that there was some diversity in the behavior of employment, on the one hand, and of wages, on the other. This result may be explained at least partly by the fact that the comparisons covered a wide variety of manufacturing industries. If the industries had been broken down into more nearly homogeneous groupings, one would expect to find a closer parallelism between employment and wage changes. There were not enough industries to make possible such a breakdown of the data for the 'thirties, so that analysis of industry groupings was attempted only for the two communities of Los Angeles and San Francisco during the period of the 'forties. Eighteen manufacturing industries were classified in three categories on the basis of similar production and/or market characteristics. Group I consisted of industries made up mostly of small firms serving predominantly local markets; Group II consisted of industries made up chiefly of large-scale enterprises and/or companies with relatively broad market areas; Group III consisted of producers' goods industries, principally in the machinery and metal trades.[9] The three industry groups were the following:

Group I	*Group II*	*Group III*
Food and kindred products	Textile mill products	Rubber products
Tobacco manufactures	Apparel	Iron and steel and their
Printing, publishing, and	Paper and allied products	products
allied industries	Petroleum products	Nonferrous metals and
Lumber and timber	Automobiles and auto-	their products
Stone, clay, and glass	mobile equipment	Electrical machinery
Leather and leather	Furniture and finished	Machinery (except
products	lumber products	electrical)
	Chemical and allied	
	products	

The results of the multisample analysis of employment and wage changes in these three industry groups for three periods, 1940–1943, 1943–1945, and 1945–1948, for both Los Angeles County and the San Francisco Bay area, are set forth in table 14. For comparison purposes, the results already given for all industries treated as a single group are also shown.

As anticipated, the divergence among industries within each of the three categories was less than among all the industries considered as a single group. Out of a total of eighteen instances, differences in rates of change in employment among industries were significant in only one period (1940–1943 for Group III in San Francisco); when the industries were treated as a single group, significant differences were found in every period but one (1943–1945 in Los Angeles). The more detailed industry grouping yielded somewhat less uniform results in interyear employment changes, significant differences occurring in five periods (two in Los Angeles and three in San Francisco). This indicates that even in similarly situated industries, changes in employment occur at quite different rates, depending on conditions prevailing at various periods of time. Differences in rates of change in wages under the three-way grouping, on the other hand, proved to be significant in about as

---

[9] A nineteenth industry, transportation equipment (except automobiles), is included in the published figures but was excluded from the three-way grouping shown here.

TABLE 14

SUMMARY OF RESULTS, ANALYSIS OF VARIANCE F TESTS, PER CENT CHANGES IN EMPLOYMENT AND AVERAGE HOURLY EARNINGS, THREE GROUPS OF MANUFACTURING INDUSTRIES, LOS ANGELES COUNTY AND SAN FRANCISCO BAY INDUSTRIAL AREA, 1940–1948.

	Source of variation	Los Angeles		San Francisco		F required for significance	
		Employment	Average hourly earnings	Employment	Average hourly earnings	$F_{.01}$	$F_{.05}$
1940–1943	Industries	S 6.10	S 1.34	S 5.49	1.35	2.49	1.90
	Years.....	1.61	S 6.54	1.31	S 13.01	5.25	3.26
Group I	Industries	2.19	1.45	2.29	S.05 3.92	5.64	3.33
	Years.....	2.95	S.05 4.29	S 8.60	S 15.47	7.56	4.10
Group II	Industries	.53	1.75	.50	.84	4.82	3.00
	Years.....	2.68	S.05 6.48	3.51	3.00	6.93	3.88
Group III	Industries	1.46	2.27	S.05 5.44	.58	7.01	3.84
	Years.....	1.10	.94	.78	S 11.07	8.65	4.46
1943–1945	Industries	2.15	S 6.25	S 3.35	S 3.77	3.13	2.22
	Years.....	S 8.66	S 42.54	S 14.27	S 14.48	8.28	4.41
Group I	Industries	4.07	S.05 5.98	1.43	.60	10.97	5.05
	Years.....	S.05 8.88	S.05 8.75	4.51	2.66	16.26	6.61
Group II	Industries	3.27	S 17.94	2.88	S.05 8.22	8.47	4.28
	Years.....	3.26	S 33.38	2.42	4.00	13.74	5.99
Group III	Industries	2.82	.84	1.80	2.79	15.98	6.39
	Years.....	S 35.95	S.05 12.30	S.05 11.17	5.59	21.20	7.71
1945–1948	Industries	S.05 2.04	S 3.27	S.05 1.98	.95	2.49	1.90
	Years.....	.54	6.58	S.05 4.56	S.05 3.77	5.25	3.26
Group I	Industries	2.94	S 9.83	.48	1.79	5.64	3.33
	Years.....	1.46	S 7.84	.64	S.05 7.07	7.56	4.10
Group II	Industries	1.81	1.01	.94	.62	4.82	3.00
	Years.....	1.75	1.69	2.91	1.72	6.93	3.88
Group III	Industries	.44	1.03	1.30	.09	7.01	3.84
	Years.....	4.07	2.20	S 11.81	.12	8.65	4.46

SOURCE: Appendix table 16.

many periods in the case of interindustry as in the case of interyear comparisons (five in the former and seven in the latter); but, as in the employment series, differences in the rates of change in wages were without significance in a substantial majority of the periods.

The foregoing evidence suggests that among industries with similar production and/or product market characteristics, changes in employment tend to occur at the same rate even over short periods of time; though less clear-cut, wage changes under these conditions exhibit a similar tendency. When all industries were grouped together, it will be recalled, no such parallelism in employment and wage behavior was found for short periods but only for the two longer periods, 1929–1939 and 1940–1948. The contrast in results points up the importance of different production and market characteristics of the three industry groups in explaining employment-wage relationships in local areas.

Conclusion

The statistical data underlying the foregoing rank correlation and multi-sample analyses were confined to manufacturing industries and to a relatively small number of communities. Although the statistical procedures employed took account of the limited character of the data, the findings cannot be accepted with as much confidence as if the coverage had been broader. The principal conclusions suggested by the data are:

1. Over the period 1929–1939, a positive association was found among industries ranked on the basis of percentage change in employment and percentage change in annual earnings. Although this was true of the individual communities, the rank correlation coefficients proved to be statistically significant only when the results for the different communities were combined in an average value. Over the period 1940–1948, on the other hand, no consistent association between rates of change in industry employment and hourly earnings levels was observed. Although the data for the two periods are not comparable, this suggests that industry employment and wage levels move together when there is a large amount of unemployment, but that these two variables bear no consistent relationship to each other when labor market conditions are generally tight.

2. Within the subperiods between 1929 and 1939, the ranked percentage changes in employment and wages of individual industries at the local level showed a closer positive correlation than over the ten-year period considered as a whole. Where the subperiods coincided with well-defined phases of the business cycle, such as 1929–1933 and 1933–1937, the association between the two series proved especially marked. This

was not true, however, of the subperiods between 1940 and 1948. Again, the major circumstance explaining the difference in local area employment and wage behavior in the 'thirties and 'forties appears to have been the high percentage of unemployment in the former period and the scarcity of labor existing in the latter.

3. The rank correlation analysis did not measure the degree to which rates of change in employment and wages varied among industries in local areas. Nor did it show the extent to which the two series' rates of change varied among areas and among years. The multisample analysis was addressed chiefly to these issues. Over the two periods, 1929–1939 and 1940–1948, interindustry differences in rates of change in employment and wages were negligible. This suggests that over fairly long periods the influences controlling employment and wages affect all industries in much the same way, and that such influences are little affected by differences in the characteristics of individual industries.

4. Interarea, as opposed to interindustry, comparisons were possible only for the period 1929–1939, but the findings were similar. Again, this suggests that over long periods the forces controlling employment and wages affect individual areas the same way and that the "area" factor is not an important influence.

5. On the other hand, differences in interyear rates of change in employment and wages were found to be significantly large over both the periods 1929–1939 and 1940–1948. In other words, the percentage changes in certain years proved to be much greater than in others, suggesting that changes in general business conditions over a period of time exert an important influence on the behavior of employment and wages in local areas.

6. Over short periods, which coincided roughly with major shifts in the general level of business activity, the multisample analysis revealed that interindustry and interarea differences in rates of change in employment and wages were more marked than over the longer periods. Under these circumstances, then, effects attributable to differences in industry and area characteristics were found to be of greater importance. Interyear differences over the short periods, on the other hand, were found to be somewhat less than over the two longer periods.

7. Although neither the factor of "industry" nor "area" exerted an important influence on the behavior of employment and wages over the two long periods, the data indicate that the industry influence was somewhat more important than the area influence. This finding is based on the fact that in the biennial periods, when the interyear influence was removed as much as possible, variations among industries with respect to employment and wages were somewhat greater than among areas.

The data are too limited, however, to justify placing much weight on this conclusion.

8. When the manufacturing industries were classified on the basis of similar production methods and/or product market characteristics, rates of change in employment and wages tended to be uniform even in short periods.

In general, the data support the view that over long periods changes in the demand for labor, as reflected in movements in employment, bear a close relationship to changes in industry and community wage levels. No less important, however, is the conclusion that over such periods variations among industries and communities with respect to changes in both employment and wages tend to be negligible. From this finding the conclusion follows that the influences controlling changes in employment and wages in different industries and areas affect both variables in a uniform manner.

VII. INVESTMENT, PRODUCTIVITY, AND WAGES

ONE OF THE circumstances shaping local wage structures discussed in the opening chapter was the influence of changes in labor productivity. This influence is examined at greater length in the present chapter, with emphasis, as before, being placed on interindustry comparisons.

Because of limitations imposed by the data, most investigations of the relationship between productivity and wages have been based on industry figures for the country as a whole.[1] Although indicative of very broad trends, national figures do not bring out local differences which may well be an important part of the problem. The view has been expressed by one authority that wages and productivity in a particular locality are likely to show a less close association than in the economy as a whole, since special circumstances may be present in local areas which alter relationships prevailing in the country at large.[2] Accordingly, to determine how important is the productivity influence on wage levels, a study of local area experience seems in order.

A difficulty that has plagued empirical investigation in this field arises from the fact that interindustry differences in productivity, whether viewed at an instant of time or over a period of time, are subject to a variety of influences. One source of influence is the product market. In automobile manufacturing, for example, it is obvious that the striking increase in output per man-hour in that industry could not have occurred except for the substantial rise in demand for the product. In explaining the wage history of the industry, then, who can say whether the rise in pay levels was due mostly to improved methods of production or to gains in market demand? Merely to measure the association between wage and productivity levels, or changes in these two variables, does not provide an answer to this question.

Other influences stem from the supply, as opposed to the demand, side of production. Gains in output per man-hour may reflect changes in the technical processes of production, in the amount or quality of

---

[1] In an investigation of manufacturing industries in the United States between 1923 and 1940, Garbarino found a rank correlation value of 0.60 between changes in hourly earnings and in output per man-hour. (With silk and rayon omitted, an industry in which output per man-hour has increased completely out of proportion to the increase in hourly earnings during this period, the rank correlation value was 0.71.) Joseph W. Garbarino, "A Theory of Interindustry Wage Structure Variation," *Quarterly Journal of Economics*, LXIV (May, 1950), 299.

[2] John T. Dunlop, in *Income, Employment and Public Policy, Essays in Honor of Alvin H. Hansen* (New York: Norton, 1948), pp. 351, 354.

worker effort, or in managerial efficiency. In analyzing the matter statistically, it again becomes difficult to determine the relative importance of these several influences. The theorist meets this problem by isolating one environmental circumstance and impounding all the others, which is to say, these other influences are assumed to remain unchanged. To secure first approximations, this procedure is satisfactory enough, but as a method for getting at the relative importance of various influences in actual market situations, the theoretical approach suffers from obvious limitations. A number of investigators accordingly have analyzed productivity phenomena by intensive study of particular plants or industries, drawing their conclusions from a relatively few, carefully chosen case studies. For some purposes this method of attack has much to recommend it, but the coverage of these inquiries is usually too narrow to make direct interindustry and interarea wage comparisons possible.

Investigations of particular localities, of which the present study is an example, fall between these approaches to the problem. Even in their case, conclusions are apt to be rather general and, where this is so, little light is thrown on the relative significance of different environmental factors. In the chapters dealing with product demand as it relates to wage behavior, an effort was made to meet this difficulty by singling out various types of product market structures for detailed examination. Using a similar device, attention is now turned to certain differences in plant operating conditions and production techniques as possible influences on interindustry and interarea wage relationships. Subsequently, the association between productivity and wages is treated in more general terms. Care should be exercised in interpreting the results of this discussion since it is based on a limited body of statistical material.

SIZE OF FIRM AND PROPORTION OF LABOR COSTS

First, attention is turned to the relationship between size of firm and industry wage levels. Even if it developed that industries in which firms are "small" tend to pay lower wages for comparable skills than those in which firms are "large," the result could not properly be attributed to smallness or largeness as such, but to certain conditions found in conjunction with differences in the average size of firms. For example, industries in which firms tend to be small may rely more on hand labor and less on mechanical processes than those in which firms are large. Although the operations may require a higher level of skill, pay for comparable work under these circumstances would tend to be less, and even the general level of wages would likely be below levels prevailing in industries in which the average size of firm is large. Similarly, value of product per man-hour would presumably be higher under the latter circumstances, and comparative wage levels would vary accordingly.

On the other hand, though indicative of the type of operations associated with differences in interindustry wage levels, size of firm is frequently found in conjunction with other and quite different environmental conditions which may be just as important. Presumably, in industries in which firms are small, product markets are more likely to be competitive than where they are large. Then, too, one can argue that under the latter conditions employers are likely to enjoy certain bargaining advantages in dealing with workers not available to small firms or, further, that the geographical scope of markets tends to be greater in industries in which firms are large, and that these circumstances have quite as much significance for wage analysis as do differences in production processes and in cost structures. Since the influences stemming from market differences were covered in earlier chapters, this aspect of the problem is not reëxamined here, but in any appraisal of the relationship between size of firm and interindustry wage levels these influences have to be kept in mind.

To measure the association between average size of firm and industry wage levels, rank correlation tests were made of a number of manufacturing industries in six industrial areas and the United States for selected years. The results, which are summarized in table 15, showed a positive relationship between average size and industry wage levels in most instances, but none of the resulting r values reached the 5 per cent significance level. In fact, in a few cases the results were actually negative.[3]

Another, and presumably related, set of circumstances is the association between interindustry differences in cost structures and wage levels. The measure of differences in cost structure most often referred to is the proportion of labor costs to total costs, the general view being that pay levels for comparable work tend to be higher in industries in which wages are a low proportion of total costs than where the opposite holds true. Again, the reason is that relatively low labor cost industries are deemed to have more capital equipment per worker than high labor cost industries, and hence higher output per man-hour. Since the measure is based directly on a comparison of industry cost structures, it has a somewhat more precise meaning than the measure of size of firm. Even so, it reflects a certain combination of operating conditions, not one

---

[3] As discussed in chap. i, other investigators have emphasized size of firm as a factor explaining interfirm wage differences *within* the same industry. W. Rupert Maclaurin and Charles A. Myers, "Wages and the Movement of Factory Labor," *Quarterly Journal of Economics,* LVII (February, 1943), 257. See also Jacob Perlman, *Hourly Earnings of Employees in Large and Small Enterprises,* T.N.E.C. Monograph no. 14 (Washington: Government Printing Office, 1941).

environmental factor alone. Manufacturing industries with relatively high labor costs generally consist of small firms engaged in active price competition and serving more limited market areas than industries with relatively low labor costs. Accordingly, it is usually assumed that this measure reflects much the same set of operating conditions as measures of size of firm.

TABLE 15

RANK CORRELATION COEFFICIENTS, SIZE OF FIRM[a] AND AVERAGE EARNINGS (ANNUAL EARNINGS, 1929, 1937, AND 1939; HOURLY EARNINGS, 1947) IN MANUFACTURING, SIX INDUSTRIAL AREAS AND UNITED STATES

	Size of firm and average annual earnings						
Year	Los Angeles	Chicago	Cleveland	Detroit	Pittsburgh	San Francisco	Significant values
1929	.155	−.127	.134	.059	.009	−.291	$r_{.01} = .735$
1939	−.200	−.400	.020	.427	.041	−.630	$r_{.05} = .602$
							11 industries

	Los Angeles County			United States		
	r	Number of industries	Significant values	r	Number of industries	Significant values
1937	.363	14	$r_{.01} = .661$	.417	14	$r_{.01} = .661$
			$r_{.05} = .532$			$r_{.05} = .532$

	Size of firm and average hourly earnings					
1947	.049	16	$r_{.01} = .623$	.247	18	$r_{.01} = .590$
			$r_{.05} = .497$			$r_{.05} = .468$

SOURCES: Calculated from:
   Philip Neff, Lisette C. Baum, and Grace E. Heilman, *Production Cost Trends in Selected Industrial Areas* (Berkeley and Los Angeles: 1948), pp. 196–201, 220, 226–231.
   Calif. State Dept. of Indus. Relations, Div. of Labor Statistics and Research, *Labor in California, 1947–1948* (June, 1949), pp. 53–54.
   U. S. Bureau of the Census, *Biennial Census of Manufactures, 1937*, p. 44; *1947 Census of Manufactures*, Vol. II, p. 22, and "California," MC 104, pp. 8–10, 15.
   U. S. Bureau of Labor Statistics, *Monthly Labor Review*, 69 (October, 1949), 455–467.
   [a] Number of workers per establishment.

As before, the wage levels of manufacturing industries in six industrial areas and the United States were analyzed by the method of rank correlation for selected years (table 16). The data show an even less consistent association between industry wage levels and relative labor cost than the analysis based on size of firm. A larger proportion of the coefficient values were negative whereas the positive r values were about the same under the two tests. None of the positive values in either case reached the 5 per cent significance level.[4] Judged by this evidence, it is clear that neither size of firm nor relative labor cost is important in explaining interindustry wage differences in local markets in this country.

TABLE 16

Rank Correlation Coefficients, Relative Labor Cost[a] and Average Earnings (Annual Earnings, 1929, 1937, and 1939; Hourly Earnings, 1947) in Manufacturing, Six Industrial Areas and United States

Relative labor cost and average annual earnings							
Year	Los Angeles	Chicago	Cleveland	Detroit	Pittsburgh	San Francisco	Significant values
1929	.159	−.073	−.248	.150	.209	.091	$r_{.01} = .735$
1939	−.223	−.455	−.189	.041	.061	−.434	$r_{.05} = .602$
							11 industries

	Los Angeles County			United States		
	r	Number of industries	Significant values	r	Number of industries	Significant values
1937	−.182	14	$r_{.01} = .661$	−.308	14	$r_{.01} = .661$
			$r_{.05} = .532$			$r_{.05} = .532$

Relative labor cost and average hourly earnings						
1947	.007	16	$r_{.01} = .623$	.007	18	$r_{.01} = .590$
			$r_{.05} = .497$			$r_{.05} = .468$

Sources: The same as for table 15.
[a] Total wages divided by total value added by manufacture.

LOCAL WAGES AND INVESTMENT

A factor which is sometimes cited as underlying industry wage levels is differences in amounts of capital equipment per worker. In fact, it is often taken for granted that wages in industries with high capital/labor ratios are substantially above wages in industries with low capital/labor ratios. Whether available data support this position has never been tested, so far as the author knows.

The question under examination here is not whether, other things

---

[4] Similarly, Ross and Goldner's study of manufacturing industry wage levels on a national basis revealed no association between labor cost as a percentage of product value and either level of earnings or increases in earnings. Their data on labor cost proportions pertained to 1939 and covered forty-eight industries. Arthur M. Ross and William Goldner, "Forces Affecting the Interindustry Wage Structure," *Quarterly Journal of Economics*, LXIV (May, 1950), 277.

TABLE 17-A

RANKINGS AND RANK CORRELATION COEFFICIENTS, AVERAGE ANNUAL EARNINGS IN MANUFACTURING, LOS ANGELES COUNTY AND UNITED STATES, AND CAPITAL PER WORKER, UNITED STATES, 1937

Industry	Los Angeles County Average annual earnings		United States Capital per worker[a]		United States Average annual earnings	
	Earnings	Rank	Amount	Rank	Earnings	Rank
Food and kindred products....	$1,180	11	$3,015	5	$1,100	11
Textile products.............	930	14	929	13	850	14
Forest products.............	1,210	9.5	1,611	11	920	13
Paper and allied products.....	1,160	12	4,818	2	1,160	9.5
Printing, publishing, and allied industries...........	1,520	2	1,844	8	1,510	3
Chemicals and allied products..	1,250	7.5	4,224	3	1,210	8
Products of petroleum and coal.	1,820	1	42,819	1	1,660	1
Rubber products.............	1,500	3	1,808	9	1,320	6
Leather and leather manufacturing.................	1,060	13	428	14	940	12
Stone, clay, and glass.........	1,210	9.5	2,976	6	1,160	9.5
Iron and steel (excluding machinery)...............	1,370	6	3,442	4	1,420	5
Nonferrous metals...........	1,250	7.5	1,622	10	1,290	7
Machinery (except transportation)...................	1,480	4	1,372	12	1,440	4
Transportation equipment.....	1,440	5	2,251	7	1,550	2

Rank correlation coefficients

Los Angeles County, average annual earnings, 1937,
   and United States, capital per worker, 1937...... $r = .361$

United States, average annual earnings, 1937,
   and United States, capital per worker, 1937..... $r = .403$

Number of industries.........................14

Significance levels.............................$r_{.01} = .661$ $r_{.05} = .532$

SOURCES: Computed from Neff, Baum, and Heilman, *op. cit.*, p. 220, and from *Biennial Census of Manufactures, 1937,* p. 44.
   Solomon Fabricant, *Employment in Manufacturing, 1899–1939* (New York: 1942), p. 257.
   [a] Coal is included in "Chemicals and allied products," not in "Products of petroleum and coal."

being equal, an industry with a large amount of capital equipment per worker would tend to pay higher wages than an industry in which the opposite were the case, but rather whether this factor is in fact more or less important than other influences in explaining actual differences in industry wage levels. Only by examining the data on interindustry wage structures is it possible to arrive at an answer to this question.

Using the same rank correlation techniques as were applied to size

TABLE 17-B

RANKINGS AND RANK CORRELATION COEFFICIENTS, AVERAGE HOURLY EARNINGS IN
MANUFACTURING, LOS ANGELES COUNTY AND UNITED STATES, AND CAPITAL PER
WORKER, UNITED STATES, 1949

Industry	Los Angeles County Average hourly earnings		United States Capital per worker		United States Average hourly earnings	
	Earnings	Rank	Amount	Rank	Earnings	Rank
Food and kindred products....	$1.532	11	$3,293	5	$1.291	13
Tobacco manufactures........	1.160	19	1,621	12	1.004	19
Textile mill products..........	1.329	18	1,751	11	1.189	16
Apparel....................	1.424	15	264	19	1.170	17
Paper and allied products.....	1.497	12	4,702	4	1.342	12
Printing, publishing, and allied industries...........	2.141	1	858	17	1.816	1
Chemicals and allied products..	1.484	14	5,759	3	1.430	10
Products of petroleum and coal.	1.817	2	42,263	1	1.791	2
Rubber products.............	1.668	4	2,598	8	1.509	7
Leather and leather products...	1.390	17	525	18	1.137	18
Lumber and wood products (except furniture)..........	1.573	9	1,521	14	1.274	14
Furniture and fixtures........	1.594	6.5	991	16	1.234	15
Stone, clay, and glass products.	1.495	13	3,234	6	1.368	11
Primary metal industries......	1.610	5	8,025	2	1.587	5
Fabricated metal products (except machinery and transportation equipment)...	1.560	10	1,913	10	1.460	8
Electrical machinery and equipment................	1.406	16	1,489	15	1.442	9
Machinery (except electrical)..	1.592	8	2,251	9	1.530	6
Transportation equipment (except automobiles)........	1.594	6.5	1,589	13	1.593	4
Automobiles and automobile equipment................	1.688	3	2,768	7	1.696	3

Rank correlation coefficients

Los Angeles County, average hourly earnings, 1949,
   and United States, capital per worker, 1949...... $r = .268$
United States, average hourly earnings, 1949,
   and United States, capital per worker, 1949...... $r = .391$
Number of industries.........................   19
Significance levels.............................$r_{.01} = .575$ $r_{.05} = .456$

SOURCES: Calif. State Dept. of Indus. Relations, Div. of Labor Statistics and Research, special release, July 5, 1950; and letter to the author, October 31, 1950.
Federal Trade Commission and Securities and Exchange Commission, *Quarterly Industrial Financial Report Series, Fourth Quarter, 1949*, pp. 8–14. These data were adjusted to include nonincorporated enterprises; see Fabricant, *op. cit.*, p. 257, and letter to the author, June 6, 1950.
U. S. Bureau of Labor Statistics, *Monthly Labor Review*, 70 (April, 1950), 443; 71 (July, 1950), 163–175.

of firm and relative labor cost, measurements were made of the degree of association between capital/labor ratios and wage levels in a number of manufacturing industries. Limitations of the data made it necessary to confine the analysis to two years, 1937 and 1949, the wage figures in the former year being average annual earnings. Comparisons were made for the United States and Los Angeles County. Information on capital/worker ratios, by industry, could not be secured for the Los Angeles area, so the ratios for United States industries were employed instead. This procedure is valid only if the industry ranking of capital/worker ratios can be assumed to be the same in both areas; since the data refer to rankings, not to absolute levels, this assumption seems warranted, though, of course, the results for the country as a whole can be regarded with more confidence than those for the single market area of Los Angeles. The findings are given in tables 17-A and 17-B.

The tables show some positive association between ratios of capital equipment per worker and industry wage levels. In the case of Los Angeles, the coefficients of rank correlation were 0.361 and 0.268 for 1937 and 1949, respectively; while in the United States as a whole, the r values were somewhat higher, 0.403 in 1937 and 0.391 in 1949. These values compare with a 5 per cent level of significance of 0.532 for the earlier year and 0.456 for the later. Although the results show a less close correspondence than might have been expected, they are not so far short of the significance levels to suggest that this factor is of little importance in explaining differences in industry wage levels. After all, capital/worker ratios constitute only one of many possible influences operating from the side of costs and production methods. For example, an industry like printing and publishing ranks comparatively low in this regard and yet its wage level is relatively high. In industries of this type there is little doubt that the skill requirements of the bulk of the jobs exert an important influence on the wage level. Indeed, if differences in the labor skill mix could be allowed for, it is safe to assume that the capital/worker rankings would yield values well above the 5 per cent significance level.

A more meaningful approach would be to study changes in these relationships over a period of time. This was the viewpoint Douglas took in his study of long-term trends in real wages for United States manufacturing as a whole.[5] But satisfactory data, by industry, are un-

---

[5] One of the major factors underlying the long-term rise in real wages in manufacturing, according to Douglas, has been the comparatively rapid increase in the supply of capital goods relative to the increase in the supply of labor. For example, between 1899 and 1922 he found that capital supply increased 331 per cent but the number of wage earners employed increased by only 61 per cent. Paul H. Douglas, *Real Wages in the United States, 1890–1926* (Boston and New York: Houghton Mifflin, 1930), p. 567.

available. Speaking of rankings only, there probably is not much variation among manufacturing industries over time in capital/worker ratios.
Industries with relatively high ratios in one decade are very likely to
have relatively high ratios in the next. To test this hypothesis, the rankings of a similar group of United States manufacturing industries were
analyzed for two sets of years, 1904 and 1937, and 1937 and 1949. The
coefficient of rank correlation obtained for the first two years was
0.838, and for the second, 0.841, compared with a 1 per cent significance
level of 0.623 in both instances. These results demonstrate beyond any
doubt that capital/worker rankings as among industries form a more
or less unchanging structure over long periods of time. This is far short
of saying, however, that interindustry rates of capital expansion are
substantially the same, or that differences in rates of capital expansion
are so small as to have little bearing on industry wage levels. Although
the influence of capital/worker ratios is probably more important in
explaining "permanent" characteristics of the interindustry wage structure, changes in the ratios over time may also have some bearing on
shifts within the structure. Further understanding of this aspect of the
subject is gained by considering the relationship between output per
worker and wages, to which attention is now turned.

VALUE ADDED PER WORKER

The analysis contained in chapter v revealed a certain association between types of product markets and local industry wage levels, but the
results were not altogether clear-cut or conclusive. Much the same conclusion has been reached in the discussion of size of firm, proportional
labor costs, and capital/worker ratios presented in the first part of this
chapter. When, however, attention was turned in the earlier analysis
to the influence on comparative wage levels of product demand in general, as reflected in employment trends, a quite different picture emerged.
A similarly broad measure of the influence of different conditions of
product supply is afforded by data on output per worker. For reasons
already cited, it is impossible to determine from statistical data alone
the exact sources of changes in worker output, but it is nonetheless
important to determine if such data show any association with changes
in wage levels.

Unfortunately, there is little material on which reliable comparisons
between worker output and wages in local communities can be based,
so that the analysis must be limited to a relatively few situations. The
best source is the United States Census of Manufactures, which contains
data on value added by manufacture for particular industries and areas.
Value added by manufacture divided by number of production workers

affords a reasonably accurate measure of value of output per worker, especially with respect to changes over time. The resulting figures, however, are not wholly satisfactory for this purpose. For one thing, "value added" is affected by the capital, labor, and other inputs for specific kinds of products as well as by the stages of manufacturing represented in a community's economic structure. Moreover, the figures do not refer to physical output alone since they also reflect changes in price. In the following discussion, therefore, it has been deemed advisable to use the term "value added per worker" (or "value added") rather than "productivity" so that the reader will keep the limitations of this measure in mind.[6]

RANK CORRELATION ANALYSIS

The relationship between value added per worker and wages can first be examined at particular points of time. The method employed in this study is to compare wage rankings of manufacturing industries with respect to this factor by calculating rank correlation coefficients and to determine by this means if the association is significantly close. Comparisons based on hourly earnings could be made for only one local area and one year (Los Angeles County in 1947), the prewar comparison (1937) having to be based on annual earnings; comparable figures were also analyzed for the country as a whole. The results are given in table 18.

The figures support the view that there is a close association between value added per worker and wages in manufacturing industries. The data for the United States in both 1937 and 1947 yielded rank correlation values above the 5 per cent level, though below the 1 per cent significance level. This was also true for Los Angeles County in 1937 but not in 1947. When compared to the results of the analysis of size of firm, percentage labor cost, and even capital/worker ratios, the findings appear all the more striking. The broader measure reveals a much closer association than was true of any of the three more narrow measures of differing output conditions, a conclusion which parallels the results obtained from the previous analysis of influences on the side of demand.

Another, and perhaps more significant, aspect of this relationship is the degree to which *changes* in value added per worker are associated with *changes* in wage levels in local areas over a period of time. Here again, the paucity of data proved a real stumbling block. The only period for which reliable comparisons could be made by individual communities was 1929–1939, and even for this period the analysis had

---

[6] The writer is indebted to Gladys L. Palmer for this suggestion.

to be based on annual, not hourly, earnings.[7] As in the discussion of employment-wage patterns, the data were studied, first, by the method of rank correlation and, second, by the method of multisample analysis.

By means of rank correlation analysis it is possible to determine how close an association, if any, there is between per cent changes in value added per worker and in the wages of industries in different communities. If the association is close, industries which experience the largest

TABLE 18

RANK CORRELATION COEFFICIENTS, VALUE ADDED PER WORKER[a] AND AVERAGE EARNINGS (ANNUAL EARNINGS, 1937; HOURLY EARNINGS, 1947) IN MANUFACTURING, LOS ANGELES COUNTY AND UNITED STATES

Year	Los Angeles County			United States		
	r	Number of industries	Significant values	r	Number of industries	Significant values
Value added per worker and average annual earnings						
1937	.594	14	$r_{.01} = .661$ $r_{.05} = .532$	.592	14	$r_{.01} = .661$ $r_{.05} = .532$
Value added per worker and average hourly earnings						
1947	.182	16	$r_{.01} = .623$ $r_{.05} = .497$	.519	18	$r_{.01} = .590$ $r_{.05} = .468$

SOURCES: The same as for Table 15.
[a] Total value added by manufacture divided by number of production workers per industry.

percentage gains in value added per worker will tend to experience the largest percentage gains in wages (in this case, annual earnings) as well. The data for eleven manufacturing industries in six industrial areas for the period 1929–1939 were analyzed in this manner, and the results are presented for each community and for all communities combined in table 19.

The data reveal a fairly close, positive association between value added and annual earnings. In two of the communities the correlation values exceeded the 5 per cent significance level, and in two others they were not much below this level. Moreover, the average r for all six com-

---

[7] Data as far back as 1899 are available from Census of Manufactures reports, but the task of rearranging industry classifications to keep the figures on a comparable basis proved too great an undertaking. As noted earlier, the staff of the Haynes Foundation had already done this work for six areas for the period 1929–1939, and this analysis is confined to the data presented in their study. Neff, Baum, and Heilman, *Production Cost Trends in Selected Industrial Areas* (Berkeley and Los Angeles: University of California Press, 1948), pp. 196–201, 226–231.

SOURCE: Calculated from Neff, Baum, and Heilman, op. cit., pp. 196–201, 226–231.

TABLE 19

RANKINGS AND RANK CORRELATION COEFFICIENTS OF PER CENT CHANGES IN AVERAGE ANNUAL EARNINGS AND VALUE ADDED PER WORKER FOR ELEVEN MANUFACTURING INDUSTRIES, SIX INDUSTRIAL AREAS, AND AVERAGE r, 1929–1939

Industry	Los Angeles County		Chicago		Cleveland		Detroit		Pittsburgh		San Francisco	
	AAE[a]	VA/W[b]	AAE	VA/W	AAE	VA/W	AAE	VA/W	AAE	VA/W	AAE	VA/W
Food and kindred products	1	2	2	1	5	5	4	2	2	2	3	7
Textiles and their products	9.5	9	7	10	9	8.5	11	6	10	11	8	3
Paper and allied products	2.5	5	4	4	2	2	5.5	4	1	1	1.5	2
Printing, publishing, and allied industries	7	11	3	5	8	11	9.5	11	7.5	8	6	10
Chemicals and allied products	2.5	3	1	2	4	8.5	1	3	7.5	5	4	4
Forest products	11	7	10	9	10	6	8	9	9	10	10	8.5
Stone, clay, and glass products	5	1	9	3	11	1	7	5	4.5	6	8	1
Iron and steel and their products, not including machinery	8	8	5	6.5	7	7	5.5	8	6	7	8	8.5
Transportation equipment, air, land, and water	6	5	8	6.5	6	10	3	10	11	3	11	11
Nonferrous metals and their products	9.5	10	6	8	3	4	2	1	4.5	9	5	5.5
Machinery, not including transportation equipment	4	5	11	11	1	3	9.5	7	3	4	1.5	5.5
Correlation coefficients	.736		.725		.243		.523		.559		.432	
Significance levels $r_{.01}$	.765		.765		.765		.765		.765		.765	
$r_{.05}$	.632		.632		.632		.632		.632		.632	

Significance levels $r_{.01}$ = .354
$r_{.05}$ = .273

Average r = .559

SOURCE: Calculated from Neff, Baum, and Heilman, op. cit., pp. 196–201, 226–231.
a AAE = Average annual earnings.
b VA/W = Value added per worker.

munities was well above even the 1 per cent significance level. Over the ten-year period, it is clear, interindustry changes in annual earnings and in value added per worker moved closely together.[8]

MULTISAMPLE ANALYSIS

Multisample analysis is used here to measure changes in value added per worker on different bases in just the same way as the data on employment and wage changes were studied in the previous chapter. Deviations of the average of per cent changes for one industry from the general average of per cent changes for all industries, or for one area from the general average of per cent changes for all areas, or for one year from the general average of per cent changes for all years, in a given period may or may not be significantly large. If they are not, we conclude that the influences controlling changes in value added affect different industries, areas, and/or years in a uniform manner. If they are, we conclude that the controlling influences operate in a nonuniform manner. This analysis augments the conclusions reached by the rank correlation analysis in a number of ways. First, it shows whether changes in value added per worker among manufacturing industries in local areas tend to be uniform or diverse, a matter on which the rank correlation analysis throws no light. Second, it breaks down the value added series into three aspects, interindustry, interarea, and interyear, and thus indicates more precisely what the major sources of change in the series are. Finally, since the data on wage changes can be analyzed in the same manner, this method of analysis makes possible direct comparisons between particular aspects of value added and wage phenomena, a type of comparison which is not feasible under the method of rank correlation analysis.

The results of the multisample analysis, which covered eleven manufacturing industries in six large urban areas between 1929 and 1939, are given in table 20. The differences in value added changes among industries and areas were found to be significantly large in only one period (1933–1937); in all others, both over the entire period and in the various subperiods, interindustry and interarea differences proved to be negligible. Differences in wage changes on these two bases of comparison, on the other hand, were significantly large in the subperiod 1929–1933, and, speaking of interindustry differences, in the subperiod 1933–1937 as well. To this extent, the data on value added per worker, on the one hand, and on wages, on the other, exhibited quite different patterns of behavior. But the point to be emphasized is that, over the ten-year

---

[8] In general, these findings tend to confirm on the local area level what Dunlop and Gabarino found on the national level. See chapter by Dunlop in *Income, Employment and Public Policy, op. cit.,* p. 350, and Gabarino, *op. cit.,* pp. 299–300.

TABLE 20

Summary of Results, Analysis of Variance *F* Tests, Per Cent Changes in Average Annual Earnings and Value Added Per Worker, Eleven Manufacturing Industries, Six Industrial Areas, 1929–1939

Period	Source of variation	Average annual earnings (b)	Average value added by manufacture per worker (c)	F required for significance $F_{.01}$ $F_{.05}$	
1929–1939	Industries....	.45	.37	(b) 2.80 (c) 2.80	2.07 2.07
	Areas........	.38	.33	(b) 4.10 (c) 4.10	2.71 2.71
	Years........	S 95.60	S.05 3.74	(b) 4.43 (c) 3.83	2.87 2.61

Phases of the business cycle

Period	Source of variation	Average annual earnings (b)	Average value added by manufacture per worker (c)	F required for significance $F_{.01}$ $F_{.05}$	
1929–1933	Industries....	S 5.70	1.74	(b) 2.49 (c) 2.70	1.91 2.02
	Areas........	S 5.04	.21	(b) 3.18 (c) 10.97	2.29 5.05
	Years........	S 51.50	.23	(b) 6.87 (c) 16.26	3.93 6.61
1933–1937	Industries....	S 3.34	S.05 2.01	(b) 2.70 (c) 2.49	2.02 1.91
	Areas........	1.17	1.95	(b) 5.64 (c) 3.18	3.33 2.29
	Years........	.49	3.86	(b) 10.04 (c) 6.87	4.96 3.93
1937–1939	Industries....	.41	1.01	2.70	2.02
	Areas........	.67	1.54	3.41	2.40
	Years........	....	....	....	....

Source: Appendix table 15.

period taken as a whole, differences among industries and areas with respect to both series were negligible.

As for year-to-year changes in value added per worker, the analysis revealed no significant variations in the three subperiods which roughly corresponded to phases of the business cycle, whereas interyear wage changes were significant in one period (1929–1933). Over the entire ten-year period, on the other hand, interyear differences in rates of change in value added per worker proved to be significant; this also was true of wages, though in the former case yearly deviations from the ten-year average reached only the 5 per cent level of significance. Speaking still of the whole ten-year period, it will be remembered that the same pat-

TABLE 21

SUMMARY OF RESULTS, ANALYSIS OF VARIANCE *F* TESTS, PER CENT CHANGES IN AVERAGE ANNUAL EARNINGS AND VALUE ADDED PER WORKER, ELEVEN MANUFACTURING INDUSTRIES, SIX INDUSTRIAL AREAS, AND FIVE TWO-YEAR PERIODS, 1929–1939

Biennial periods	Source of variation	Average annual earnings	Average value added by manufacture per worker	*F* required for significance	
				$F_{.01}$	$F_{.05}$
1929–1931	Industries..............	S 7.08	S 3.55	2.70	2.02
	Areas.................	S 6.98	S 3.79	3.41	2.40
1931–1933	Industries..............	S.₀₅ 2.35	S 4.29	2.70	2.02
	Areas.................	.97	1.27	3.41	2.40
1933–1935	Industries..............	S.₀₅ 2.13	S.₀₅ 2.07	2.70	2.02
	Areas.................	S 7.14	1.90	3.41	2.40
1935–1937	Industries..............	S.₀₅ 2.36	1.73	2.70	2.02
	Areas.................	.16	1.62	3.41	2.40
1937–1939	Industries..............	.41	1.01	2.70	2.02
	Areas.................	.67	1.54	3.41	2.40

SOURCE: Appendix table 15.

tern of interindustry, interarea, and interyear behavior was exhibited by the data on employment (tables 11 and 12).

To remove the interyear influence to the greatest possible extent so as to focus attention on the influences of industry and area alone, the value added and wage data were analyzed on a biennial basis, the same method that was used in connection with the analysis of employment-wage patterns. The results are summarized in table 21.

When studied on a two-year basis, changes in value added per worker showed a greater tendency toward significant differences among industries and areas than in the longer periods. Thus the variations in value added were found to exhibit much the same pattern as annual earnings, the two magnitudes failing to parallel one another in only two periods. Again, it will be recalled that the data on employment and annual earnings also showed greater similarity of behavior in the biennial period analysis than in the phases of the cycle (tables 11 and 13).

To summarize, in very short periods value added per worker and annual earnings tend to vary widely among industries and areas. In periods corresponding to phases of the cycle, both vary less widely, value added varying least. Over long periods the variations tend to be without significance in either case. It appears, then, that though short-term variations in value added and wages among industries and areas are likely to be significantly large, over longer periods the forces controlling both magnitudes tend to eliminate marked variations. This squares with the view that in short periods the influences making for diversity outweigh those making for similarity, whereas in long periods (of ten years or more) the reverse holds true. This also supports the view that over long periods of time the forces controlling changes in annual earnings and value added per worker affect different industries and areas in a uniform manner. In changes in the general level of these two variables one year to the next, however, no consistent pattern of behavior was observed.

CONCLUSION

The foregoing analysis failed to disclose any close association in local areas between type of firm or type of cost structure and interindustry wage levels. Thus, neither size of firm nor the proportion of labor cost to total cost was found to bear a consistent relation to differences in annual earnings in various manufacturing fields. Ratios of the amount of capital to the work force revealed a much closer association, but even in this case the results were not as clear-cut as might have been expected. When the influence of product supply conditions was studied from the broader viewpoint of differences in value added per worker, however, a much closer association was found. Generally speaking, industries in which increases in value added between 1929 and 1939 were substantial experienced the greatest rise in average annual earnings, whereas those in which value added gains were small registered the lowest wage gains.

This, of course, should not be interpreted to mean that over this period there were substantial differences among industries with respect to changes either in value added per worker or in annual earnings. As a matter of fact, judging from the multisample analysis, neither magnitude was marked by significant differences among industries or among areas. Variations between years, on the other hand, were found to be significantly large.

The picture which emerges is that of a closely knit interindustry and interarea structure in which the influences controlling value added per worker and average annual earnings affected individual industries and areas in a fairly uniform manner; but no such uniformity was exhibited on an interyear basis, the two variables moving at different rates of change in different years. When the ten-year period was broken up into shorter periods, significant differences were observed among industries and areas in a number of instances, indicating that in such periods, even on these two bases of comparison, value added per worker and average annual earnings tend to behave in a dissimilar manner.

VIII. UNIONS AND LOCAL WAGE
BEHAVIOR

PREVIOUS CHAPTERS reviewed some of the major economic influences which have shaped the interindustry wage structure of Los Angeles and other large urban areas. This chapter considers the major effects on local wage relationships in the Los Angeles area which can be attributed to the spread of trade unionism. Contrary to the earlier discussion, this part of the analysis does not lend itself to precise statistical measurement. Examination of certain general facts about local market developments in the area yields a few important conclusions, but mostly the analysis must rely on case study materials drawn from particular industries. These materials were secured from records obtained from unions, employers, and government agencies and through interviews with many persons working in this general field. Although a voluminous amount of case data was gathered, space limitations permit only a brief summarization of these materials here.[1]

UNIONS IN LOS ANGELES

The wage effects of trade unions cannot be understood apart from the particular environment surrounding their activities. In addition to economic influences, conditions of an institutional and even of a political nature are no less important. The Los Angeles experience affords a striking illustration of this proposition.

At the beginning of the 'forties comparatively few industries in the area were covered by union agreements. During the previous two decades even labor organizations in the building and printing trades had lost much of their strength, and outside these two traditional strongholds unions were practically nonexistent. Numerous organizing campaigns were launched as early as 1933, following the National Industrial Recovery Act, and sizable gains in membership were quickly made among the teamsters, clothing workers, street railway workers, bakers, butchers, cleaners and dyers, culinary workers, printing craftsmen, glass workers, barbers, and laundry workers. At the height of this activity, however, paid-up membership in Los Angeles unions probably did not exceed 25,000 to 30,000, and even this total was reduced after the breakdown of the NIRA program in 1934.

In large measure the failure of the unions to maintain membership gains at this time was due to the effective opposition of various employer

---

[1] Some observations of a more general nature on the influence exerted by unions on wage movements in this area will be found on pp. 39–40, 60, 67, 69.

groups. This was an outgrowth of the open-shop program sponsored for many years by the Merchants and Manufacturers Association and the *Los Angeles Times*. During the 'twenties management had been able to eliminate almost all unions in the area, and though some adaptations were made during the 1933–1934 period to comply with the federal government's labor policies, the methods used by employers in the later period to block unionization proved hardly less effective. Other factors were also involved, such as geographical remoteness, limited industrial development, the importance of agriculture and the transient character of much of the area's labor force, internal union dissension, and inept union leadership. What set off the Los Angeles experience from other large cities, however, was the extent and effectiveness of employer organization to combat the spread of trade unionism.

In 1934 and 1935, union organizing efforts were continued, though at a slower tempo. Passage of the Wagner Act in 1935 gave added protection to labor organizations in their dealings with employers, but some time elapsed before the effects of this legislation were felt in the Los Angeles area. Beginning in 1936, union membership campaigns made more headway, notable gains being won in most of the industries cited earlier as well as among aircraft, rubber, motion picture, brewery, fishing, cannery, and fur workers and in certain branches of the metal trades. In 1937, aided by the CIO Los Angeles Industrial Union Council, which was established on June 14 of that year, membership drives were also launched in automobiles, basic steel, and steel fabricating, as well as among oil and newspaper workers.

Opposition by employer groups, coupled with the sharp business recession which began in the latter part of 1937, brought these campaigns to a temporary halt, but the drives were pushed with redoubled vigor the next year. At the same time the employer groups stepped up their efforts to maintain open-shop conditions, chief emphasis being placed on enactment of a local antipicketing ordinance and on the formation of a number of citizens' groups. In some industries, especially furniture, restaurants, aircraft, and automobiles, union organizing efforts met with little success, but in many others, such as steel, trucking, wholesale and retail food distribution, and cleaning and dyeing, substantial progress was made. In 1939, the status of unions remained pretty much unchanged, only organizations in building construction, trucking, and retail meat shops making much headway.[2]

Thus, 1940 was the first year that the organized labor movement was

---

[2] The foregoing account of recent trade union history in this area is largely based on a doctoral dissertation by Louis B. Perry, "A Survey of the Labor Movement in Los Angeles, 1933–1939" (University of California, Los Angeles, 1950), especially chaps. ii, iii, vii, and x.

in a position to exert a significant influence, by reason of its own strength, on the community's economic and political affairs. The major branches of building construction, trucking, motion pictures, longshoring, and the printing trades were well organized, and important "islands of control" were established in the mass-production industries, in almost all of the light manufacturing fields, and in many branches of trade and related consumer service fields. In certain branches of almost every industry, however, the majority of employers continued to operate nonunion. This was not only true of such industries as restaurants, furniture, clothing, machinery, and the metal trades, but it even plagued the building crafts, teamsters, and printers. Similarly, a number of larger firms in aviation, automobiles, and steel remained outside the orbit of trade unionism. After 1940, organization spread much further as the pressure on available labor supplies mounted and the bargaining power of labor groups increased. In a relatively short time after 1940, the community shifted from a predominantly nonunion to a predominantly union economy. At the end of the 'forties there were still some fields, such as retail trade (other than food distribution), finance, real estate, and insurance, personal and business services, and repair shops, in which unions enjoyed little or no strength. Most workers in white-collar jobs and the professions were also nonunion. Unions, however, had gained enough strength generally to exert an important, though indirect, influence on labor relations policies even in nonunion fields.

BARGAINING MAP OF LOS ANGELES

With the spread of trade unionism, local wages became a more closely knit structure both as among industries in the area and among other areas. The high level of business activity, locally and nationally, also contributed to this result, but it is safe to say that wage developments over the decade of the 'forties as a whole would have been very different if no unions had been in existence. During the war years, the extreme scarcity of labor, coupled with government controls over wage increases, makes it almost impossible to isolate the wage effects of unions from other environmental factors, but these matters become much clearer when attention is focused on the postwar period.

Generally speaking, with the advent of unionism, wage relationships became more subject to a common set of rules, differences in wage rates among industries and areas becoming more the result of conscious design than of impersonal market forces or employer choice. In fields like motion picture production and metal fabricating, postwar unemployment in the local area had an important impact on wage levels but not nearly so much as might have been expected. Unions in consumer service industries, on the other hand, were quick to secure substantial wage gains as the postwar expansion in these fields gained momentum.

A review of collective bargaining patterns in the Los Angeles area shows the extent to which industry wage levels have been affected by the advent of trade unionism. Collective wage agreements in the community reflect two major influences, one stemming directly from sources outside the immediate area, and the other from sources more local in character. To some degree the wage bargain in every industry bears the imprint of both influences, but one or the other tends to be dominant. Using this basis of distinction, there appear to be five industry groupings in this community, each of which exhibits certain well-defined characteristics. The first consists of mass-production industries, like steel, automobiles, and rubber tires, in which there are a few large firms and in which decisions about wages are made outside the local area. Coupled with this group are a few local industries, mostly in the metal trades, which are intimately associated with mass-production manufacturing. The influences controlling wages in these fields are predominantly nonlocal in character. The second group is made up of manufacturing firms which, though of large size and serving broad market areas, are nevertheless locally managed. Examples are aircraft, shipbuilding, oil refining, and motion picture production. In their case, influences from outside the Los Angeles market, though somewhat less controlling than in the first group, still predominate.

A third category consists of a number of light manufacturing industries in which firms are typically small and numerous, and in which wage issues are determined at the local level. In these fields the local market absorbs a much larger share of total output than is characteristic of large-scale industry, but sales competition and, to a lesser degree, competition for labor extend well beyond the immediate vicinity. Consequently, though local conditions usually are the more important, influences from outside the area are hardly less significant in determining wage levels. Members of this group are such industries as furniture, clothing, and commercial printing. The fourth category consists of certain nonmanufacturing fields in which there are many small employers, wage decisions tend to be worked out at the local level, and product market competition from outside the immediate area is negligible. The two most important fields in this group are construction and local trucking, but there are many others such as hotels and restaurants, building services, laundering, cleaning, and dyeing, and various branches of the wholesale and retail trades. As would be expected, wages in these fields reflect local market developments more than do wages in industries in the other three groups.[3]

---

[3] The statistical data on industry wage levels in this area were analyzed on the basis of type of product and type of product market area in chap. v.

Finally, there are certain nonmanufacturing industries which are subject to close government regulation or are considered to be in a special public service category. These include rail and water transportation, over-the-road trucking, street railways and buses, and other types of public utilities. For obvious reasons, it seems appropriate to include government work in this public service group. Longshoring, on the other hand, defies easy classification. It has close affiliations with such local nonmanufacturing fields as warehousing and the distributing trades, but it also is linked to water transportation, bargaining is conducted on a coast-wide basis, and negotiations are more affected by developments on the East Coast as well as by government policies than most other nonmanufacturing industries. There are other borderline cases as well, indicating that the distinctions made here are suggestive only, and not to be applied in any rigid or mechanical way.

Local Wage Patterns Under Collective Bargaining

These five categories of collective bargaining form a complicated network of wage relationships, and the transmission of wage changes within and between the groupings does not always follow the same channels. An industry may play an active role at one time and a passive role at another. Similarly, relationships between two or more industries may be mutually influencing rather than one directional only. Nonetheless, interindustry wage levels in unionized fields in this community form a unified structure, changes in the structure following fairly well defined and readily distinguishable patterns. These conclusions are supported by such wage data as are available for the period since World War II. The figures, which consist of hourly wage rate increases under major union agreements in selected industries, are given in table 22 for the five industry groups already described.

Of wage negotiations which are primarily the result of national industry settlements, the most important locally is the agreement between the United States Steel Corporation and the United Steelworkers. This settlement, which sets the pattern for other basic steel companies throughout the country, is followed by the subsidiaries of U. S. Steel and of the other steel firms in the Los Angeles area. Differences in job content and the prevalence of incentive pay systems make exact comparisons impossible, but at present the wage rates in such local firms as Columbia Steel (a U. S. Steel subsidiary in basic steel) and Consolidated Steel (a U. S. Steel subsidiary in steel fabrication) are on a par with Pittsburgh rates.

The influence of the settlements reached by the major steel companies is felt directly by two major groups in the local area: subsidiaries of

TABLE 22

GENERAL CHANGES IN UNION WAGE RATES, FIVE INDUSTRY GROUPS,
LOS ANGELES AREA, 1946–1949

(Increases in cents per hour unless otherwise noted)

Industry	1946	1947	1948	1949[a]
Group I				
"National" large-scale manufacturing and related fields				
Basic steel (steelworkers)	18½	12½	13	0
Automobiles (automobile workers)	18½	11½	11	0[b]
Rubber tires (rubber workers)	18½	11½	11	0
Electrical equipment (electrical workers, Ind.)	18½	11½	8% or 9c	0 ½–
Meat packing (packinghouse workers)	16	13½	13	15
Steel fabrication (steelworkers)	18½	12½	13	0
Steel foundries (steelworkers)	18½	12½	12	0
Grey iron foundries (molders)	18½	10–12	8–12	0
Nonferrous foundries (steelworkers)	15	5	0	10
Group II				
"Locally controlled" large-scale manufacturing				
Aircraft (machinists)	15%	5	10	5
Oil refining (oil workers)	18%	20	10	12½
Shipbuilding (shipbuilding workers)	18	12c	8	0
Motion pictures (theatrical and stage workers)	45[d]	25	0	0
Group III				
Small-scale manufacturing				
Commercial printing (typographical workers)	20	45⅔	27⅔	13⅓
Paper products (paper mill workers)	19%	10%+ 7½c	9% or 15c	0
Furniture				
furniture workers, CIO	18½	12½	10	5
upholsterers, AFL	18½	12½	11½	0
Clothing (amalgamated clothing)	12½	12½	0	0
Bakeries (bakery workers)	18½	20½	12	10
Group IV				
Nonmanufacturing				
Construction (6 basic trades)	16	20	14	8
Trucking, food distribution (teamsters)	20	15	10	15
Meat, retail (butchers)	20⅘	40	10	25
Clerks, retail (retail clerks)	16⅝	37½	6¼	7½
Hotels and restaurants (culinary workers)	..[e]	0	10	0
Group V				
Public utilities				
Street railway (street railway workers)	26	11	5	7
Over-the-road trucking (teamsters)	18½	15	12½	5
Electric light and power (electrical workers, AFL)	10%	8%	5%	5%

SOURCE: Major agreements of the principal unions as indicated.
[a] In industries where negotiations began in 1949 but agreements were not reached until 1950, the 1949 settlements are shown as zero.
[b] An increase of 3 cents per hour was granted under the General Motors agreement in 1949.
[c] Larger increases were granted on nonrepair jobs to eliminate the repair work differential.
[d] At the same time, the workday was increased from 6 to 8 hours for computing overtime.
[e] In 1946 the settlement continued existing rates, but wages had risen substantially during the war.

national companies in the other mass-production industries (auto-mobiles, rubber tires, electrical equipment, and meat packing) and the various branches of the local metal trades and machinery industries. For the first group, the general wage adjustments in recent years have typically been the same as in the major companies, the local subsidiaries consistently granting the same wage adjustments as their companies' plants in the East. Within individual companies, however, the absolute level of rates is not in every case uniform throughout the country. Of the three major automobile producers, only Ford pays identical rates in all its plants. Differences among the 100-odd General Motors plants do not exceed 5 or 10 cents per hour on individual jobs, and for the most part its rates are on a par. Rate differences among the Chrysler plants have been greater, though the differential East and West has been far less than North and South. The automobile workers union secured a national agreement covering all Chrysler plants for the first time after the 1950 strike, and as a result interplant differentials have been sub-stantially lessened.

The rubber workers union has national agreements with all the major rubber tire manufacturers, General Tire having been the last to sign a nation-wide agreement. Some interplant rate differences still exist, though they are being steadily reduced. As of 1950, rates in the Los Angeles area were roughly 10 per cent below pay levels in the Akron area. The major meat-packing companies also sign agreements covering all their plants, but some interplant differences in wage rates nonethe-less exist. In the case of the agreements between the Big Four packers and the CIO Packinghouse Workers, for example, ever since the first agreements were signed in 1936, rates in the Los Angeles branch plants have been 10 cents an hour higher than in the Midwest plants. Because of differences in job content, similar comparisons cannot be made for electric equipment manufacturing. However, the General Electric plant in the Los Angeles area, which produces flatirons for the national mar-ket, has granted the same general pay increases as the company's other plants since the end of World War II.

The figures on union wage rate increases in the five industries in the Los Angeles area comprising Group I of table 22 show a high degree of similarity. Of the first four postwar years, 1946 was marked by the most uniformity, and 1949 by the least. Meat packing followed a slightly different pattern from the other four industries, a result one would expect from a comparison of the production and marketing character-istics of these fields. During this period inflationary influences were of major importance in keeping wage changes uniform; nonetheless, dif-ferences in wage behavior among these industries, both interarea and intra-area, would have been greater between 1946 and 1949 if unions had not become so powerful in this region.

The various branches of the metal trades and machinery industries, the second local group directly affected by the settlements in steel, follow a far less consistent pattern than the plants in the mass-production group. Not all firms in any one branch of the industry pay the same wage increase, much less the same absolute scale, nor is the average change among the different branches of the field always the same. Wage rate levels in machine shops are especially diverse, so much so that even rough estimates of recent wage changes are impossible. This is due to the fact that the shops are typically small, many hiring five employees or less, a substantial number are nonunion, and, even in the unionized sector of the industry, differences are aggravated by the presence of several unions. What is as important as any of these factors, machine shops service a wide variety of industries, each with different production requirements and profit prospects. As a consequence, wage rates in any one category of machine shops are as likely to be influenced by the settlements in aircraft, shipbuilding, oil refining, or even construction, as in basic steel. These conditions are less true of steel fabricating, gray iron foundries, steel foundries, and nonferrous foundries, and in their case estimates of general wage changes are possible. Wage increases in all four of these metal trades industries followed much the same course between 1946 and 1949. The greatest deviations occurred in nonferrous foundries, but even in this industry the changes paralleled the "steel pattern" fairly closely. Although economic conditions after World War II were conducive to this result, it seems clear that the similarity would have been less marked if the unions in these fields had not become so strongly established locally.

Another cluster of industries (Group II), which is nearly as much affected by the wage settlements in steel as those in the first category, consists of large-scale, but "locally controlled," manufacturing firms. The principal members of this group are the oil refining, aircraft, shipbuilding, and motion picture companies. Although their production and market conditions differ from the other mass-production industries discussed above, in many important respects they are similar. This applies even to the type of union organization which has developed in these fields. What demarcates them from the other mass-production industries is that major decisions regarding wages and other issues are worked out locally, the spokesmen who represent the employers and unions in the area having authority to agree on terms. Also, they form a less homogeneous group of industries than those in the first category, the markets for their products being quite dissimilar.

One would suppose, then, that though union rates in these firms would behave in much the same way as in the nationally controlled plants, certain differences would be observed. The data for these industries for the years 1946–1949 (Group II in table 22) support this supposition. A degree of uniformity among the industries, as well as between the group as a whole and the nationally controlled firms, is evident in the figures for 1946 and 1948, though even in these two years wage rate adjustments in motion pictures formed a quite separate pattern. On the other hand, in 1947 and 1949, union rate levels in these four fields pulled widely apart and, when taken together, showed little similarity to the pattern established by the Group I industries. During the latter part of this period, economic conditions were most favorable in oil refining and least favorable in shipbuilding and motion pictures. Although union wage levels, as table 22 shows, reflected these divergent developments, they did so to a much less degree than could reasonably have been expected. Some part of the explanation, exactly how much one cannot say, may properly be attributed to the influence of unions.

In assessing the role of unions in this group of industries, comparisons with other major industrial centers are of interest. Despite the difficulties besetting the shipbuilding industry which were particularly marked on the West Coast, wage rates in the Los Angeles area in the postwar period remained as high as in most other localities. In aircraft and oil refining, local rates were not the highest in the country at this time but they equaled or surpassed the levels prevailing in most eastern plants. The fact that, in spite of diverse economic developments in these fields, interarea wage relationships remained substantially unchanged in these industries testifies to the importance of trade union policies.

Union wages in small-scale manufacturing fields in the Los Angeles area (Group III) are also largely influenced by the steel and other national industry settlements. In some industries like furniture and paper products, wage changes during the first four postwar years displayed a striking parallelism. In certain others, like commercial printing and men's clothing, wages behaved quite differently. There are a number of reasons for this divergent wage pattern in small-scale industry. Generally speaking, the most important consideration was whether sales volume in a given industry moved closely with fluctuations in the national, mass-production industries (Group I). Business trends in some small-scale manufacturing lines, especially those selling most of their output to the construction industry or some other strictly local field, diverged from trends in other lines for extended periods, and the effect was carried over into these industries' wage structures. True, even though most of an industry's output was sold locally, sales sometimes closely paralleled business fluctuations in large-scale industry. In Los Angeles, however, an area in which growth has been very rapid, sales trends in these fields have frequently followed an independent course, with corresponding effects on wage movements.

Similarly, conditions in the small-scale manufacturing industries of this community varied widely as to the extent their methods had been mechanized and labor skills "diluted." In industries like clothing, use of machine equipment remained quite limited, and hand skills continued to be important, since at this time Los Angeles was still a relatively new and undeveloped clothing center. The closer production methods in a given industry approximated those prevailing in the mass-production fields, the greater the similarity in wage structures and wage behavior tended to be. As these industries develop in the Los Angeles area and machine equipment is more extensively employed, these tendencies will become increasingly evident.

The diversity of wages among small-scale manufacturing fields also reflected differences in degrees of product market competition, especially in interarea market rivalry. In industries like bread baking, intercity cost comparisons were much less significant for local producers than in industries like furniture or commercial printing. Consequently, union rates in the latter industries were noticeably more influenced by wage scales paid by competing firms in other centers than by prevailing local area rates, whereas the reverse held true for industries oriented toward the local market. In a period such as 1946–1949 and in a community like Los Angeles, this distinction was probably less important than would generally be true, since in many instances both the local area settlements and settlements in other centers of an industry were closely tied to the wage patterns established by steel and by other national mass-production industries; again, the local furniture manufacturing industry affords a good example. To the extent this was true, the local area, interindustry influence and the interarea, intra-industry influence led to the same result. But where this was not true, as, for example, in the local commercial printing industry, rates were pulled well above, or held well below, local area rates.

These environmental influences were modified, but certainly not eliminated, by the existence of trade unions. Labor organizations doubtless made for greater uniformity of wage behavior among small-scale manufacturing fields in the postwar period, but the conditions described above placed severe limitations on their activities. This was apparent enough in those fields in which a substantial part of local production was nonunion, a circumstance which was itself related to the environmental circumstances described earlier. Less apparent, but hardly less significant in many instances, was the ability of nonunion firms in other areas to "out compete" local firms in their own market. In a few cases this even applied to unionized competitors in other cities, though their advantage usually extended only to other market centers and not to the southern California market. Thus, during the war and early postwar boom, local companies in furniture and clothing found it easy enough to match the wage increases in large-scale industries in the area, since demand conditions for their products were extremely favorable. By 1948 and 1949, however, these firms found themselves in serious difficulties because the "area" influence had pulled their rates out of line with those paid by competitors in other regions. These conditions had a direct bearing on local wages under collective bargaining, so much so that unions had no recourse but to adjust their wage policies accordingly.

The impact of postwar market forces on union wage programs is clearly seen in the men's clothing industry. The war boom brought an extraordinary expansion in the industry's output in the Los Angeles area, the rise being greater locally than in most of the older centers. As shown in an earlier section of this study, wage levels during this period moved up quickly as employers sought to check the loss of their manpower. After the war, in 1946 and 1947, the expansion in business continued, local manufacturers of men's sportswear finding an especially ready market for their output. During these two years, wage rates in the local industry continued their rapid climb, and thus were kept fully abreast of gains elsewhere. Despite the production record of the 1940's, however, Los Angeles remained predominantly an import market, sportswear being the only branch in which local manufacturers had substantial sales in other markets. So long as general business conditions remained extremely favorable, continued growth was possible, but as soon as there was some decline, the position of Los Angeles manufacturers proved to be particularly weak. Thus, the slight letdown experienced in most clothing markets in 1948 and 1949 had serious repercussions in this West Coast center and further gains in wage rates became out of the question. These developments are directly reflected in the local industry's wage structure as shown in table 22 above.

Much of what has been said about union wage rates in small-scale manufacturing applies to local nonmanufacturing fields (Group IV) as well. In fact, union scales in nonmanufacturing displayed much more diversity of structure and behavior than union rates in small-scale manufacturing as a whole. Such unity or similarity as obtained can be largely attributed to the agreements signed by the building trades and teamster unions. Thus, the wage settlements in building construction had immediate effects on wages in a number of closely allied industries like sand and gravel and other building supply fields; they also provided a general standard for wage negotiations in further removed industries like building services, public utilities, certain branches of motion picture production, and even various manufacturing lines. The teamster union influenced the wage structures of a wide range of nonmanufacturing and small-scale manufacturing industries, including warehousing, wholesale and retail food distribution, dairies, bakeries, breweries, and other food processing trades, automotive repair, laundries, and similar service fields. Although the teamster union was concerned primarily with the trucking and delivery branches of these industries, it frequently organized on a plant-wide basis and in some cases even represented clerical employees. As in construction agreements, the wage adjustments secured by the teamster union served as a general standard for a number of other craft groups in the same or other industries. Moreover, the teamster union agreements provided a connecting link between the settlements in the construction trades and elsewhere, since they covered the delivery of supplies in building and most other industries.

In spite of these unifying tendencies, it has already been mentioned that union wage rates in nonmanufacturing industries exhibit little coherence. The adjustments since 1946, shown in table 22 for selected fields, exhibit no consistent behavior, whereas comparisons of absolute rate levels present an even more haphazard picture. A number of circumstances explain this lack of cohesion. On the institutional level, it should be said that the unions in these fields are mostly AFL craft organizations and, though today these unions usually have broad jurisdictions, their primary concern is still the winning of gains for specific skilled groups. This deserves particular emphasis in a community like Los Angeles where there is an extremely large number of labor organizations in nonmanufacturing fields, each affiliated with different national bodies. Furthermore, wide differences in wages are also to be found among locals of the same union where membership cuts across different industries. The teamster union, for example, follows a highly decentralized wage policy in this area, wage scales for trucking varying between fields almost as much as do rates for other jobs. Most of the other major unions, even though representing single crafts like the operative engineers, allow for wage rate differences where the industries are clearly not the same.

A related circumstance is that there are wide differences in the relative strength of labor organizations in this part of the local economy. In some instances, as in construction, unionization is almost complete but in others, as in most branches of retail trade, organization is extremely limited. The presence of nonunion firms, except under extreme boom conditions, tends to hold union scales down, since there is always the danger that rates, if raised too high, will be undercut. In a number of these fields the problem of establishing and maintaining effective labor organizations is made difficult by the fact that most firms are extremely small and are frequently shifting their locations. In others, such as the restaurant field, much of the work requires little skill, many of the workers are women or of foreign extraction, and labor turnover is high. On the other hand, once a strong organization is established and competition in the local labor market is brought under control, conditions in many nonmanufacturing fields redound to the unions' favor. Because of their size and the nature of their operations, employers are frequently in a poor position to resist wage demands. More important, competition in many nonmanufacturing industries is confined to a particular community or local geographical area, so that limitations exerted by lower-wage producers in other centers, such as are found in most manufacturing fields, are conspicuously absent. The upshot is that certain of these unions find themselves in a highly favorable position to raise their wage standards but others do not, a distinction which is reflected in the wage scales of these organizations.

Underlying many of these circumstances is the fact that nonmanufacturing industries, both in operating methods and marketing conditions, are heterogeneous in the extreme. In the Los Angeles area, these fields range all the way from large-scale construction projects to one-man retail stores, and the influences bearing on wage levels are correspondingly varied. To the degree wage uniformity has been achieved under unionism, it has usually been confined to various branches of a single closely related field, such as the construction trades, whereas substantial differences between major industry categories continue to be recognized. During the first half of the 'forties, conditions in Los Angeles served to modify these influences, but after World War II the economic fortunes of local nonmanufacturing industries became more diverse again.

PUBLIC UTILITIES

Wage settlements in Los Angeles public utilities, as in other communities, bear little relation to agreements reached in other industries in the area. Probably the most important local influence is the building trades agreement, since utility companies engage in some construction work and, more important, they deal with unions like the teamsters and AFL electrical workers which operate in both spheres. However, the dominant concerns in the public utility field are large in size and their operations often extend far beyond the local area. Moreover, they frequently enjoy a monopolistic position and competitive cost considerations have little bearing on wage policies. As a consequence, wage adjustments in other industries in the immediate area, except when conditions of labor supply change markedly, exert only a minor influence.

In a number of the major utilities, notably street railways and bus transportation, changes in wage rates have become linked rather closely to wage changes in the same industry in other large urban areas. The tendency to follow rates in other cities has, of course, found much support in labor circles but it should not be thought of as wholly an outgrowth of trade unionism. The size and prominence of the companies involved would make it difficult, under any circumstance, to disregard key settlements elsewhere in the industry.

In one sense, the salient feature of collective bargaining in all public utility fields, whether it be over-the-road trucking or gas and electric power distribution, is that the price of the product is subject to government regulation. Nonetheless, though this factor has important indirect effects, it seems to have little direct bearing on wage settlements in these fields. For the most part, wage adjustments are made on the best "bargained" basis possible and then, if price relief is felt to be necessary, appeal is made to the proper rate regulatory body. Since the latter bodies generally grant higher rates whenever a substantial increase in labor costs has occurred, the effect of rate regulation is to facilitate rather than impede wage increases. On the other hand, it would be erroneous to assume that the criterion of profits and ability to pay has no effect on wage settlements. Investigation of recent wage settlements in these fields shows that the financial outlook for the companies played a highly important part in the bargaining process. If on no other grounds, employers in rate-regulated fields oppose increases in labor costs because sooner or later consumer resistance will set in and any gains from higher prices may well be lost.

To sum up, because of the special circumstances surrounding government-regulated fields, wage rate adjustments in local utilities are likely to bear little similarity to rate changes in other industries in the immediate area. In postwar Los Angeles some parallelism can be detected in the figures presented in table 22, but only of a general nature. Wage rate changes in over-the-road trucking showed rather close conformity to rate adjustments in construction and other fields in which the teamsters held important agreements, but some marked differences nonetheless appeared. In electric utilities, rates for the key job of linesman behaved about the same way as general construction rates, though again some differences occurred. In street railways, postwar wage changes reflected local area influences hardly at all. Since the circum-

TABLE 23

Average Hourly Rates, Four Unionized Trades, Los Angeles and Other Cities, Prewar and Postwar

| Trade | Number of cities | Year | Prewar | | | Postwar (1949)[a] | |
			Average rate, all cities	Average rate, Los Angeles	Rank, Los Angeles	Average rate, all cities	Average rate, Los Angeles	Rank, Los Angeles
Book and job printing trades.........	67	1940[b]	1.000	1.041	25	1.911	2.311	4
Journeymen, building trades.........	68	1940[c]	1.291	1.189	53	2.218	2.202	33
Helpers and laborers, building trades.....	63	1940[c]	.734	.710	35	1.455	1.586	20
Motortruck drivers..............	68	1942[d]	.793	.998	5	1.352	1.653	6
Bread and cake machine shops.........	56	1941[e]	.700	.852	9	1.251	1.655	2

[a] Source of all data for 1949 is *Handbook of Regional Statistics*, 81st Cong., 2d sess. (Washington: 1950), pp. 431–433.
[b] *Monthly Labor Review*, 51 (December, 1940), 1500, table 11.
[c] *Monthly Labor Review*, 51 (November, 1940), 1245, table 9.
[d] U.S. Bureau of Labor Statistics, Bull. no. 732, table 8, p. 7.
[e] *Monthly Labor Review*, 54 (January, 1942), 182, table 7.

stances controlling wage rates in these fields were found to be so different from those in other industries, it was decided not to go into these matters in the present study in any detail. For the same reason no attempt has been made to analyze wage changes in government agencies and other nonprofit bodies.

INTERAREA UNION WAGE COMPARISONS

The extent to which unions have narrowed wage rate differences between industries in the Los Angeles area and the reasons why dissimilarities in wage behavior persist have thus far been the focus of discussion. Attention is now turned to the effects of unions on interarea wage relationships. As in the earlier discussion, it is impossible to measure the interarea influence of unionism precisely because it cannot be separated from other influences which were operating during the war and postwar periods. Again, generalizations must depend primarily on case materials drawn from individual industries.

The data presented in chapter iii, however, indicated that wage rates in the Los Angeles area, after the advent of unionism in the late 'thirties, generally rose more rapidly than in traditionally higher-paying centers. Since the economic expansion of the area was also relatively more rapid during most of the 'forties, this change in the community's general wage level can hardly be attributed to the spread of unionism alone. However, it seems safe to conclude that labor organizations at least played a facilitating role in the development. Unions, in other words, served as transmittal agencies, carrying wage increases that were reached in key settlements to industries and groups which would otherwise have hardly been touched. There also can be no doubt that, in the period after World War II, the pressure of unions was the main factor causing hourly rates to rise as much as they did in the local area.

As for interarea comparisons of union rates in these and other industries, adequate data are lacking. Such authoritative information as there is, is summarized in table 23. The data afford striking testimony to the influence which unions can exert on interarea wage rate relationships when surrounding conditions are favorable. In the early 'forties, when unions had just achieved a position of importance in the local community, Los Angeles was well down in the list of cities in three of the four industries. By 1949, it had moved up sharply in every one of these fields. In the fourth industry, motor trucking, rates in the earlier period were relatively high locally, and they stood at about the same level in 1949.

At the same time the data underline the importance of economic trends and industry characteristics in the determination of relative wage levels. In the early 'forties, wage rates in Los Angeles were relatively high in motor trucking and in bread and cake shops, industries in which unions had enjoyed little strength locally, though they were relatively low in book and job printing and building construction, industries in which unions had been much stronger. Apparently, economic conditions with respect to changes in the demand for and supply of labor were more favorable at this time in the former industries than in the latter. With the subsequent spread of unionism, coupled with the general expansion of the war period and the pressure on employers to compete for scarce labor supplies, such differences became of less moment and union rates in the lower ranking industries moved up rapidly.

Viewing the matter in broader perspective, there can be no doubt that interarea differences in union strength will be of diminishing importance as unionization becomes more nearly universal. The bargaining advantage unions enjoy may still vary, city to city, though among communities of about the same size such differences are more likely to follow industry than area lines. Moreover, under conditions of "universal unionism," differences in bargaining strength will be more likely to depend on such economic circumstances as relative employment trends and capital growth rates than on the organizational status of unions as such. In accordance with the industry groupings suggested above, it follows that in mass-production industries which serve national markets, interarea differences in union rates will tend to disappear. In industries serving local markets, on the other hand, union wage scales will reflect variations in the economic conditions of individual communities. Thus, although the spread of unionism will entail a further narrowing of interarea rate differentials, it will probably cause less change on this score than is commonly supposed.

Local Industry Rate Standardization

If the effects of unionism on most aspects of the community's wage structure are obscure, one result is abundantly clear: interfirm rate differences within individual industries in the area have been greatly reduced and in some instances virtually eliminated. A variety of programs for standardizing job rates have been introduced, some quite elaborate and far-reaching in scope. The most widely publicized was the plan adopted in the southern California aircraft industry during World War II. This plan was formally dropped after the war but the essential features of the scheme are still in existence.[4] Another ambitious

---

[4] The plan is described in Robert D. Gray, *Systematic Wage Administration in the Southern California Aircraft Industry* (New York: Industrial Relations Counselors, 1943). For an appraisal of the plan and its administration, see Clark Kerr and Lloyd H. Fisher, "Effect of Environment and Administration on Job Evaluation," *Harvard Business Review*, XXVII May, 1950), 77–96.

program for stabilizing job rates has been in effect since 1941 in the southern California building construction industry.[5] In certain mass-production industries, such as basic steel, local branch plants have been parties to national programs to standardize pay rates throughout a given company.

In most industries, less formal and comprehensive plans have been attempted, but at bottom they are much the same. For example, in the section of the metal trades where it has a substantial membership, the steelworkers union has endeavored to apply the same principles of job rate uniformity as in basic steel. The various AFL unions which have jurisdiction in the metal trades (notably the machinists, molders, and boilermakers) have also actively sought to establish uniform rate conditions in the shops and for the jobs they control. To prevent the various AFL unions from working at cross-purposes and thus defeating these efforts, the unions have established a Metal Trades Council to coördinate their activities where overlapping occurs. In hotels and restaurants, the organizations representing the different culinary crafts have formed a joint board, one of its principal purposes being to establish uniform rates for major jobs throughout the local industry. Similar bodies have been established in most other fields, such as motion picture production, clothing, printing, and food distribution, in which the presence of a number of union groups has prompted the formation of coördinating bodies. So far as rate standardization is concerned, it appears to be of little moment whether the unions are all-inclusive, industrial organizations or are built along relatively narrow, craft lines. In either case, vigorous measures have been undertaken to prevent inter-firm wage competition.

Intensive study of these wage standardization programs yields a number of conclusions which are of interest to students of local wage structures. First, among large-scale enterprises, initiation and formulation of the plans have come as much (if not more) from employers as from unions, whereas in small-scale, highly competitive industries, the reverse has tended to be true. In the case of the southern California aircraft industry, for instance, the program to make job rates uniform was really an extension of individual company job evaluation studies initiated in the early 'forties. It is doubtful, however, whether these companies would have launched such an undertaking if their workers had remained unorganized. Even in the face of the labor pirating of the early war period, it required the presence of a "common enemy" to overcome their preference for individual action. But once having made

---

[5] For a detailed discussion of this program, see Frank C. Pierson, "Building Trades Bargaining Plan in Southern California," *Monthly Labor Review*, 70 (January, 1950), 14–18.

the basic decision to merge their several job evaluation programs into a single, area-wide plan, responsibility for its execution rested largely with the employers. It hardly comes as a surprise, then, to find that in scope and content the scheme bore many similarities to conventional job evaluation plans, with jobs carefully defined, evaluated in terms of a system of factor weights, and grouped into certain general labor grades. No less understandable is the fact that from the outset the air-craft unions had many misgivings about the scheme and that after the war the idea of complete job rate uniformity was modified in some important respects.

The rate standardization plans in small-scale industries, being chiefly the product of union effort, bear unmistakable evidence of their origin. In their case, attention is focused almost exclusively on establishing and enforcing uniform minimum rates for key jobs among competing firms, the purpose being not to check an upward spiraling of labor costs but to prevent rate cutting "below scale." Unions which have dealings with hundreds of small employers and which have members who are continually shifting from firm to firm, such as the building trades and, to a less extent, the culinary unions, have no recourse but to develop machinery for securing area-wide rate uniformity. By the same token, investigation shows that care is exercised in the union-sponsored programs not to deal with detailed matters of job content or work conditions, questions which call for individual management-union negotiation. Although employer participation in the early stages of these programs tends to be passive, if not actually hostile, the active support of at least some of the larger and more influential firms has had to be secured to insure success. Once their coöperation has been won, most of the other employers have found it desirable, if not necessary, to go along.

Second, in the large-scale industries, the industry-area boundary lines of these plans are clear-cut and reasonably well fixed, the type and location of firms which are covered being evident from the nature of the industry involved. In the small-scale industries, on the other hand, the coverage of the programs is usually narrow at first, broadening by successive stages subsequently. The stabilization program of the southern California building trades, for example, was first confined to the immediate Los Angeles area but soon was extended to cover the entire southern half of the state. The area of standardization has also been steadily broadened in hotels and restaurants and a number of other industries. The various unions in the metal trades, on the other hand, have not only extended the programs geographically but industrially as well. Today, the same increases are applied to most branches of the industry, and in a number of instances the absolute level of rates for key jobs is even the same. A similar broadening process has occurred in industries which have dealings with the teamsters and other unions in wholesale and retail distribution.

Both of these types of expansion reflect, in part, the time and effort normally required to extend union organization in small-scale industries. A related factor is the increased bargaining strength which labor groups in newly organized sections of an industry may derive from merging forces with more securely established bodies. Sometimes the ambitions and rivalries of local labor leaders are also a factor, though the interplay of personalities can lead to quite opposite results in different industries. The most important influence leading to wider coverage stems from the fact that lower wage standards in one part of a union's jurisdiction constitute a serious threat to standards achieved elsewhere. This is made abundantly clear in situations where members of the same union are moving from job to job within a broad area, as in the southern California construction industry, or are shifting from industry to industry, which to some extent is true of journeymen in the metal trades. The same lesson is driven home wherever an employer has operations in a number of different areas or fields. Chain organizations in hotels, restaurants, and food distribution afford good examples, though, in fact, multi-unit companies are to be found in almost every industry. For these and other reasons the effects of wage differentials (or, more particularly, a change in established differentials) spread quickly throughout a given area or industry, an advantage enjoyed by one group being taken up, or insisted on, by the next. By broadening the area of bargaining, unions are better able to see to it that the "advantages" passed from group to group are in labor's favor rather than the other way around.

A third characteristic of the wage standardization plans in this locality, which is related to the question just discussed, is their impact on the community's general level of wage rates. Judging from the evidence presented in this and earlier chapters, these programs certainly exerted little if any inhibiting effect on the upward movement of rates. True, there are some instances where a particular labor group (or section of an industry) would doubtless have gained (or conceded) more than was finally agreed upon, but by and large negotiations appear to have been closely geared to the objectives and strategies of the most powerfully placed bargaining groups. At the same time, as long as employment was rising rapidly, wage rates were hardly made higher by reason of the fact that negotiations covered broad industrial or geographical areas. Some "fringe groups" who might otherwise not have been affected were brought into line, but for the majority of employees and firms there is reason to believe the results would have been much the same. Perhaps area-wide bargaining had some effects on general wage rate levels immediately after World War II and again in 1948 and 1949, two periods when unemployment was mounting in particular industries and business prospects were none too favorable locally. Under such conditions, some lowering of wage standards, as a result of competitive undercutting of rates, was to be expected. Instead, not only were wage scales maintained but further increases were secured. It therefore appears that the machinery for standardizing interfirm wage levels played a part in this development. However, since business activity was expanding during most of the 'forties, this was not too important in the immediate situation.

Fourth, and last, these programs increase the degree to which wages are subject to deliberate, centralized control. The element of unpredictability inherent in markets where rates are set by individual employee-employer agreement is eliminated. The possibility that the wages paid by one firm will soon be undercut by competing firms is ruled out, the bargaining spokesman knowing in advance of a settlement what its coverage will be. As a result, the parties are in a position to base wage rate changes on conscious policy considerations. Whether over-all wage levels or even the relationships between industry wage levels are much different under these circumstances is open to question. Judging from the evidence presented in this and earlier chapters, the Los Angeles experience suggests that the influence exerted by unions is extremely limited. As stated above, the major change has been reflected in interfirm wage relationships within particular industries or industry groups, a single uniform scale taking the place of a wide variety of rates for similar work. On the other hand, even though the general structure of industry wage levels has been little affected by the advent of trade unionism, it is of great importance that this structure is the result of deliberate choice by spokesmen for worker and employer organizations. That their decisions seem to be in accord with competitive market principles should not be construed to mean that wages are controlled by impersonal market forces but, on the contrary, by policy decisions in which market developments are only one of many factors that are taken into account.

IX. CONCLUSIONS

THIS INVESTIGATION points to a number of conclusions about the behavior of wages in local areas, which can usefully be summarized here. The study has been focused on the Los Angeles area, but though the economic and social characteristics of this community are in many respects unusual, certain inferences can be drawn from its experience which are applicable to other large population centers as well. Data on wage movements in additional areas have also been examined to determine what are the major forces controlling relative wage levels within and between communities.

On balance, the findings support the view that wages in different industries and localities form a well-knit structure largely controlled by economic and social forces operating on a broad regional and national basis. Even in the case of Los Angeles the general level of wages did not change materially in relation to the rest of the country over long periods, not even during the years when this area was moving from a sparsely settled, frontier community to a large and complex metropolis. During its early settlement, hourly rates in Los Angeles were well above wage rates for comparable work in most other communities, a product of the labor scarcity normally experienced in remote, frontier areas. As settlement proceeded and the dearth of labor became less severe, hourly rates moved somewhat closer to the national level. This narrowing tendency was subject, however, to powerful counter influences, all related directly or indirectly to the community's phenomenal economic growth. During most of the period since 1900, demand for labor remained high in relation to available man power and, instead of depressing wages, the rapid increase in population served only to raise the demand for labor in the area still further. Between 1920 and 1940, for example, there was little change in the relative wage rate position of Los Angeles, and the upheaval resulting from the armament program of the early 'forties only pushed the community somewhat nearer the position it had occupied in the national wage structure some fifty or sixty years before. Wage comparisons covering many decades are admittedly hazardous, especially in view of changes in prices, in kinds of goods produced, and in types of industries in a given area. Nonetheless, the weight of the evidence clearly indicates that the general wage rate level of this community has been subject to little change in relation to the rest of the country for long periods of time.

This investigation shows further that as the Los Angeles area became more fully developed economically, its wages became geared more closely to wage trends in the nation as a whole. Common sources of material supplies, common market outlets for products, common labor organizations, and, to some degree, common corporate managements have been the major influences binding wage rate movements in this and other large population centers closely together. These findings suggest that under present-day circumstances any marked shift in the relative wage position of a community can come about only as a result of fundamental readjustments in economic and social relationships.

At the same time, fluctuations in business conditions, since they affect different areas at different times and in different degrees, can cause short-term changes in a community's relative wage position. During the boom of the 'twenties, for example, the record shows that wages in Los Angeles rose somewhat faster than in most large population centers, whereas during the 'thirties its wage level changed to about the same extent as elsewhere. The rapid growth of its armament trades in the early 'forties again pushed up this area's wage level, but in the postwar period wages did not rise quite so fast locally as nationally.

The Los Angeles experience of the 'forties also shows that absolute changes in a community's wage level are closely related to changes in local business activity, though during the years 1946–1949 the upward movement of wages was at a steadier rate than the rise in the volume of business would have led one to expect. Generally speaking, during periods of general labor scarcity such as the early 'forties, wage rates in lower-paying areas tend to rise more rapidly than in higher-paying areas, but in periods of widespread unemployment such as the 'thirties the wage levels of different localities tend to move in parallel fashion. The presence of trade unionism modifies but does not change this conclusion fundamentally.

A locality's internal (or interindustry) wage structure, as opposed to the general level of its wages, is, of course, more likely to exhibit distinctive characteristics, depending in part on what its major industries are and how they are affected by changing economic conditions.[1] Until recently, due to the rapid growth in its population, the greatest expansion among Los Angeles industries occurred in consumer services and the manufacture of light consumers' goods. Wages in these fields have been correspondingly high in relation to other communities, the contrast between the relative wage levels of nondurable and durable goods manufacturing being especially marked. Despite the increased importance of heavy manufacturing in the Los Angeles area as a result

---

[1] As used in this discussion, the wage level of an industry refers to its average hourly earnings unadjusted for overtime, shift differentials, and the like. Because of the nature of the data, however, industry wage comparisons appearing in this study for the period 1929–1939 had to be based on average annual earnings.

of World War II, these relationships were little changed by developments during the 'forties.

Nonetheless, even the interindustry wage structures within different
communities exhibit many similar characteristics. In Los Angeles, as
elsewhere, the highest and lowest industry wage levels in manufacturing
are found in fields producing nondurable consumption goods, with
durable consumers' goods and producers' goods tending to occupy a
middle position. Comparable data on nonmanufacturing could not be
secured, but these fields being more heterogeneous, it is safe to assume
that earnings levels in them form a wider variety of structures in different communities.

In addition to considering local industry wage structures at different
points in time, study was also made of similarities and differences in
the behavior of industry earnings levels over time. In this phase of the
investigation, the results of which are set forth in chapter vi, percentage
changes in earnings in manufacturing were compared on an interindustry, interarea, and interyear basis for six industrial areas between 1929
and 1939 and on an interindustry and interyear basis for two industrial
areas (Los Angeles and San Francisco) between 1940 and 1948. Although
the evidence was limited, the analysis revealed that over these periods
differences among industries and areas with respect to rates of change
in earnings levels were negligible, thus supporting the view that the
forces controlling general wage movements affect all manufacturing
industries and areas in a uniform manner. On the other hand, earnings
levels were found to move at widely varying rates in different years,
reflecting the effects of variations in business conditions on local area
wage levels. Differential effects from the latter source were, of course,
greatly reduced when the longer periods were broken down into intervals
coinciding with shifts in general business activity, but differences among
industries and areas in the shorter periods were somewhat increased.

Although this investigation has uncovered basic similarities in the
structure and behavior of wages at the community level, certain differences were found as well. Industry wage relationships and wage movements in the Los Angeles area (in terms of both earnings and rates)
illustrate this clearly. A review of its wage history shows, further, that
these differences resulted from certain environmental conditions which
distinguish the area from most other large communities. Since this part
of the study bears directly on the concepts developed by wage economists discussed in the opening chapter, the findings on this point
deserve particular emphasis.

One important influence stems from the physical characteristics of
the area. Productive soil, favorable climate, and a few outstanding re-

sources such as crude oil have made higher rates and earnings possible not only in the industries immediately concerned but throughout the area as well. On the other hand, certain deficiencies, notably in water and basic minerals, have militated against the growth of heavy manufacturing and related fields, so that this customary source of wage gains has been generally precluded. Similarly, the factor of geographical location has had mixed wage effects. Since Los Angeles is the center of a new and relatively undeveloped region, its wages reflect the community's increasing importance in commerce and trade, but its remoteness from major consumption and industrial markets has exerted a serious counteracting influence on local wage levels. Because physical characteristics such as these have largely determined what industries would locate and thrive in the area, their significance in explaining the level and structure of the community's wages needs no further elaboration.

Another major influence has had to do with the supply of labor. In the period of early settlement the scarcity of man power was great enough in itself to explain the high-wage position of the community. In succeeding decades, the fact that there was no ready source of labor to draw from in the surrounding region, and that workers had to migrate many hundreds of miles to move to this market, exerted a continuous upward pressure on wages in relation to pay levels elsewhere. There is no evidence that the quality of labor available in terms of training, efficiency, or general background had any marked influence on the community's wage level, though the presence of foreign-born labor had observable effects at one end of the scale and the absence of certain highly skilled artisans, at the other. The importance of labor supply as a factor distinguishing the wage history of this area from longer-settled communities steadily lessened as migration into the area proceeded, just as the influence exerted by physical resources became less significant as ties with the rest of the national economy became stronger.

During the years immediately before and after World War I, the economic expansion of the area was rapid enough to prevent any narrowing of interarea wage relationships which otherwise would have occurred. Subsequent shifts in the wage position of Los Angeles were largely determined by comparative changes in the demand for labor, locally and nationally. During most years the rate of increase in the demand for labor (as reflected in comparative figures on output and employment) was well above the rest of the country and the high wage position of the community was fully maintained. In the brief periods when the rate of increase in demand approached rates elsewhere, the change was quickly reflected in the data on comparative wage movements.

Demand influences also largely shaped the interindustry structure of hourly earnings within the Los Angeles area. In the decade after World War I, the increase in the community's labor requirements was largely confined to construction, motion picture production, and consumer services. Although the skills involved were in some instances high, many of these fields had a preponderance of low-skilled jobs and hourly earnings levels were correspondingly low. By the late 'thirties the local and regional market had expanded enough to induce the development of a number of manufacturing lines producing goods for immediate consumption, notably clothing, furniture, and a variety of processed foods. These industries, though not utilizing as much capital equipment as heavy manufacturing, were partly mechanized. Finally, with the armament boom of the 'forties, some heavy industry came into the area, and earnings levels locally were quick to reflect the higher output per man-hour made possible by machine processes.

A detailed investigation, such as this, of the circumstances controlling interindustry wage levels within particular communities indicates that some influences are definitely more important than others. Thus, the data on Los Angeles manufacturing industries given in chapter v show a close relationship between the geographical scope of product markets and comparative wage levels. In 1940 and 1949, industries selling in broad regional or national markets ranked highest on the average in hourly earnings, industries selling in the local market ranked lowest, and those selling in both markets tended to rank midway between the other two. The local market group, however, contained the highest ranking industry in the local area (printing and publishing) and one of the lowest (textiles). Expressed as ratios to wages in the rest of the country, the order of ranking was reversed, with the middle position still held by industries serving both local and nonlocal markets. A breakdown of Los Angeles manufacturing into capital vs. consumption goods and durable vs. semidurable vs. nondurable goods gave similar though less clear-cut results.

Data on manufacturing in six industrial areas and the United States, set forth in chapter vii, revealed a positive association between industry rankings based on size of firm and level of earnings, but the correlation values fell below the level of significance. The association between rankings based on labor as a proportion of total cost and level of earnings proved even less clear. A closer relationship was found between rankings based on amount of capital equipment per worker and industry wage levels, the data in this case being limited to Los Angeles and the United States. Although the rank correlation values did not quite reach the significance level, they were high enough to indicate that differences in capital equipment per worker are one of the factors which help to explain differences in interindustry earnings levels. The closest association of all was found between rankings based on value added per worker and industry wage levels, the results being well above the 5 per cent level of significance.[2]

To generalize from these findings, when the analysis was confined to narrow comparisons such as durability of product or size of firm, no consistent association was found, but when broader comparisons were introduced, more consistent results were obtained. Thus, wage levels in local manufacturing industries were found to be closely associated with differences in types of product market and in value added per worker, two measures closely related to broad demand influences, on the one hand, and to general production-cost differences, on the other.

These findings pertain to local interindustry wage structures considered at moments of time, not to *changes* in interindustry wage relationships over periods of time. In chapter v, the data on industry wage changes in Los Angeles manufacturing between 1940 and 1949 were studied to determine if there were any observable patterns of behavior. The most striking finding, already noted by other investigators, was the inverse relation between hourly earnings levels prevailing at the outset of the period and subsequent percentage wage increases, a rank correlation value of -0.792 being obtained. No consistent association was found between relative wage changes and product durability, on the one hand, or product use (capital vs. consumption goods), on the other. Type of product market area had a somewhat greater effect, average hourly earnings in industries serving the local area rising more sharply than in either of the other two industry groups, though the initial wage level of these industries was higher than that of one of the groups (industries serving both local and nonlocal markets) and slightly below that of the other (industries serving regional or national markets). Again, the data indicate that shifts in local industry wage levels are not to be explained in simple or narrow terms, but are the result of broad changes in the economic position of different fields.

With this in mind, an investigation was made of the relationship between changes in industry earnings levels and changes in the demand for labor, the latter measured by industry employment data. Rank correlation tests were made covering Los Angeles and San Francisco

---

[2] As in the analysis dealing with capital equipment per worker, the data on value added per worker referred only to Los Angeles and the United States. The latter data provide a rough measure of changes in productivity over a period of time but, of course, they do not measure differences in productivity among industries at a given point in time. Throughout this discussion the term "value added per worker" rather than "productivity" is employed.

manufacturing industries between 1940 and 1948 and six industrial areas between 1929 and 1939. No consistent pattern was found in the two-city analysis but in the six industrial areas the average r value obtained approximated the 5 per cent level of significance (0.261 as against 0.273). Similar calculations were made for periods coinciding with major shifts in business conditions, and the contrast between the period of the 'thirties and the 'forties proved even sharper. These findings suggest that under conditions of general unemployment, industry wage levels in local areas tend to move in association with interindustry shifts in employment and with changes in the relative demand for labor among different fields, but that no such association obtains under conditions of general labor scarcity.

As for influences in local areas operating on the side of output and costs, a close association was found between changes in manufacturing industry earnings levels and value added per worker, the r value for six industrial areas during the period 1929–1939 exceeding the 1 per cent level of significance (0.559 as against 0.354). Data for the period of the 'forties were not available. The evidence, though scanty, clearly supports the view that over a period as long as ten years, local industries which enjoy the greatest gains in value added per worker tend to experience the greatest increases in wage levels, and industries with the smallest gains in value added per worker tend to experience the smallest wage increases. Thus, of the many variables studied in the course of this investigation, the two which were found to bear the closest association with changes in industry earnings levels were employment and value added per worker. It need hardly be added that these two variables are themselves closely related, industries which experience the greatest gains in employment also frequently experiencing the greatest increases in value added per worker.

These findings are placed in a rather different perspective when considered within the framework of the multisample analysis in chapter vi. As already stated, this analysis revealed that over fairly long periods earnings in manufacturing tend to move at uniform rates among industries and areas but at widely varying rates one year to the next. A similar analysis of rates of change in employment and in value added per worker yielded similar findings, both variables changing at uniform rates on an interindustry and interarea basis but at dissimilar rates on an interyear basis. The nature of our economy appears to be such that though changes in wages, employment, and value added per worker are much greater in some years than in others, the forces which control their movement in different industries and areas affect all three variables in substantially the same way.

The institutions and environment of modern society also make for similarities rather than for differences in wage movements between industries and areas. The growth of trade unions is perhaps the most powerful pressure working in this direction, but influences on the side of management and employer groups are hardly less significant. At the same time, intraunion and interunion relations are such as to allow for some diversity in wage trends within and between individual industries and areas. Study of the impact of collective bargaining on the Los Angeles wage structure clearly shows both effects. The spread of unionism in the early 'forties greatly facilitated the process of gearing wage changes in this community to wage changes in other large urban areas, at the same time that it led to more uniform rate structures within and between local industries. Nonetheless, the evidence revealed a number of industry groupings, each with its own pattern of wage structure and wage behavior, in the period after World War II. If labor surpluses were to supplant conditions of general labor scarcity, differences in local wage behavior under local bargaining systems would doubtless increase; as this study has clearly demonstrated, it is the economic environment, not the institution of collective bargaining, which largely controls wage relationships at the community level.

APPENDIX TABLES

TABLE 1

INDEXES OF WAGE RATES IN MANUFACTURING, TWENTY URBAN AREAS IN THE
UNITED STATES, JANUARY, 1941–APRIL, 1948[a]

Urban area	Index number			
	January, 1941	April, 1943	April, 1945	April, 1948
Detroit.........................	133	131	127	176
Seattle.........................	114	116	110	159
Pittsburgh......................	113	113	108	156
Milwaukee......................	110	102	100	150
San Francisco...................	109	114	106	155
Philadelphia....................	108	107	105	155
Cleveland......................	102	111	112	161
Indianapolis....................	102	101	98	146
Buffalo.........................	101	99	103	150
Kansas City....................	100	100	98	149
Los Angeles....................	96	103	104	152
Chicago........................	96	99	99	147
Baltimore......................	93	94	90	128
St. Louis.......................	89	87	89	137
Houston........................	88	90	84	123
Providence.....................	87	92	89	137
Louisville.......................	85	92	92	139
Boston.........................	84	86	88	122
Dallas..........................	72	76	79	119
Atlanta.........................	68	70	71	116

SOURCE: Ruth Macfarlane, *Wage Rate Differentials: Comparative Data for Los Angeles and Other Urban Areas* (Los Angeles: 1946), pp. 97, 104. The indexes are based on figures published by the U. S. Bureau of Labor Statistics.

[a] 1943 average wage rate index for twenty-six urban areas = 100. 1941 indexes were estimated by using 1943 indexes and January, 1941–April, 1943 per cent increases.

TABLE 2

AVERAGE ANNUAL EARNINGS OF PRODUCTION WORKERS IN MANUFACTURING, LOS
ANGELES COUNTY, SIX INDUSTRIAL AREAS, AND UNITED STATES, 1919–1939[a]

Year	Los Angeles County[b]	Buffalo	Chicago	Cleveland	Detroit	New York	San Francisco	United States
1919......	$1,170	$1,261	$1,257	$1,339	$1,469	$1,261	$1,230	$1,158
1921......	1,388	1,290	1,427	1,287	1,579	1,421	1,452	1,180
1923......	1,469	1,378	1,482	1,451	1,653	1,470	1,407	1,254
1925......	1,478	1,454	1,523	1,515	1,702	1,568	1,463	1,280
1927......	1,499	1,495	1,549	1,534	1,678	1,637	1,459	1,299
1929......	1,535	1,490	1,578	1,562	1,744	1,543	1,472	1,315
1931......	1,308	1,272	1,307	1,199	1,321	1,372	1,359	1,102
1933......	1,005	1,022	1,026	949	1,077	1,072	1,073	869
1935......	1,130	1,202	1,179	1,184	1,408	1,155	1,191	1,023
1937[c].....	1,281	1,461	1,374	1,424	1,594	1,233	1,390	1,180
1939......	1,318	1,392	1,324	1,423	1,644	1,227	1,453	1,153

SOURCES: Fourteenth Census of the United States, 1920, Vol. VIII, *Manufactures, 1919*, pp. 171, 224, 226, 230, 232, 233, 234.

Fifteenth Census of the United States, 1930, *Manufactures, 1929*, Vol. III, pp. 17, 61, 139, 250, 352, 397.

Sixteenth Census of the United States, 1940, *Manufactures, 1939*, Vol. III, pp. 44, 80, 232, 478, 678, 766.

U. S. Bureau of the Census, *Biennial Census of Manufactures, 1921*, pp. 1269, 1530, 1533, 1539, 1545, 1553, 1563, 1587; *1923*, pp. 1211, 1397, 1400, 1405, 1410, 1418, 1426, 1445; *1927*, pp. 1311, 1423, 1426, 1431, 1437, 1448, 1460, 1486; *1931*, p. 34; *1933*, p. 37; *1935*, p. 39; *1937*, p. 40.

[a] Use of Census data to compute average annual earnings raises certain questions which are discussed in the "General Explanations" section of the *Biennial Census of Manufactures, 1935*, p. 8. The Census note states, in part: "The quotient obtained by dividing the amount of wages (the total amount paid to wage earners during the year) by the average number of wage earners cannot . . . be accepted as representing the average wage received by full time wage earners." The reasons given for this statement are: (1) Average number of wage earners as reported is greater than the number which would be required to do the same amount of work with all workers on a full-time basis, because the reported figure includes an unspecified number of part-time workers. (2) Average number of wage earners as reported includes figures from plants which did not work over the complete periods (e.g., monthly) on which their reports of employment totals were based. Since the sampling is done in these plants during only a fraction of the period reported, the figures so reported either overestimate or underestimate the actual average number of wage earners per month.

Data for Los Angeles County and the six other urban areas herein consist of "Industrial Area" statistics for 1929–1931, inclusive. Data for 1919–1927, when "Industrial Area" statistics were not yet published, consist of statistics for Los Angeles and the six "cities" as such.

[b] Los Angeles data for 1929–1939, inclusive, do not include motion picture industry figures.

[c] The 1937 Biennial Census discontinues the treatment of "Gas, manufactures, illuminating and heating" and "Railroad repair shops" as manufacturing industries; 1937 wage and wage-earner figures reflect this change.

TABLE 3

DISTRIBUTION OF EMPLOYMENT BY MAJOR INDUSTRY GROUP, LOS ANGELES COUNTY AND UNITED STATES, 1920–1940

	Los Angeles County						United States					
	1920[a]		1930[b]		1940[c]		1920		1930		1940	
	Number of employed persons (in thous.)	Per cent of total	Number of employed persons (in thous.)	Per cent of total	Number of employed persons (in thous.)	Per cent of total	Number of employed persons (in thous.)	Per cent of total	Number of employed persons (in thous.)	Per cent of total	Number of employed persons (in thous.)	Per cent of total
Agriculture	10	3.8	19	2.6	35	3.4	10,953	26.3	10,722	22.0	8,475	18.8
Mining	2	.8	9	1.2	13	1.2	1,070	2.6	984	2.0	913	2.0
Construction	11	4.0	24	3.3	65	6.3	977	2.4	1,097	2.3	2,056	4.6
Manufacturing	75	28.3	163	22.5	205	19.8	11,931	28.7	13,016	26.7	10,573	23.4
Transportation, communication, and other public utilities	23	8.6	52	7.2	75	7.2	3,064	7.4	3,843	7.9	3,113	6.9
Wholesale and retail trade	50	18.6	98	13.5	249	24.0	4,243	10.2	5,334	10.9	7,539	16.7
Finance, insurance, and real estate	8	3.0	62	8.6	59	5.6	446	1.1	748	1.5	1,468	3.2
Business and repair services	d	d	d	d	32	3.1	d	d	d	d	864	1.9
Personal services	33	12.2	103	14.2	110	10.6	3,405	8.2	4,952	10.1	4,009	8.9
Amusement, recreation, and related services	2	.6	10	1.4	43	4.2	46	.1	130	.3	343	.9
Professional and related services	29	11.0	80	11.0	94	9.1	2,144	5.2	3,124	6.4	3,318	7.3
Government	5	2.0	14	1.9	47	4.5	770	1.9	856	1.8	1,753	3.9
Industry not reported	19	e	91	e	10	e	2,564	e	4,023	e	689	e
Total[f]	266		724		1,037		41,614		48,830		45,166	

SOURCE: Frank L. Kidner and Philip Neff, *A Statistical Appendix to an Economic Survey of the Los Angeles Area* (Los Angeles: 1945), pp. 414–415, 428–429.
a Los Angeles City only.
b Figures include: Alhambra, Glendale, Long Beach, Los Angeles, Pasadena, and Santa Monica.
c Figures include: Alhambra, Beverly Hills, Burbank, Glendale, Huntington Park, Inglewood, Long Beach, Los Angeles, Pasadena, Santa Monica, and South Gate.
d Data not available.
e This group includes sundry items which make calculations based upon them irrelevant.
f Items will not add to total, due to lack of data and rounding.

TABLE 4-A

GROSS AND REAL AVERAGE HOURLY EARNINGS IN MANUFACTURING, LOS ANGELES COUNTY, SAN FRANCISCO BAY INDUSTRIAL AREA, AND UNITED STATES, 1940-1949

Manufacturing	Gross average hourly earnings			Real[a] average hourly earnings		
	Los Angeles	San Francisco	United States	Los Angeles	San Francisco	United States
Total manufacturing[b]						
1940	$ .736	$ .820	$ .661	$ .736	$ .820	$ .661
1941	.826	.918	.729	.787	.870	.694
1942	.995	1.155	.853	.843	.977	.733
1943	1.113	1.285	.961	.898	1.021	.779
1944	1.206	1.333	1.019	.958	1.034	.814
1945	1.220	1.319	1.023	.942	.996	.799
1946	1.308	1.316	1.084	.938	.920	.780
1947	1.415	1.466	1.237	.900	.910	.778
1948	1.518	1.591	1.350	.903	.914	.790
1949	1.582	1.649	1.401	.948	.956	.830
Nondurable goods						
1940	.715	.781	.602	.715	.781	.602
1941	.765	.817	.640	.729	.774	.610
1942	.864	.920	.723	.732	.778	.622
1943	.998	1.033	.803	.805	.820	.651
1944	1.093	1.083	.861	.868	.840	.688
1945	1.145	1.120	.904	.884	.846	.706
1946	1.290	1.267	1.012	.925	.885	.728
1947	1.431	1.433	1.171	.910	.890	.737
1948	1.544	1.564	1.278	.919	.899	.748
1949	1.586	1.633	1.325	.950	.947	.794
Durable goods						
1940	.750	.872	.724	.750	.872	.724
1941	.852	1.007	.808	.811	.955	.770
1942	1.030	1.242	.947	.873	1.051	.814
1943	1.138	1.342	1.059	.918	1.066	.858
1944	1.235	1.398	1.117	.981	1.085	.892
1945	1.248	1.405	1.111	.964	1.061	.867
1946	1.319	1.370	1.156	.946	.957	.832
1947	1.405	1.498	1.292	.893	.930	.813
1948	1.500	1.620	1.410	.892	.931	.825
1949	1.580	1.669	1.469	.947	.968	.870

SOURCES: Calif. State Dept. of Indus. Relations, Div. of Labor Statistics and Research, *Estimated Employment, Total Wages, and Average Earnings and Hours Worked, Production and Related Workers, Manufacturing Industries, California and Los Angeles and San Francisco Bay Industrial Areas, 1940-1948* (May 1949), pp. 26-40.
    U. S. Bureau of Labor Statistics:
        Employment, Hours and Earnings, special release, September, 1949.
        Handbook of Labor Statistics, 1947 Edition, pp. 54-79, 110, 112.
        Hours and Earnings, February, 1950, p. 16.
        Monthly Labor Review, 66 (February, 1948), 236; 68 (February, 1949), 261; 70 (February, 1950), 240; 70 (June, 1950), 703.
    [a] 1940 cost-of-living index = 100.
    [b] Figures include production and related workers only. 1940 figures are not strictly comparable with figures for 1941-1949, due to BLS revisions in September, 1949, of the Employment and Hours and Earnings series. Revised figures for 1941-1949, to provide comparability with the new series, were prepared by the BLS. For further explanation of these revisions, see the introductory notices to the July, 1949, issues of *Hours and Earnings* and *Employment and Pay Rolls*, both published by the BLS.

TABLE 4-B

GROSS AND REAL AVERAGE HOURLY EARNINGS IN SELECTED NONMANUFACTURING
INDUSTRIES,[a] LOS ANGELES COUNTY AND UNITED STATES, 1940-1949

	Gross average hourly earnings		Real[b] average hourly earnings	
	Los Angeles	United States	Los Angeles	United States
Six nonmanufacturing industries[c]				
1940	.655	.578	.655	.578
1941	.681	.609	.649	.580
1942	.757	.659	.642	.567
1943	.853	.718	.688	.582
1944	.916	.773	.728	.617
1945	.962	.821	.743	.641
1946	1.105	.925	.792	.665
1947	1.258	1.049	.780	.660
1948	1.317	1.133	.783	.663
1949	1.361	1.183	.815	.701
Selected consumer services[d]				
1940	.600	.573	.600	.573
1941	.627	.604	.597	.575
1942	.701	.654	.594	.562
1943	.797	.712	.643	.577
1944	.859	.767	.682	.613
1945	.905	.815	.699	.636
1946	1.042	.918	.747	.660
1947	1.183	1.042	.752	.656
1948	1.258	1.124	.748	.658
1949	1.303	1.173	.781	.695

SOURCES: Calif. State Dept. of Indus. Relations, Div. of Labor Statistics and Law Enforcement, *Labor in California, 1943-1944* (May, 1945), p. 59.

Calif. State Dept. of Indus. Relations, Div. of Labor Statistics and Research:
Labor in California, 1945-1946 (June, 1947), p. 50.
Labor in California, 1947-1948 (June, 1949), p. 75.
Special releases, July 21, 1950, August 11, 1950, and August 21, 1950.

U. S. Bureau of Labor Statistics:
Employment and Pay Rolls, February, 1949, p. 30.
Hours and Earnings, February, 1950, pp. 16, 23.
Handbook of Labor Statistics, 1947 Edition, pp. 24-5, 81-3, 110, 112.
Employment, Hours and Earnings, special release, September, 1949.
Monthly Labor Review, 66 (February, 1948), 236; 68 (February, 1949), 261; 70 (February, 1950), 240; 70 (June, 1950), 703; 71 (July, 1950), 152.

National Industrial Conference Board, *Economic Almanac for 1950* (New York: 1950), p. 302.

U. S. Bureau of the Census, *Statistical Abstract of the United States, 1944-1945*, p. 160; and *Statistical Abstract . . . 1949*, p. 206.

[a] Figures for laundries, cleaning, and dyeing, crude petroleum producing, and motion picture producing include production and related workers; figures for wholesale trade, retail trade, and hotels include nonsupervisory employees and working supervisors. United States data for 1947-1949 are not strictly comparable with 1940-1946 data, due to BLS revisions in the Employment and Hours and Earnings series, September, 1949. For further explanation of these revisions, see the introductory notices to the July, 1949, issues of *Hours and Earnings* and *Employment and Pay Rolls*, both published by the BLS. 1949 figures for Los Angeles are subject to a downward bias but the revised data were not available at the time of writing.

[b] 1940 cost-of-living index = 100.

[c] Figures for Los Angeles consist of weighted averages of the following industries: wholesale trade, retail trade, laundering, cleaning, and dyeing, hotels (cash payments only; additional value of board, room, and tips excluded), crude petroleum producing, and motion picture producing. Figures for United States consist of weighted averages of the following industries: wholesale trade, retail trade, laundries, cleaning, and dyeing, hotels, year-round (cash payments only; additional value of board, room, uniforms, and tips excluded), and crude petroleum producing.

[d] Figures for Los Angeles and United States consist of weighted averages of the following industries: wholesale trade, retail trade, laundering, cleaning, and dyeing, and hotels (see footnote [c] above).

TABLE 4-C

Gross and Real Average Hourly Earnings in Wholesale and Retail Trade, Los Angeles County, San Francisco Bay Industrial Area, and United States, 1940–1949

Industry[b]	Gross average hourly earnings			Real[a] average hourly earnings		
	Los Angeles	San Francisco	United States	Los Angeles	San Francisco	United States
Wholesale trade						
1940	.769	.864	.739	.769	.864	.739
1941	.818	.914	.793	.779	.866	.755
1942	.925	.984	.860	.784	.832	.739
1943	1.034	1.086	.933	.834	.863	.756
1944	1.096	1.150	.985	.871	.892	.787
1945	1.134	1.182	1.029	.876	.893	.803
1946	1.272	1.327	1.144	.912	.927	.823
1947	1.426	1.483	1.268	.907	.921	.798
1948	1.524	1.559	1.359	.907	.896	.795
1949	1.577	1.644	1.414	.945	.953	.838
Retail trade						
1940	.589	.688	.542	.589	.688	.542
1941	.611	.717	.568	.582	.680	.541
1942	.678	.773	.614	.575	.654	.528
1943	.774	.846	.670	.624	.672	.543
1944	.837	.901	.724	.665	.699	.578
1945	.886	.935	.773	.684	.706	.603
1946	1.034	1.062	.878	.741	.742	.632
1947	1.178	1.196	1.009	.749	.742	.635
1948	1.243	1.294	1.088	.739	.744	.637
1949	1.288	1.360	1.137	.772	.788	.674

Sources: Calif. State Dept. of Indus. Relations, Div. of Labor Statistics and Law Enforcement, *Labor in California, 1943–1944* (May, 1945), p. 59.
 Calif. State Dept. of Indus. Relations, Div. of Labor Statistics and Research:
  Labor in California, 1945–1946 (June, 1947), p. 50.
  Labor in California, 1947–1948 (June, 1949), p. 75.
  Special release, July 21, 1950.
 U. S. Bureau of Labor Statistics:
  Handbook of Labor Statistics, 1947 Edition, pp. 82, 110, 112.
  Hours and Earnings, February, 1950, p. 23.
  Monthly Labor Review, 66 (February, 1948), 236; 68 (February, 1949), 261; 70 (February, 1950), 240; 70 (June, 1950), 703.
 [a] 1940 cost-of-living index = 100.
 [b] Figures include nonsupervisory employees and working supervisors. United States data for 1947–1949 are not strictly comparable with 1940–1946 data, due to BLS revisions in the Employment and Hours and Earnings series, September, 1949. For further explanation of these revisions, see the introductory notices to the July, 1949, issues of *Hours and Earnings* and *Employment and Pay Rolls*, both published by the BLS. 1949 figures for Los Angeles are subject to a downward bias but the revised data were not available at the time of writing.

TABLE 5

AVERAGE HOURLY EARNINGS IN MANUFACTURING, PHILADELPHIA AND
PITTSBURGH INDUSTRIAL AREAS, 1940–1949

Year	Philadelphia area[a]	Pittsburgh area[b]
1940	$ .725	$ .883
1941	.793	.908
1942	.933	.997
1943	1.050	1.086
1944	1.125	1.142
1945	1.132	1.140
1946	1.155	1.220
1947	1.275	1.336
1948	1.380	1.497
1949	1.460	1.573

SOURCE: Research Department, Federal Reserve Bank of Philadelphia.
[a] Counties included: Bucks, Chester, Delaware, Montgomery, and Philadelphia.
[b] Counties included: Allegheny, Armstrong, Beaver, Butler, Fayette, Greene, Washington, and Westmoreland.

TABLE 6

INDEXES OF WAGE RATES IN SELECTED NONMANUFACTURING INDUSTRIES,
TWENTY URBAN AREAS, APRIL, 1943–APRIL, 1948[a]

Urban area	Index number		
	April, 1943	April, 1945	April, 1948
Seattle	136	122	187
San Francisco	135	123	202
Detroit	116	124	189
Buffalo	115	106	165
Los Angeles	114	109	191
Chicago	112	117	188
Cleveland	110	109	161
Milwaukee	106	108	175
Pittsburgh	105	98	167
Philadelphia	103	105	169
Providence	102	95	158
Boston	100	97	155
Minneapolis	100	94	152
Baltimore	93	92	145
Denver	90	87	143
St. Louis	88	89	147
Kansas City	88	89	148
Louisville	86	90	142
Houston	83	87	135
New Orleans	73	77	117

SOURCE: Macfarlane, *op. cit.*, p. 115.
[a] 1943 average wage rate index for thirty-one urban areas = 100.

TABLE 7

AVERAGE SPENDABLE REAL WEEKLY EARNINGS, SINGLE AND MARRIED WORKERS IN
MANUFACTURING, LOS ANGELES COUNTY AND UNITED STATES, 1940–1949

	Gross average weekly earnings of production workers	Net spendable average weekly earnings			
		Worker with no dependents		Worker with 3 dependents	
		Current dollars	1940 dollars	Current dollars	1940 dollars
Los Angeles					
1940.	$28.56	$27.54	$27.54	$27.99	$27.99
1941.	33.95	31.45	29.95	33.27	31.69
1942.	44.24	37.49	31.77	42.63	36.13
1943.	50.23	39.46	31.82	46.43	37.44
1944.	54.53	44.34	35.22	50.13	39.82
1945.	53.28	43.42	33.53	49.19	37.98
1946.	51.74	43.69	31.32	49.17	35.25
1947.	55.63	46.82	29.76	52.32	33.26
1948.	59.39	50.73	30.18	56.43	33.57
1949.	61.38	52.95	31.73	58.65	35.14
United States					
1940.	25.20	24.69	24.69	24.95	24.95
1941.	29.58	28.05	26.73	29.28	27.90
1942.	36.65	31.77	27.33	36.28	31.21
1943.	43.14	36.01	29.21	41.39	33.57
1944.	46.08	38.29	30.57	44.06	35.17
1945.	44.39	36.97	28.84	42.74	33.35
1946.	43.74	37.65	27.09	43.13	31.03
1947.	49.97	42.76	26.92	48.24	30.37
1948.	54.14	47.43	27.76	53.17	31.12
1949.	54.92	48.09	28.50	53.83	31.90

SOURCES: Calif. State Dept. of Industrial Relations, *Estimated Employment, Total Wages, and Average Earnings . . . , California and Los Angeles and San Francisco Bay Industrial Areas, 1940–1948* (May, 1949), p. 26; and special release, July 5, 1950.
U. S. Bureau of Labor Statistics, *Handbook of Labor Statistics, 1947 Edition*, p. 110; and *Monthly Labor Review*, 66 (February, 1948), 236; 68 (February, 1949), 261; 70 (February, 1950), 240; 71 (July, 1950), 178.

TABLE 8

EMPLOYMENT AND UNEMPLOYMENT, LOS ANGELES COUNTY AND UNITED STATES,
APRIL, 1940, AND APRIL, 1949
(in thousands)

	Los Angeles County		United States	
	April, 1940	April, 1949	April, 1940	April, 1949
Civilian labor force...........	1,199	1,789	49,492	60,835
Employment...............	1,037	1,597	45,166	57,819
Unemployment.............	162	192	4,326	3,016

SOURCES: Calif. State Dept. of Employment, Area V and VI, unpublished material.
Sixteenth Census of the United States, 1940, *Population*, Vol. II, pt. 1, p. 558; Vol. III, pt. 1, p. 11.
U. S. Bureau of Labor Statistics, *Monthly Labor Review*, 70 (April, 1950), 442.

TABLE 9

TOTAL CIVILIAN LABOR FORCE, EMPLOYMENT, AND UNEMPLOYMENT, LOS ANGELES
COUNTY, APRIL, 1940, AND 1947–1949
(in thousands)

	Total civilian labor force[a]	Employment	Unemployment
1940			
April	1,199	1,037	162
1947			
January	1,751	1,601	150
March	1,750	1,597	153
May	1,727	1,578	149
July	1,732	1,566	166
September	1,714	1,587	127
November	1,714	1,614	100
1948			
January	1,736	1,604	132
March	1,749	1,602	147
May	1,737	1,606	131
June	1,744	1,606	138
July	1,757	1,624	133
August	1,749	1,627	122
September	1,762	1,642	120
October	1,756	1,639	117
November	1,777	1,642	135
December	1,794	1,646	148
1949			
January	1,788	1,618	170
February	1,786	1,601	185
March	1,789	1,595	194
April	1,789	1,597	192
May	1,786	1,596	190
June	1,781	1,593	188
July	1,797	1,602	195
August	1,795	1,603	192
September	1,786	1,612	174
October	1,760	1,580	180
November	1,771	1,603	168
December	1,791	1,623	168

SOURCE: Calif. State Dept. of Employment, Area V and VI, unpublished material.
[a] Items do not necessarily total, due to rounding.

TABLE 10-A

Distribution of Employment, Los Angeles County and United States, April, 1940 and February, 1950

Industry	Los Angeles County				United States			
	April, 1940		February, 1950		April, 1940		February, 1950	
	Number employed (in thousands)	Per cent of total	Number employed (in thousands)	Per cent of total	Number of wage earners (in thousands)	Per cent of total	Number of wage earners (in thousands)	Per cent of total
Total employment[a].........	1,037		1,584		33,965		44,857	
Construction, agriculture, forestry, and mining...	113	10.9	125	7.9	4,570	13.5	3,635	8.1
Manufacturing............	205	19.8	396	25.0	10,291	30.3	13,996	31.2
Durable goods...........	102	9.8	232	14.6	4,651	13.7	7,325	16.3
Nondurable goods.........	103	9.9	164	10.4	5,640	16.6	6,671	14.9
Nonmanufacturing.........	719	69.3	1,064	67.2	19,105	56.2	27,226	60.7

Sources: Calif. State Dept. of Employment, Area V and VI, unpublished material.
U. S. Bureau of the Census, *Current Population Reports*, "Labor Force," Series P-57, no. 92 (March 10, 1950), p. 9.
Sixteenth Census of the United States, 1940. *Population*, Vol. II, pt. 1, pp. 558–559; Vol. III, pt. 1, pp. 194–195.
U. S. Bureau of Foreign and Domestic Commerce, *Survey of Current Business*, 30 (June, 1950), S-10.
U. S. Bureau of Labor Statistics, *Monthly Labor Review*, 70 (June, 1950), 674–676.
a Items do not necessarily total, owing to rounding.

TABLE 10-B

DISTRIBUTION OF EMPLOYMENT BY MAJOR INDUSTRY, LOS ANGELES COUNTY AND UNITED STATES, APRIL, 1940, AND FEBRUARY, 1950

Industry	Los Angeles County[a] April, 1940 Number employed (in thousands)	April, 1940 Per cent of total	February, 1950 Number employed (in thousands)	February, 1950 Per cent of total	United States[b] April, 1940 Number of wage earners (in thousands)	April, 1940 Per cent of total	February, 1950 Number of wage earners (in thousands)	February, 1950 Per cent of total
Total employment[c]	1,037		1,584		33,965		44,857	
Agriculture, forestry, and fishing	35	3.4	32	2.0	2,130	6.3	1,174[d]	2.6
Mining	13	1.3	14	.9	874	2.6	601	1.3
Construction	65	6.3	79	5.0	1,566	4.6	1,860	4.1
Manufacturing	205	19.8	396	25.0	10,291	30.3	13,996	31.2
Transportation equipment	40	3.9	91	5.7	876	2.6	1,091	2.4
Electrical machinery	4	.4	16	1.0	372	1.1	770	1.7
Machinery (except electrical)	15	1.4	30	1.9	683	2.0	1,261	2.8
Metal fabrication	23	2.2	45	2.8	977	2.9	852	1.9
Chemicals	7	.7	11	.7	432	1.3	664	1.5
Rubber	2	.2	11	.7	158	.5	234	.5
Textiles and apparel	21	2.0	51	3.2	1,916	5.6	2,453	5.5
Food and kindred products	26	2.5	40	2.5	1,051	3.1	1,410	3.1
Other	67	6.5	100	6.3	3,825	11.3	5,261	11.7
Transportation, communication, and utilities	75	7.2	120	7.6	2,919	8.6	3,841	8.6
Trade	249	24.0	421	26.6	5,528	16.3	9,154	20.4
Finance, real estate, and insurance	59	5.7	83	5.2	1,274	3.8	1,777	4.0
Service, including domestic	279	26.9	340	21.5	6,983	20.6	6,712	15.0
All other	57	5.5	100	6.3	2,401	7.1	5,742	12.8

SOURCES: Calif. State Dept. of Employment, Area V and VI, unpublished material.
U. S. Bureau of the Census, *Current Population Reports*, "Labor Force," Series P-57, no. 92 (March 10, 1950), p. 9.
Sixteenth Census of the United States, 1940, *Population*, Vol. II, pt. 1, pp. 558–559; Vol. III, pt. 1, pp. 194–195.
U. S. Bureau of Labor Statistics, *Monthly Labor Review*, 70 (June, 1950), 674–676.
a The figures for Los Angeles include proprietors and self-employed persons.
b The figures for United States exclude proprietors and self-employed persons.
c Items do not necessarily total, due to rounding.
d Figure includes agricultural wage earners only.

TABLE 11

AVERAGE HOURLY EARNINGS OF PRODUCTION WORKERS IN MAJOR MANUFACTURING INDUSTRY GROUPS WITH INDUSTRY RANKINGS, LOS ANGELES COUNTY AND UNITED STATES, 1940 AND 1949; RATIOS OF LOS ANGELES TO UNITED STATES EARNINGS, 1940 AND 1949; AND PER CENT CHANGES IN EARNINGS, 1940–1949

Industry	1940 Los Angeles County Earnings	Rank	1940 United States Earnings	Rank	1940 LA/US ratio	Rank	1949a Los Angeles County Earnings	Rank	1949a United States Earnings	Rank	1949a LA/US ratio	Rank	Per cent changes 1940–1949 Los Angeles County Earnings	Rank	Per cent changes 1940–1949 United States Earnings	Rank
Food and kindred products	.681	13	.616	12	1.110	7	1.532	11	1.291	13	1.186	5	125.1	5	109.6	5
Textile mill products	.598	16	.482	18	1.241	2	1.329	18	1.189	15	1.118	7	122.2	6	146.7	1
Apparel	.552	18	.544	15	1.015	13	1.424	15	1.072	18	1.328	3	158.0	1	97.1	16
Paper and allied products	.692	12	.613	13	1.129	5	1.497	12	1.342	12	1.115	8	116.3	8	118.9	4
Printing, publishing, and allied industries	.980	1	.882	3	1.111	6	2.141	1	1.816	1	1.178	6	118.5	7	105.9	10
Chemicals and allied products	.725	10	.676	10	1.072	9	1.484	14	1.430	10	1.038	12	104.7	11	111.5	6
Petroleum products	.963	2	.887	2	1.086	8	1.817	2	1.791	2	1.015	15	88.7	16	101.9	12
Rubber products	.906	4	.766	5	1.183	4	1.668	4	1.509	7	1.105	9	84.1	17	97.0	17
Leather and leather products	.561	17	.549	14	1.022	12	1.390	17	1.137	16	1.223	4	147.8	2	107.1	9
Lumber and timber	.772	6	.511	17	1.511	1	1.573	9	1.136	17	1.385	1	103.8	12	122.3	3
Furniture and finished lumber products	.658	14	.536	16	1.228	3	1.594	5.5	1.195	14	1.334	2	142.2	3	122.9	2
Stone, clay, and glass products	.656	15	.654	11	1.003	14	1.495	13	1.368	11	1.093	10	127.9	4	109.2	8
Iron and steel and their products	.755	8	.755	7	1.000	15	1.581	8	1.528	6	1.035	13.5	109.4	10	102.4	11
Transportation equipment (except automobiles)	.750	9	.795	4	.943	18	1.594	5.5	1.593	4	1.001	16	112.5	9	100.4	14
Nonferrous metals and their products	.761	7	.711	9	1.070	10	1.546	10	1.493	8	1.035	13.5	103.2	13	110.0	7
Electrical machinery and equipment	.722	11	.728	8	.992	16	1.406	16	1.442	9	.975	18	94.7	15	98.1	15
Machinery (except electrical)	.787	5	.761	6	1.034	11	1.592	7	1.530	5	1.041	11	102.3	14	101.1	13
Automobiles and automobile equipment	.921	3	.948	1	.972	17	1.688	3	1.696	3	.995	17	83.3	18	78.9	18

Sources: Calif. State Dept. of Indus. Relations, Estimated Employment, Total Wages, and Average Earnings . . . California and Los Angeles and San Francisco Bay Industrial Areas, 1940–1948 (May, 1949), pp. 26–32; and special release, July 5, 1950.
U. S. Bureau of Labor Statistics:
Handbook of Labor Statistics, 1947 Edition, pp. 54–79.
Employment, Hours and Earnings, special release, September, 1949.
Monthly Labor Review, 71 (July, 1950), 163–175.

a In the case of six industries for the United States (apparel, automobiles and automobile equipment, furniture and finished lumber products, iron and steel and their products, lumber and timber, and transportation equipment, except automobiles), the figures for 1948 and 1949 were not found to be sufficiently comparable with prior years because of revisions in the series. Therefore, the per cent changes in the revised series in 1948 and 1949 were applied to the 1947 (unrevised series) to put the hourly earnings for 1948 and 1949 on a comparable basis.

TABLE 12

Per Cent Changes in Employment, Los Angeles County and United States, April, 1940–April, 1949, and Distribution of Employment, April, 1940, and April, 1949.

Industry (ranked by Los Angeles per cent changes)	Los Angeles County			United States		
	Per cent changes 1940–1949	April 1940	April 1949	Per cent changes 1940–1949	April 1940	April 1949
		(in thousands)	(in thousands)		(in thousands)	(in thousands)
Shipbuilding and repairing....	1100.0	1	12	−28.8	153	109
Rubber products............	400.0	2	10	49.7	159	238
Electrical machinery.........	225.0	4	13	105.3	375	770
Lumber and timber..........	150.0	2	5	1.0	712	719
Aircraft and parts...........	140.0	30	72	142.1	107	259
Wholesale trade.............	135.4	48	113	107.5	1,207	2,504
Machinery (except electrical)..	133.3	15	35	98.4	698	1,385
Apparel....................	127.8	18	41	43.5	781	1,121
Stone, clay, and glass products.................	114.3	7	15	43.6	337	484
Communication..............	114.3	14	30	77.6	393	698
Government.................	106.4	47	97	229.4	1,753	5,775
Leather and leather products..	100.0	2	4	6.9	364	389
Primary and fabricated metal products.............	100.0	23	46	33.6	1,543	2,062
Automobiles and automobile equipment.................	85.7	7	13	35.3	575	778
Food and kindred products...	73.1	26	45	28.9	1,094	1,410
Chemicals and allied products	71.4	7	12	53.4	440	675
Petroleum and coal products..	60.0	10	16	22.4	201	246
Retail trade.................	59.2	201	320	10.1	6,332	6,974
Utilities...................	52.9	17	26	− 1.8	542	532
Finance, insurance, and real estate....................	44.1	59	85	19.7	1,468	1,757
Furniture and fixtures........	36.4	11	15	37.6	226	311
Forestry and fishing.........	33.3	3	4	a	103	a
Service....................	31.7	224	295	b	6,260	4,768
Printing, publishing, and allied industries...........	27.7	18	23	14.4	631	722
Textile mill products.........	25.0	4	5	1.5	1,170	1,188
Construction................	12.3	65	73	− 1.0	2,056	2,036
Mining....................	7.7	13	14	7.8	913	984
Paper and allied products....	0	4	4	34.8	328	442
Agriculture.................	− 3.0	32	31	− 6.6	8,372	7,820
Miscellaneous manufacturing	− 8.3	12	11	24.7	526	656
Domestic service............	−12.7	55	48	−21.7	2,327	1,821
Other transportation equipment.....................	−100.0	2	1	113.3	45	96
Industry not reported........	a	10	a	a	689	a
Tobacco manufactures.......	a	a	1	−16.7	108	90
Total employment⁰........		1,037	1,597		45,166	57,819

Sources: Calif. State Dept. of Employment Area V and VI, unpublished material.
U. S. Bureau of the Census, *Current Population Reports*, "Labor Force," Series P-57, no. 82 (May 6, 1949), p. 9.
Sixteenth Census of the United States, 1940, *Population*, Vol. II, pt. 1, p. 558; Vol. III, pt. 1, pp. 180–181.
U. S. Bureau of Labor Statistics, *Monthly Labor Review*, 69 (December, 1949), 696–699.
a Data not available.
b Data not comparable.
⁰ Data will not total, due to omissions.

TABLE 13

PER CENT CHANGES IN EMPLOYMENT AND AVERAGE HOURLY EARNINGS OF PRODUCTION
WORKERS IN MANUFACTURING INDUSTRIES, RANKED BY EMPLOYMENT CHANGES,
LOS ANGELES COUNTY, 1940–1948

Industry	1940–1948 per cent changes	
	Employment	Average hourly earnings
Electrical machinery and equipment.............	168.0	96.4
Stone, clay, and glass products.................	113.0	115.9
Automobiles and automobile equipment.........	110.6	74.2
Rubber products.............................	109.1	76.7
Machinery (except electrical).................	105.7	93.9
Chemicals and allied products.................	96.9	96.6
Leather and leather products.................	91.7	144.2
Petroleum products...........................	90.7	81.1
Paper and allied products....................	64.3	109.7
Nonferrous metals and their products...........	56.5	97.6
Furniture and finished lumber products.........	54.9	128.0
Apparel......................................	54.6	162.0
Iron and steel and their products..............	53.1	199.5
Textile mill products.........................	40.9	119.1
Transportation equipment.....................	36.1	99.3
Printing, publishing, and allied industries........	35.1	109.3
Lumber and timber...........................	27.8	103.1
Food and kindred products....................	25.3	115.9
Tobacco manufactures........................	−25.0	106.3

SOURCE: Calif. State Dept. of Indus. Relations, *Estimated Employment, Total Wages, and Average Earnings..., California and Los Angeles and San Francisco Bay Industrial Areas, 1940–1948* (May, 1949), pp. 26–32.

TABLE 14

Per Cent Changes in Employment and Average Hourly Earnings of Production Workers in Manufacturing Industries, Ranked by Employment Changes, United States, 1940–1948

Industry	1940–1948 per cent changes	
	Employment	Average hourly earnings
Machinery (except electrical)....................	92.5	93.0
Chemicals and allied products...................	83.7	101.9
Electrical machinery and equipment.............	83.0	91.9
Lumber and timber............................	79.2	120.2
Miscellaneous manufacturing...................	66.8	97.6
Automobiles and automobile equipment.........	65.8	70.5
Transportation equipment......................	62.9	90.8
Rubber products..............................	56.7	90.9
Nonferrous metals and their products...........	50.6	95.5
Petroleum products............................	48.2	88.4
Stone, clay, and glass products.................	47.6	99.2
Food and kindred products.....................	46.3	96.9
Iron and steel and their products...............	43.6	93.9
Apparel.......................................	42.8	99.3
Paper and allied products......................	41.7	110.8
Furniture and finished lumber products..........	36.7	115.1
Printing, publishing, and allied industries........	32.5	89.0
Textile mill products...........................	13.5	140.2
Leather and leather products...................	12.8	104.7
Tobacco manufactures.........................	− 5.4	101.4

Sources: Table 11.
U. S. Bureau of the Census, *Statistical Abstract of the United States, 1948*, p. 200.
U. S. Bureau of Labor Statistics, *Hours and Earnings*, February, 1949, pp. 15–19.

TABLE 15

SUMMARY OF RESULTS, ANALYSIS OF VARIANCE F TESTS, PER CENT CHANGES IN EM-
PLOYMENT, AVERAGE ANNUAL EARNINGS, AND AVERAGE VALUE ADDED BY MANU-
FACTURE PER WORKER, ELEVEN MANUFACTURING INDUSTRIES, SIX INDUSTRIAL AREAS,
AND FIVE TWO-YEAR PERIODS, 1929–1939

Period	Source of Variation	Employment (a)	Average annual earnings (b)	Average value added by manufacture per worker (c)	F required for significance	
					$F_{.01}$	$F_{.05}$
1929–1939	Industries	.61	.45	.37	(a) 2.80 (b) 2.80 (c) 2.80	2.07 2.07 2.07
	Areas.....	1.46	.38	.33	(a) 3.11 (b) 4.10 (c) 4.10	2.26 2.71 2.71
	Years.....	S 8.60	S 95.60	S.05 3.74	(a) 3.83 (b) 4.43 (c) 3.83	2.61 2.87 2.61

Phases of the business cycle

Period	Source of Variation	Employment (a)	Average annual earnings (b)	Average value added by manufacture per worker (c)	F required for significance	
1929–1933	Industries	.72	S 5.70	1.74	(a) 2.49 (b) 2.49 (c) 2.70	1.91 1.91 2.02
	Areas.....	.83	S 5.04	.21	(a) 3.18 (b) 3.18 (c) 10.97	2.29 2.29 5.05
	Years.....	2.94	S 51.50	.23	(a) 6.07 (b) 6.87 (c) 16.26	3.93 3.93 6.61
1933–1937	Industries	1.36	S 3.34	S.05 2.01	(a) 4.85 (b) 2.70 (c) 2.49	2.97 2.02 1.91
	Areas.....	S.05 2.47	1.17	1.95	(a) 3.41 (b) 5.64 (c) 3.18	2.40 3.33 2.29
	Years.....	S 11.00	.49	3.86	(a) 10.04 (b) 10 04 (c) 6.87	4.96 4.96 3.93
1937–1939	Industries	S 2.90	.41	1.01	2.70	2.02
	Areas.....	1.19	.67	1.54	3.41	2.40
	Years.....	....	....	....	....	....

TABLE 15—*Continued*

Biennial periods

Period	Source of variation	Employment (a)	Average annual earnings (b)	Average value added by manufacture per worker (c)	F required for significance $F_{.01}$	$F_{.05}$
1929–1931	Industries	S 4.41	S 7.08	S 3.55	2.70	2.02
	Areas.....	S.05 2.69	S 6.98	S 3.79	3.41	2.40
1931–1933	Industries	.83	S.05 2.35	S 4.29	2.70	2.02
	Areas.....	.85	.97	1.27	3.41	2.40
1933–1935	Industries	S 4.39	S.05 2.13	S.05 2.07	2.70	2.02
	Areas.....	S.05 2.63	S 7.14	1.90	3.41	2.40
1935–1937	Industries	S 4.76	S.05 2.36	1.73	2.70	2.02
	Areas.....	.82	.16	1.62	3.41	2.40
1937–1939	Industries	S 2.90	.41	1.01	2.70	2.02
	Areas.....	1.19	.67	1.54	3.41	2.40

SOURCE: Computed from Philip Neff, Lisette C. Baum, and Grace E. Heilman, *Production Cost Trends in Selected Industrial Areas* (Berkeley and Los Angeles: 1948), pp. 196–231, as shown in table 18.

TABLE 16

SUMMARY OF RESULTS, ANALYSIS OF VARIANCE F TESTS, PER CENT CHANGES IN EMPLOYMENT AND AVERAGE HOURLY EARNINGS, NINETEEN MANUFACTURING INDUSTRIES AND THREE INDUSTRY GROUPS, LOS ANGELES COUNTY AND SAN FRANCISCO BAY INDUSTRIAL AREA, 1940–1948 AND SUBPERIODS[a]

Group	Source of variation	Los Angeles		San Francisco		F required for significance	
		Employment	Average hourly earnings	Employment	Average hourly earnings	$F_{.01}$	$F_{.05}$
1940–1948							
All industries	Industries.........	S .45	S .65	1.00	S .63	2.09	1.69
	Years.........	3.48	8.88	1.74	25.68	2.79	2.08
1940–1943							
All industries	Industries.........	S 6.10	S 1.34	S 5.49	S 1.35	2.49	1.90
	Years.........	1.61	6.54	1.31	13.01	5.25	3.26
Group I	Industries.........	2.19	S.05 1.45	2.29	S 3.92	5.64	3.33
	Years.........	2.95	4.29	S 8.60	15.47	7.56	4.10
Group II	Industries.........	.53	S.05 1.75	.50	.84	4.82	3.00
	Years.........	2.68	6.48	3.51	3.00	6.93	3.88
Group III	Industries.........	1.46	2.27	S.05 5.44	S .58	7.01	3.84
	Years.........	1.10	.94	.78	11.07	8.65	4.46

[a] This is a summary of the analyses of the data in table 17.

1943–1945

	1	2	3	4	5	6
All industries						
Industries	S 2.15	S 6.25	S 3.35	S 3.77	3.13	2.22
Years	8.66	S 42.54	S 14.27	S 14.48	8.28	4.41
Group I						
Industries	S.05 4.07	S.05 5.98	1.43	.60	10.97	5.05
Years	8.88	S.05 8.75	4.51	2.66	16.26	6.61
Group II						
Industries	3.27	S 17.94	2.88	S.05 8.22	8.47	4.28
Years	3.26	S 33.38	2.42	4.00	13.74	5.99
Group III						
Industries	S 2.82	S.05 .84	S.05 1.80	2.79	15.98	6.39
Years	35.95	S.05 12.30	11.17	5.59	21.20	7.71

1945–1948

	1	2	3	4	5	6
All industries						
Industries	S.05 2.04	S 3.27	S.05 1.98	S.05 .95	2.49	1.90
Years	.54	S 6.58	S.05 4.56	S.05 3.77	5.25	3.26
Group I						
Industries	2.94	S 9.83	.48	S.05 1.79	5.64	3.33
Years	1.46	S 7.84	.64	S.05 7.07	7.56	4.10
Group II						
Industries	1.81	1.01	.94	.62	4.82	3.00
Years	1.75	1.69	2.91	1.72	6.93	3.88
Group III						
Industries	.44	1.03	S 1.30	.09	7.01	3.84
Years	4.07	2.20	11.81	.12	8.65	4.46

TABLE 17

SUMS OF PER CENT CHANGES IN EMPLOYMENT AND AVERAGE HOURLY EARNINGS, NINETEEN MANUFACTURING INDUSTRIES AND THREE INDUSTRY GROUPS, LOS ANGELES COUNTY AND SAN FRANCISCO BAY INDUSTRIAL AREA, 1940–1948 AND SUBPERIODS

Los Angeles—Individual industries, industry groups, and periods of time

Industry	1940–1948 E[a]	1940–1948 AHE[b]	1940–1943 E	1940–1943 AHE	1943–1945 E	1943–1945 AHE	1945–1948 E	1945–1948 AHE
All industries	1376	1467	1185	705	−77	247	268	515
Group I								
Food and kindred products	23	82	6	40	2	6	15	36
Tobacco manufactures	−25	81	0	41	0	36	−25	4
Printing, publishing, and allied industries	35	80	−11	16	4	13	42	51
Lumber and timber	28	76	6	39	−5	9	27	28
Stone, clay, and glass	89	82	11	43	2	12	76	27
Leather and leather products	74	97	50	56	15	23	9	18
	224	498	62	235	18	99	144	164
Group II								
Textile mill products	44	84	26	46	−31	11	49	27
Apparel	46	104	16	54	0	29	30	21
Paper and allied products	53	78	38	31	3	10	12	37
Chemicals and allied products	80	71	69	32	24	10	−13	29
Petroleum products	73	63	26	24	51	5	−4	34
Automobiles and automobile equipment	167	58	−3	26	−12	6	182	26
Furniture and finished lumber products	48	89	28	41	2	14	18	34
	511	547	200	254	37	85	274	208
Group III								
Rubber products	104	60	139	14	−12	13	−23	33
Iron and steel and their products	55	73	78	43	−26	7	3	23
Nonferrous metals	76	73	133	38	−38	10	−19	25
Electrical machinery	142	71	159	33	4	12	−21	26
Machinery (except electrical)	92	70	109	40	−8	10	−9	20
	469	347	618	168	−80	52	−69	127
Transportation equipment (except autos)	172	75	305	48	−52	11	−81	16

Los Angeles—Individual years, periods of time, and industry groups

	Period	E	AHE	Period	E	AHE	Period	E	AHE
All industries	1940–1941	476	163	1943–1944	61	169	1945–1946	167	185
	1941–1942	281	263	1944–1945	−138	78	1946–1947	64	198
	1942–1943	428	279				1947–1948	37	132
	1940–1943	1185	705	1943–1945	−77	247	1945–1948	268	515
Group I	1940–1941	60	43	1943–1944	−3	66	1945–1946	87	52
	1941–1942	−2	89	1944–1945	21	33	1946–1947	27	76
	1942–1943	4	103				1947–1948	30	36
	1940–1943	62	235	1943–1945	18	99	1945–1948	144	164
Group II	1940–1941	91	52	1943–1944	53	57	1945–1946	206	80
	1941–1942	−19	85	1944–1945	−16	28	1946–1947	42	70
	1942–1943	128	117				1947–1948	26	58
	1940–1943	200	254	1943–1945	37	85	1945–1948	274	208
Group III	1940–1941	182	52	1943–1944	−25	36	1945–1946	−70	46
	1941–1942	190	67	1944–1945	−105	16	1946–1947	12	49
	1942–1943	246	49				1947–1948	−11	32
	1940–1943	618	168	1943–1945	−80	52	1945–1948	−69	127
Transportation equipment (except autos)	1940–1941	143	16	1943–1944	−14	10	1945–1946	−56	7
	1941–1942	112	22	1944–1945	−38	1	1946–1947	−17	3
	1942–1943	50	10				1947–1948	−8	6
	1940–1943	305	48	1943–1945	−52	11	1945–1948	−81	16

a E = Employment.
b AHE = Average hourly earnings.

TABLE 17—Continued

SUMS OF PER CENT CHANGES IN EMPLOYMENT AND AVERAGE HOURLY EARNINGS, NINETEEN MANUFACTURING INDUSTRIES AND THREE INDUSTRY GROUPS, LOS ANGELES COUNTY AND SAN FRANCISCO BAY INDUSTRIAL AREA, 1940–1948 AND SUBPERIODS

San Francisco—Individual industries, industry groups, and periods of time

Industry	1940–1948		1940–1943		1943–1945		1945–1948	
	E^a	AHE^b	E	AHE	E	AHE	E	AHE
All industries	1274	1309	1145	603	−63	147	192	559
Group I	191	426	67	179	−16	48	140	199
Food and kindred products	23	74	21	36	4	6	−2	32
Tobacco manufactures	43	65	37	24	−14	10	20	31
Printing, publishing, and allied industries	22	73	−14	17	2	10	34	46
Lumber and timber	16	74	−17	38	−8	7	41	29
Stone, clay, and glass	64	70	29	32	0	6	35	32
Leather and leather products	23	70	11	32	0	9	12	29
Group II	276	474	44	197	58	54	174	223
Textile mill products	−1	63	3	22	−18	2	14	39
Apparel	35	87	6	38	−5	22	34	27
Paper and allied products	36	73	10	28	−8	10	18	35
Chemicals and allied products	29	69	17	28	−2	7	14	34
Petroleum products	33	64	16	25	19	2	−2	37
Automobiles and automobile equipment	79	53	−35	32	56	0	58	21
Furniture and finished lumber products	65	65	27	24	0	11	38	30
Group III	275	343	317	188	−42	38	0	117
Rubber products	−11	73	3	34	17	15	−31	24
Iron and steel and their products	42	65	29	36	−11	4	24	25
Nonferrous metals	40	70	52	40	−15	9	3	21
Electrical machinery	124	71	152	35	−21	10	−7	26
Machinery (except electrical)	80	64	81	43	−12	0	11	21
Transportation equipment (except autos)	532	66	717	39	−63	7	−122	20

San Francisco—Individual years, periods of time, and industry groups

	Period	E	AHE	Period	E	AHE	Period	E	AHE
All industries	1940–1941	562	149	1943–1944	70	96	1945–1946	26	179
	1941–1942	419	258	1944–1945	−133	51	1946–1947	224	224
	1942–1943	164	196				1947–1948	−58	156
	1940–1943	1145	603	1943–1945	−63	147	1945–1948	192	559
Group I	1940–1941	93	35	1943–1944	7	29	1945–1946	65	65
	1941–1942	−8	78	1944–1945	−23	19	1946–1947	59	85
	1942–1943	−18	66				1947–1948	16	49
	1940–1943	67	179	1943–1945	−16	48	1945–1948	140	199
Group II	1940–1941	102	48	1943–1944	58	34	1945–1946	99	70
	1941–1942	−56	78	1944–1945	0	20	1946–1947	77	92
	1942–1943	−2	71				1947–1948	−2	61
	1940–1943	44	197	1943–1945	58	54	1945–1948	174	223
Group III	1940–1941	133	48	1943–1944	−20	28	1945–1946	−58	43
	1941–1942	77	87	1944–1945	−62	10	1946–1947	−92	38
	1942–1943	107	53				1947–1948	−34	36
	1940–1943	317	188	1943–1945	−42	38	1945–1948	0	117
Transportation equipment (except autos)	1940–1941	234	18	1943–1944	−15	5	1945–1946	−80	1
	1941–1942	406	15	1944–1945	−48	2	1946–1947	−4	9
	1942–1943	77	6				1947–1948	−38	10
	1940–1943	717	39	1943–1945	−63	7	1945–1948	−122	20

Source: Computed from Calif. State Dept. of Indus. Relations, *Estimated Employment, Total Wages, and Average Earnings . . . , California and Los Angeles and San Francisco Bay Industrial Areas, 1940–1948* (May, 1949), pp. 26–39.

TABLE 18
Completed Analyses of Variance
Part I: 1929–1939

Employment

Source of variation	Degrees of freedom	Sum of squares	Mean square
Industries.......................	10	50,933	5,093.3
Areas........................	5	35,837	7,167.4
Years........................	4	287,453	71,863.3
I × A interaction...............	50	207,833	4,156.7
I × Y interaction...............	40	334,200	8,355.0
A × Y interaction...............	20	94,404	4,720.2
I × A × Y interaction...........	200	980,487	4,902.4

For industries: $F = 5,093.3/8,355.0 = .61$
For areas: $F = 7,167.4/4,902.4 = 1.46$
For years: $F = 71,863.3/8,355.0 = 8.60$

Average annual earnings

Source of variation	Degrees of freedom	Sum of squares	Mean square
Industries.......................	10	1,007	100.7
Areas........................	5	455	91.0
Years........................	4	92,499	23,124.8
I × A interaction...............	50	1,531	30.6
I × Y interaction...............	40	9,025	225.6
A × Y interaction...............	20	4,838	241.9
I × A × Y interaction...........	200	25,982	129.9

For industries: $F = 100.7/225.6 = .45$
For areas: $F = 91.0/241.9 = .38$
For years: $F = 23,124.8/241.9 = 95.60$

Value added by manufacture per worker

Source of variation	Degrees of freedom	Sum of squares	Mean square
Industries.......................	10	2,133.74	213.4
Areas........................	5	869.14	173.8
Years........................	4	85,490.47	21,372.6
I × A interaction...............	50	3,504.47	70.1
I × Y interaction...............	40	22,863.62	571.6
A × Y interaction...............	20	10,671.28	533.6
I × A × Y interaction...........	200	55,079.10	275.4

For industries: $F = 213.4/571.6 = .37$
For areas: $F = 173.8/533.6 = .33$
For years: $F = 21,372.6/571.6 = 3.74$

Employment

Source of variation	Degrees of freedom	Sum of squares	Mean square
Industries......................	10	62,491	6,249.1
Areas........................	5	35,946	7,189.2
Years........................	1	25,371	25,371.0
I × A interaction...............	50	374,134	7,482.7
I × Y interaction...............	10	90,571	9,057.1
A × Y interaction..............	5	40,051	8,010.2
I × A × Y interaction...........	50	487,165	9,743.3
Pooled interaction...............	115	991,921	8,625.4

For industries: $F = 6,249.1/8,625.4 = .72$
For areas: $F = 7,189.2/8,625.4 = .83$
For years: $F = 25,371.0/8,625.4 = 2.94$

Average annual earnings

Source of variation	Degrees of freedom	Sum of squares	Mean square
Industries......................	10	2,629	262.9
Areas........................	5	1,162	232.4
Years........................	1	2,376	2,376.0
I × A interaction...............	50	1,427	28.5
I × Y interaction...............	10	987	98.7
A × Y interaction..............	5	334	66.8
I × A × Y interaction...........	50	2,558	51.2
Pooled interaction...............	115	5,306	46.1

For industries: $F = 262.9/46.1 = 5.70$
For areas: $F = 232.4/46.1 = 5.04$
For years: $F = 2,376.0/46.1 = 51.50$

Value added by manufacture per worker

Source of variation	Degrees of freedom	Sum of squares	Mean square
Industries......................	10	3,406.85	340.7
Areas........................	5	1,482.86	296.6
Years........................	1	330.28	330.3
I × A interaction...............	50	3,864.81	77.3
I × Y interaction...............	10	2,384.77	238.5
A × Y interaction..............	5	7,063.69	1,412.7
I × A × Y interaction...........	50	9,791.77	195.8

For industries: $F = 340.7/195.8 = 1.74$
For areas: $F = 296.6/1,412.7 = .21$
For years: $F = 330.3/1,412.7 = .23$

Employment

Source of variation	Degrees of freedom	Sum of squares	Mean square
Industries.......................	10	69,987	6,998.7
Areas..........................	5	22,678	4,535.6
Years..........................	1	56,710	56,710.0
I × A interaction................	50	44,375	887.5
I × Y interaction................	10	51,564	5,156.4
A × Y interaction...............	5	8,948	1,789.6
I × A × Y interaction...........	50	91,970	1,839.4

For industries: $F = 6,998.7/5,156.4 = 1.36$
For areas: $F = 4,535.6/1,839.4 = 2.47$
For years: $F = 56,710.0/5,156.4 = 11.00$

Average annual earnings

Source of variation	Degrees of freedom	Sum of squares	Mean square
Industries.......................	10	4,027	402.7
Areas..........................	5	1,693	338.6
Years..........................	1	142	142.0
I × A interaction................	50	5,905	118.1
I × Y interaction................	10	1,428	142.8
A × Y interaction...............	5	1,451	290.2
I × A × Y interaction...........	50	6,020	120.4

For industries: $F = 402.7/120.4 = 3.34$
For areas: $F = 338.6/290.2 = 1.17$
For years: $F = 142.0/290.2 = .49$

Value added by manufacture per worker

Source of variation	Degrees of freedom	Sum of squares	Mean square
Industries.......................	10	6,321.71	632.2
Areas..........................	5	3,070.42	614.1
Years..........................	1	1,212.73	1,212.7
I × A interaction................	50	12,259.51	245.2
I × Y interaction................	10	4,959.93	496.0
A × Y interaction...............	5	2,138.46	427.7
I × A × Y interaction...........	50	16,771.45	335.4
Pooled interaction...............	115	36,129.35	314.2

For industries: $F = 632.2/314.2 = 2.01$
For areas: $F = 614.1/314.2 = 1.95$
For years: $F = 1,212.7/314.2 = 3.86$

TABLE 18—Continued

COMPLETED ANALYSES OF VARIANCE, PART I—Concluded

Source of variation	1929-1931			1931-1933			1933-1935			1935-1937			1937-1939		
	d.f.	Sum of squares	Mean square	d.f.	Sum of squares	Mean square	d.f.	Sum of squares	Mean square	d.f.	Sum of squares	Mean square	d.f.	Sum of squares	Mean square
Employment															
Industries............	10	12,403	1,240.3	10	140,659	14,065.9	10	99,014	9,901.4	10	22,537	2,253.7	10	110,519	11,051.9
Areas.................	5	3,783	756.6	5	72,214	14,442.8	5	29,682	5,936.4	5	1,944	388.8	5	22,616	4,523.2
I X A interaction......	50	14,054	281.1	50	847,245	16,944.9	50	112,678	2,253.6	50	23,667	473.3	50	190,678	3,813.6
For industries: $F=$		1,240.3/281.1=4.41			14,065.9/16,944.9=.83			9,901.4/2,253.6=4.39			2,253.7/473.3=4.76			11,051.9/3,813.6=2.90	
For areas: $F=$		756.6/281.1=2.69			14,442.8/16,944.9=.85			5,936.4/2,253.6=2.63			388.8/473.3=.82			4,523.2/3,813.6=1.19	
Average annual earnings															
Industries............	10	2,610	261.0	10	1,006	100.6	10	1,731	173.1	10	3,747	374.7	10	938	93.8
Areas.................	5	1,287	257.4	5	208	41.6	5	2,902	580.4	5	128	25.6	5	766	153.2
I X A interaction......	50	1,844	36.9	50	2,142	42.8	50	4,063	81.3	50	7,952	159.0	50	11,513	230.3
For industries: $F=$		261.0/36.9=7.08			100.6/42.8=2.35			173.1/81.3=2.13			374.7/159.0=2.36			93.8/230.3=.41	
For areas: $F=$		257.4/36.9=6.98			41.6/42.8=.97			580.4/81.3=7.14			25.6/159.0=.16			153.2/230.3=.67	
Value added by manufacture per worker															
Industries............	10	5,996.51	599.7	10	4,474.02	447.4	10	7,533.87	753.4	10	3,747.77	374.8	10	3,245.19	324.5
Areas.................	5	3,205.59	641.1	5	662.03	132.4	5	3,459.00	691.8	5	1,749.89	350.0	5	2,461.91	492.8
I X A interaction......	50	8,447.80	169.0	50	5,208.79	104.2	50	18,221.55	364.4	50	10,809.40	216.2	50	16,000.42	320.0
For industries: $F=$		599.7/169.0=3.55			447.4/104.2=4.29			753.4/364.4=2.07			374.8/216.2=1.73			324.5/320.0=1.01	
For areas: $F=$		641.1/169.0=3.79			132.4/104.2=1.27			691.8/364.4=1.90			350.0/216.2=1.62			492.8/320.0=1.54	

TABLE 18—*Continued*

COMPLETED ANALYSES OF VARIANCE, PART 2
1940–1948

Source of variation	Los Angeles						San Francisco					
	Employment			Average hourly earnings			Employment			Average hourly earnings		
	d.f.	Sum of squares	Mean square	d.f.	Sum of squares	Mean square	d.f.	Sum of squares	Mean square	d.f.	Sum of squares	Mean square
All industries—1940–1948												
Industries........	18	5,441	302.3	18	301	16.7	18	30,690	1,705.0	18	103	5.7
Years............	7	16,220	2,317.1	7	1,583	226.1	7	20,643	2,949.0	7	1,651	235.8
I × Y interaction..	126	83,673	664.1	126	3,209	25.5	126	212,799	1,688.9	126	1,157	9.2
For industries: $F=$		$302.3/664.1 = .45$			$16.7/25.5 = .65$			$1,705.0/1,688.9 = 1.00$			$5.7/9.2 = .63$	
For years: $F=$		$2,317.1/664.1 = 3.48$			$226.1/25.5 = 8.88$			$2,949.0/1,688.9 = 1.74$			$235.8/9.2 = 25.68$	
All industries—1940–1943												
Industries........	18	36,931	2,051.7	18	772	42.9	18	161,403	8,966.8	18	295	16.4
Years............	2	1,086	543.0	2	416	208.0	2	4,279	2,139.5	2	315	157.5
I × Y interaction..	36	12,100	336.1	36	1,143	31.8	36	58,775	1,632.6	36	434	12.1
For industries: $F=$		$2,051.7/336.1 = 6.10$			$42.9/31.8 = 1.34$			$8,966.8/1,632.6 = 5.49$			$16.4/12.1 = 1.35$	
For years: $F=$		$543.0/336.1 = 1.61$			$208.0/31.8 = 6.54$			$2,139.5/1,632.6 = 1.31$			$157.5/12.1 = 13.01$	

Group I—1940–1943

Group II—1940-1943

	df	SS	MS	df	SS	MS	df	SS	MS	df	SS	MS
Industries...........	6	964	160.7	6	245	40.8	6	789	131.5	6	59	9.8
Years...............	2	1,670	835.0	2	302	151.0	2	1,843	921.5	2	70	35.0
I × Y interaction....	12	3,735	311.3	12	279	23.3	12	3,144	262.0	12	140	11.7

For industries: $F=$ 160.7/311.3 = .53 ; 40.8/23.3 = 1.75 ; 131.5/262.0 = .50 ; 9.8/11.7 = .84

For years: $F=$ 835.0/311.3 = 2.68 ; 151.0/23.3 = 6.48 ; 921.5/262.0 = 3.51 ; 35.0/11.7 = 3.00

Group III—1940-1943

	df	SS	MS	df	SS	MS	df	SS	MS	df	SS	MS
Industries...........	4	1,290	322.5	4	177	44.3	4	4,374	1,093.5	4	19	4.8
Years...............	2	486	243.0	2	37	18.5	2	314	157.0	2	180	90.0
I × Y interaction....	8	1,762	220.3	8	156	19.5	8	1,608	201.0	8	65	8.1

For industries: $F=$ 322.5/220.3 = 1.46 ; 44.3/19.5 = 2.27 ; 1,093.5/201.0 = 5.44 ; 4.8/8.1 = .58

For years: $F=$ 243.0/220.3 = 1.10 ; 18.5/19.5 = .94 ; 157.0/201.0 = .78 ; 90.0/8.1 = 11.07

All industries—1943-1945

	df	SS	MS	df	SS	MS	df	SS	MS	df	SS	MS
Industries...........	18	4,653	258.5	18	573	31.9	18	4,588	254.9	18	249	13.8
Years...............	1	1,042	1,042.0	1	217	217.0	1	1,085	1,085.0	1	53	53.0
I × Y interaction....	18	2,164	120.2	18	91	5.1	18	1,368	76.0	18	66	3.7

For industries: $F=$ 258.5/120.2 = 2.15 ; 31.9/5.1 = 6.25 ; 254.9/76.0 = 3.35 ; 13.8/3.7 = 3.77

For years: $F=$ 1,042.0/120.2 = 8.66 ; 217.0/5.1 = 42.54 ; 1,085.0/76.0 = 14.27 ; 53.0/3.7 = 14.48

Group I—1943-1945

	df	SS	MS	df	SS	MS	df	SS	MS	df	SS	MS
Industries...........	5	110	22.0	5	311	62.2	5	119	23.8	5	9	1.8
Years...............	1	48	48.0	1	91	91.0	1	75	75.0	1	8	8.0
I × Y interaction....	5	27	5.4	5	52	10.4	5	83	16.6	5	15	3.0

For industries: $F=$ 22.0/5.4 = 4.07 ; 62.2/10.4 = 5.98 ; 23.8/16.6 = 1.43 ; 1.8/3.0 = .60

For years: $F=$ 48.0/5.4 = 8.88 ; 91.0/10.4 = 8.75 ; 75.0/16.6 = 4.51 ; 8.0/3.0 = 2.66

TABLE 18—*Concluded*

Source of variation	Los Angeles						San Francisco					
	Employment			Average hourly earnings			Employment			Average hourly earnings		
	d.f.	Sum of squares	Mean square	d.f.	Sum of squares	Mean square	d.f.	Sum of squares	Mean square	d.f.	Sum of squares	Mean square
Group II—1943–1945												
Industries................	6	2,050	341.7	6	194	32.3	6	1,717	286.2	6	173	28.8
Years....................	1	340	340.0	1	60	60.1	1	241	241.0	1	14	14.0
I × Y interaction........	6	625	104.2	6	11	1.8	6	596	99.3	6	21	3.5
For industries: *F*=		341.7/104.2=3.27			32.3/1.8=17.94			286.2/99.3=2.88			28.8/3.5=8.22	
For years: *F*=		340.0/104.2=3.26			60.1/1.8=33.38			241.0/99.3=2.42			14.0/3.5=4.00	
Group III—1943–1945												
Industries................	4	532	133.0	4	11	2.8	4	434	108.5	4	67	16.8
Years....................	1	1,690	1,690.0	1	40	40.0	1	673	673.0	1	33	33.0
I × Y interaction........	4	188	47.0	4	13	3.3	4	241	60.3	4	24	6.0
For industries: *F*=		133.0/47.0=2.82			2.8/3.3=.84			108.5/60.3=1.80			16.8/6.0=2.79	
For years: *F*=		1,690.0/47.0=35.95			40.0/3.3=12.31			673.0/60.3=11.17			33.0/6.0=5.50	
All industries—1945–1948												
Industries................	18	16,827	934.8	18	578	32.1	18	8,651	480.6	18	287	15.9
Years....................	2	495	247.5	2	129	64.5	2	2,206	1,103.0	2	126	63.0
I × Y interaction........	36	16,440	456.7	36	353	9.8	36	8,704	241.8	36	602	16.7
For industries: *F*=		934.8/456.7=2.04			32.1/9.8=3.27			480.6/241.8=1.98			15.9/16.7=.95	
For years: *F*=		247.5/456.7=.54			64.5/9.8=6.58			1,103.0/241.8=4.56			63.0/16.7=3.77	

Group I—1945-1948

	df			df			df			df		
Industries	5	1,915	383.0	5	423	84.6	5	448	89.6	5	69	13.8
Years	2	381	190.5	2	135	67.5	2	238	119.0	2	109	54.5
I × Y interaction	10	1,300	130.0	10	86	8.6	10	1,843	184.3	10	77	7.7

For industries: $F=$ 383.0/130.0=2.94 | 84.6/8.6=9.83 | 89.6/184.3=.48 | 13.8/7.7=1.79
For years: $F=$ 190.5/130.0=1.46 | 67.5/8.6=7.84 | 119.0/184.3=.64 | 54.5/7.7=7.07

Group II—1945-1948

	df			df			df			df		
Industries	6	8,784	1,464.0	6	63	10.5	6	786	131.0	6	79	13.2
Years	2	2,836	1,418.0	2	35	17.5	2	806	403.0	2	73	36.5
I × Y interaction	12	9,695	807.9	12	124	10.3	12	1,658	138.2	12	253	21.2

For industries: $F=$ 1,464.0/807.9=1.81 | 10.5/10.3=1.01 | 131.0/138.2=.94 | 13.2/21.2=.62
For years: $F=$ 1,418.0/807.9=1.75 | 17.5/10.3=1.69 | 403.0/138.2=2.91 | 36.5/21.2=1.72

Group III—1945-1948

	df			df			df			df		
Industries	4	157	39.3	4	31	7.8	4	572	143.0	4	7	1.8
Years	2	716	358.0	2	33	16.5	2	2,597	1,298.5	2	5	2.5
I × Y interaction	8	705	88.1	8	60	7.5	8	879	109.9	8	162	20.3

For industries: $F=$ 39.3/88.1=.44 | 7.8/7.5=1.03 | 143.0/109.9=1.30 | 1.8/20.3=.09
For years: $F=$ 358.0/88.1=4.07 | 16.5/7.5=2.20 | 1,298.5/109.9=11.81 | 2.5/20.3=.12

TABLE 19

DATA FOR ANALYSIS OF VARIANCE

THREE TWO-WAY TABLES, SUMMARY OF PER CENT CHANGES IN EMPLOYMENT FOR ELEVEN MAJOR INDUSTRY GROUPS, SIX INDUSTRIAL AREAS, AND FIVE TWO-YEAR PERIODS, 1929–1939[a]

Area	Industry											Total
	Food and kindred products	Textiles and their products	Forest products	Paper and allied products	Printing, publishing, and allied industries	Chemicals and their products	Stone, clay, and glass products	Iron, steel, and their products	Nonferrous metals and their products	Machinery, not including transportation equipment	Transportation equipment, air, land, and water	
	1	2	3	4	5	6	7	8	9	10	11	
Los Angeles	27	62	15	125	9	78	56	23	84	269	63	811
Chicago	9	40	−2	27	6	37	90	16	94	84	26	427
Cleveland	2	25	42	61	−16	40	94	−28	123	107	−19	431
Detroit	26	374	15	133	12	224	454	46	26	217	41	1,568
San Francisco	14	95	−12	126	−3	45	128	119	43	88	95	738
Pittsburgh	14	253	108	99	0	39	−3	6	342	54	1,033	1,945
Total	92	849	166	571	8	463	819	182	712	819	1,239	5,920

Industry

Years	1	2	3	4	5	6	7	8	9	10	11	Total
1929–1931	− 91	− 2	−241	−110	− 79	−114	−230	−166	−194	−229	−287	−1,743
1931–1933	24	− 63	−170	− 2	−110	12	−270	− 81	− 2	− 94	843	87
1933–1935	108	420	266	226	124	196	559	252	343	926	574	3,994
1935–1937	68	−153	174	177	121	53	181	225	133	266	13	1,258
1937–1939	− 17	647	137	280	− 48	316	579	− 48	432	− 50	96	2,324
Total	92	849	166	571	8	463	819	182	712	819	1,239	5,920

Area

Years	Los Angeles	Chicago	Cleveland	Detroit	San Francisco	Pittsburgh	Total
1929–1931	− 392	− 354	− 309	− 279	− 127	− 282	−1,743
1931–1933	− 71	− 134	− 66	− 184	− 271	813	87
1933–1935	815	529	410	1,107	620	513	3,994
1935–1937	285	172	133	293	172	203	1,258
1937–1939	174	214	263	631	344	698	2,324
Total	811	427	431	1,568	738	1,945	5,920

ᵃ An additional figure (beyond the decimal point) was used in this table because value added by manufacture per worker was computed from the figures for value added by manufacture and the figures for employment, in an effort to preserve the number of significant figures given in the original data.

TABLE 19—Continued

Area	Industry											Total
	Food and kindred products	Textiles and their products	Forest products	Paper and allied products	Printing, publishing, and allied industries	Chemicals and their products	Stone, clay, and glass products	Iron, steel, and their products	Nonferrous metals and their products	Machinery, not including transportation equipment	Transportation equipment, air, land, and water	
	1	2	3	4	5	6	7	8	9	10	11	
Los Angeles........	13.6	−14.0	−1.9	16.8	−21.3	21.3	21.9	−9.9	−11.9	12.2	8.3	35.1
Chicago............	21.7	−29.1	−22.3	−14.1	−25.7	9.2	3.8	−12.2	−17.5	−20.6	−3.4	−110.2
Cleveland..........	2.4	−6.3	2.2	20.0	−18.6	−6.8	63.0	−0.3	3.5	10.0	4.9	74.0
Detroit............	9.0	9.5	−10.6	2.5	−26.3	23.8	11.1	−3.8	24.8	−5.1	−25.0	9.9
San Francisco......	14.4	40.0	3.3	27.0	−9.7	17.1	45.7	−8.2	16.3	19.7	−13.6	168.4
Pittsburgh.........	26.4	−56.9	−16.7	23.4	−21.4	21.4	4.9	−12.0	6.1	68.3	58.1	125.6
Total............	87.5	−56.8	−46.0	75.6	−123.0	86.0	150.4	−6.0	21.3	84.5	29.3	302.8

Industry

Years	1	2	3	4	5	6	7	8	9	10	11	Total
1929–1931	−38.2	−126.7	−140.8	−100.4	−74.1	−77.6	−129.1	−193.1	−176.9	−76.7	12.6	−1,121.0
1931–1933	−129.0	−147.0	−136.8	5.8	−93.6	−133.3	−122.1	−104.5	−100.0	−179.3	−190.0	−1,329.8
1933–1935	28.8	144.1	72.6	39.1	32.7	151.6	119.3	71.0	188.1	235.0	104.2	1,186.5
1935–1937	79.8	36.9	90.8	56.0	−33.9	70.6	124.8	150.1	53.3	83.2	74.8	786.4
1937–1939	146.1	35.9	68.2	75.1	45.9	74.7	157.5	70.5	56.8	22.3	27.7	780.7
Total	87.5	−56.8	−46.0	75.6	−123.0	86.0	150.4	−6.0	21.3	84.5	29.3	302.8

Area

Years	Los Angeles	Chicago	Cleveland	Detroit	San Francisco	Pittsburgh	Total
1929–1931	−162.9	−186.6	−236.7	−254.6	−32.3	−247.9	−1,121.0
1931–1933	−195.9	−265.6	−258.8	−171.6	−238.8	−199.1	−1,329.8
1933–1935	129.7	160.2	176.2	181.7	166.8	371.9	1,186.5
1935–1937	107.0	143.1	229.0	120.1	38.8	148.4	786.4
1937–1939	157.2	38.7	164.3	134.3	233.9	52.3	780.7
Total	35.1	−110.2	74.0	9.9	168.4	125.6	3,028

TABLE 19—Concluded

Area	Industry											Total
	Food and kindred products	Textiles and their products	Forest products	Paper and allied products	Printing, publishing, and allied industries	Chemicals and their products	Stone, clay, and glass products	Iron, steel, and their products	Nonferrous metals and their products	Machinery, not including transportation equipment	Transportation equipment, air, land, and water	
	1	2	3	4	5	6	7	8	9	10	11	
Los Angeles	3	—17	—10	—1	—16	2	3	—9	—14	3	—7	—61
Chicago	—1	—24	—30	—10	—10	0	—20	—5	—22	—30	—25	—177
Cleveland	0	—5	—4	6	—9	—1	7	3	5	14	3	5
Detroit	2	—33	—5	5	—17	12	13	2	17	—11	7	—12
San Francisco	14	0	—3	15	0	5	1	—2	6	19	—42	13
Pittsburgh	6	—59	—15	23	—13	8	6	—8	11	27	—11	—25
Total	24	—138	—67	40	—65	10	—4	—7	3	22	—75	—257

Industry

Years	1	2	3	4	5	6	7	8	9	10	11	Total
1929–1931	− 45	−102	−124	− 72	− 29	− 35	−110	−141	−112	−111	−127	−1,008
1931–1933	−119	−144	−178	−107	−134	−128	−193	−139	−150	−141	−135	−1,568
1933–1935	82	99	126	100	63	64	111	145	136	160	130	1,216
1935–1937	99	44	118	77	12	112	170	145	104	142	56	1,079
1937–1939	7	− 35	− 9	42	23	− 3	18	− 17	25	− 28	1	24
Total	24	−138	− 67	40	− 65	10	− 4	− 7	3	22	− 75	− 257

Area

Years	Los Angeles	Chicago	Cleveland	Detroit	San Francisco	Pittsburgh	Total
1929–1931	−119	−174	−200	−244	− 98	−173	−1,008
1931–1933	−254	−271	−248	−297	−235	−263	−1,568
1933–1935	120	178	239	336	130	213	1,216
1935–1937	172	166	213	177	177	174	1,079
1937–1939	20	− 76	1	16	39	24	24
Total	− 61	−177	5	− 12	13	− 25	− 257

Source: Computed from Neff, Baum, and Heilman, op. cit., pp. 196–231. Data for "Transportation equipment, air, land, and water" in Pittsburgh, 1937 and 1939, were interpolated.

INDEX

INDEX

Alchian, Armen, 101 n.

Analysis of variance
  of employment, Los Angeles and 5 industrial areas, 1929–1939, 105–118; Los Angeles and San Francisco, 1940–1948, 105–118
  of value added per worker, Los Angeles and 5 industrial areas, 1929–1939, 131–135
  of wages, Los Angeles and 5 industrial areas, 1929–1939, 105–118, 131–135; Los Angeles and San Francisco, 1940–1948, 105–118

Annual earnings
  and capital per worker, Los Angeles and United States, 1937, 123–127
  and employment, Los Angeles and 5 industrial areas, 1929–1939, 98–104, 107–113, 116–118
  and labor costs, Los Angeles, 5 industrial areas, and United States, 1929–1939, 121–123
  Los Angeles, 6 industrial areas, and United States, 1919–1939, 27–29
  and size of firm, Los Angeles, 5 industrial areas, and United States, 1929–1939, 120–122
  and value added per worker, Los Angeles and 5 industrial areas, 1929–1939, 128–135; Los Angeles and United States, 1937, 128–129

Bank deposits per capita, Los Angeles and United States, 1940–1949, 65, 67

Baum, Lisette C., 13 n., 24 n., 34 n., 36 n., 98 n., 100, 122, 129 n., 130

Belloc, Nedra B., 50 n.

Big Four packers, 142

Blair, John M., 10 n.

Boulding, Kenneth E., 9 n.

Buffalo, 26–29

Business activity, level of, 9–10, 110–111, 117; and wages in Los Angeles, 43, 55–57, 60–69, 158

Business enterprises, southern California, 1940–1949, 64–65

Business loans, Los Angeles and United States, 1940–1949, 63, 65

Cairnes, J. E., 8 n.

Capital equipment and investment, 13–14, 38, 62, 64, 123–127, 161–162

Capital/worker ratios. *See* Capital equipment and investment

Chicago, 24, 26–29, 33–34, 48–50, 100, 101, 122, 123, 130

Chrysler Corp., 142

CIO Los Angeles Industrial Union Council, 137

Cleveland, 24, 26–29, 33–34, 36, 38, 48–50, 99–101, 122, 123, 130

Collective bargaining
  and community wage structures, 18–20
  Los Angeles history, 39–40, 136–138
  Los Angeles patterns, 138–140
  Los Angeles wages under, 140–152; industry rate standardization, 152–156

Columbia Steel, 140

Community wage structures, 1–21
  capital equipment and investment, 13–14
  controlling influences, 6–7
  cost influences, 12–13
  distribution of productive gains, 17–18
  economists' view of, 6–20
  industry wage comparisons, 7–10
  man-land ratio, 10–12
  nature of, 3–6
  product demand and markets, 15–16
  skill mix, 10
  summary, 20–21
  union and employer organizations, 18–20

Comparison of community wage levels, limitations on, 5–6, 22. *See also* Community wage structures

Consolidated Steel, 140

Cost of living, 8; in Los Angeles, pre-1940, 38; 1940–1949, 50–51, 56, 59–60, 61

Daily wages, 1885, 31

Demand for labor, 1, 8–9, 14, 53, 98, 162–163; in Los Angeles, 23, 32, 41, 43, 58, 160–161

Detroit, 24, 26–29, 33–34, 36, 38, 48–50, 57, 99–101, 122, 123, 130

Douglas, Paul H., 126

Dunlop, John T., 2 n., 7 n., 10 n., 55 n., 82 n., 119 n., 131 n.

Employer associations, 2, 9, 18–19, 39–40, 136–137

Employment
  in Los Angeles, 1929–1939, 34; 1940–1949, 58, 71

FACULTY ADVISORY COMMITTEE

NEIL H. JACOBY, Dean, School of Business Administration (Chairman)

JOSEPH A. GENGERELLI, Chairman, Department of Psychology

J. A. C. GRANT, Professor, Department of Political Science, and Divisional Dean of Social Sciences, College of Letters and Science

HARRY HOIJER, Chairman, Department of Anthropology and Sociology

PAUL T. HOMAN, Chairman, Department of Economics

DONALD S. HOWARD, Dean, School of Social Welfare

PAUL H. SHEATS, Associate Director, University Extension, and Associate Professor, Department of Education

INSTITUTE STAFF
SOUTHERN DIVISION

1952–1953

EDGAR L. WARREN, Director

ABBOTT KAPLAN, Associate Director

ROBERT B. BUCHELE, Assistant Director, Management Programs

ARTHUR CARSTENS, Assistant Director, Labor Programs

NANCY TAYLOR, Administrative Assistant

HUGH G. LOVELL, Principal Extension Representative.

BENJAMIN AARON, Research Associate

IRVING BERNSTEIN, Research Associate

WALTER R. GOLDSCHMIDT, Research Associate

PHILIP NEFF, Research Associate

JOHN J. SCHWARZ, Research Associate

ROBERT TANNENBAUM, Research Associate

IRVING R. WESCHLER, Research Associate

RICHARD BAISDEN, Research Assistant

PAULA BROWN, Research Assistant

GRACE E. HEILMAN, Research Assistant

FRED MASSARIK, Research Assistant

FRED ROTHFARB, Research Assistant

ROBERT E. THOMASON, Librarian

ANNE P. COOK, Editor

www.ingramcontent.com/pod-product-compliance
Lightning Source LLC
Chambersburg PA
CBHW031130270326
41929CB00011B/1563